Portraits of Thought

Mon pere sest servi de ce corps
de droit pour son ouvrage
des loix civiles
portrai de Mr pascal fai par mon pere

Buford Norman

Portraits of Thought

Knowledge, Methods, and Styles in Pascal

Ohio State University Press
Columbus

Library of Congress Cataloging-in-Publication Data

Norman, Buford.

Portraits of thought : knowledge, methods, and styles in Pascal / Buford Norman.

p. cm.

Bibliography: p.

Includes index.

ISBN 0–8142–0464–3 (alk. paper)

1. Pascal, Blaise, 1623–1662. I. Title.

B1903.N66 1988 88–12026

194—dc19 CIP

The paper in this book meets the guidelines for permanence and durability of the Committee on Production Guidelines for Book Longevity of the Council on Library Resources.

Printed in the U.S.A.

To my parents

Contents

Acknowledgments

This book has been a long time in the making, and there are many people to thank, from undergraduate mentors to current colleagues. Hal Walker first showed me what literary scholarship is all about and has been generous with his advice ever since. My professors at Yale helped me create a distant cousin of this book, and though there is not a sentence of that dissertation here, *Portraits of Thought* would not exist without them. Jean Boorsch, with his personal distrust and professional admiration of Pascal, was the perfect director; Henri Peyre and Tim Reiss gave and continue to give valuable advice.

Among the many Pascal scholars around the world, I owe special thanks to Jean Mesnard and Philippe Sellier in France and to Hugh Davidson and Robert Nelson in this country. I am thankful to have them as friends as well as colleagues, and the many references to their work only begin to show what I owe them. Robert in particular gave my manuscript a careful and wise reading that has had a profound effect on the finished product.

It would tax even the generosity and understanding of Ohio State University Press to list all the colleagues at Iowa State University and at the University of South Carolina whose wisdom has found its way into these pages. Special thanks are due to James Dow, James Ruebel, and Robert Hatch at Iowa State, and to the participants in the many interdisciplinary discussions that contributed so much to my understanding of Pascal's scientific works. The seventeenth-century seminar at USC has played a similar role; my French colleagues Elizabeth Joiner, William Mould, and Philip Wadsworth have been particularly helpful. I am also grateful to Paula Feldman, whose writing skills have helped me portray my own thoughts; to Greg Jay, who guided me through the complexities of Paul de Man's writing; and to Don Edwards, my guide to the equally daunting world of statistics. The staff of the Humanities and Social Sciences Computer Lab probably wish that the programming language was the only Pascal they had to deal with.

It is by no means *pro forma* that I thank everyone at Ohio State University Press. Alex Holzman, Kate Capps, and Charlotte Dihoff—to mention only those with whom I have been in direct contact—have been a true joy to work with and have shown a remarkable combination of friendliness, understanding and high professional standards. I am especially grateful to the anonymous "ED," a skillful copyeditor who has shown a remarkable understanding of what I am trying to say.

Iowa State University, the University of South Carolina, and the American Council of Learned Societies have provided financial support for research and travel. Finally, to the wonderful friends who, from the softball field to a refined table, have kept me going all these years: "*Un vrai ami est une chose si avantageuse. . . .*" Pascal, as usual, understood.

Introduction

Je ne puis concevoir l'homme sans pensée. (143/111)

Le moi consiste dans ma pensée. (167/135)

Cette partie même de moi qui pense ce que je dis. . . . (681/427)

L'éloquence est une peinture de la pensée. Et ainsi ceux qui, après avoir peint, ajoutent encore, font un tableau au lieu d'un portrait. (481/578)[1]

Il est peu important d'examiner si c'est à la Grammaire ou à la Logique d'en traiter. . . . Or certainement il est de quelque utilité pour la fin de la Logique, qui est de bien penser, *d'entendre les divers usages des sons qui sont destinés à signifier les idées.*[2]

It is hard to read Pascal dispassionately. The nature of the subject matter, especially in the *Pensées*, his direct and often arrogant approach, his skillful, persuasive use of language, and his place in the classical canon rarely leave readers indifferent. The ideas of the man behind the author (554/675) leave us fascinated, if not exasperated, and this is as it should be for a writer

[1]Pascal, *Pensées*, ed. Philippe Sellier (Paris: Mercure de France, 1976), fragment 481. All references to the *Pensées* will be to this edition unless otherwise noted and will include the fragment number from this edition and from the Lafuma edition (*Oeuvres complètes*, Paris: Seuil, 1963), such as 481/578 in the present case. The spelling and punctuation have been modernized in these and other editions. I sometimes follow the text of the manuscript where Pascal's intentions are clearer. References to other works by Pascal will be to this Lafuma edition, identified only by page number: 123A, for example, will refer to the left-hand column on page 123.

[2]Antoine Arnauld and Pierre Nicole, *La Logique ou l'art de penser*, 5th ed., ed. Pierre Clair and François Girbal (1683; Paris: P.U.F., 1965), 103. The first edition appeared in 1662. References to this work will be in the form of "*Logique*"; spelling has not been modernized.

who could not conceive of a person without thought. However, Pascal also realized that he could not express his thoughts, his conceptions, without language. The end result of his thought is "ce que je dis," the language that has preserved his thoughts and made him famous both as a thinker and as a writer.

What we have of Pascal's writings is not so much *pensées* as *paroles.* There are only two direct ways to approach his literal *pensée,* or thought process—through the words he wrote about thought (in general or his own) and through the way he wrote, that is, how he used words to express his thoughts and bring them into existence for the rest of the world. My study will thus deal with two aspects of Pascal's writings and will pay particular attention to the *Pensées*—the content of the fragments which discuss thought, language, knowledge and method, and the styles of certain fragments as they reflect Pascal's methods and his thought. One of the main goals of my study is an understanding of what I call Pascal's methods in the *Pensées.* My subject is not his apologetic method per se nor the plan of a projected apology, but rather the relationship between thought and language, between what went on in his mind (or in the *moi* which "consiste dans ma pensée" [167/135]) and what appears in the text before us as the manuscript of the *Pensées.*

We must remember that this manuscript, these often almost illegible jottings, is *all* we have. We do not have an apology for the Christian religion, nor a definitive plan for one, and Pascal never wrote that he intended to write one. There is no reason to doubt that he thought about the possibility of writing an apology, but a careful study of his thought processes and styles suggests that Pascal would never have written anything like what was then known as an apology, that is, a complete, ordered, linear presentation where each argument is intended to support the following ones. Therefore, any references here to an apology or to apologetics should be understood as references to a *projected* work or plan; I will not use *"Apologie"* as a title, since Pascal never used it and since such a work does not exist.[3]

[3]Edouard Morot-Sir pointed out the absence of the term "apologie" in Pascal in "Du Nouveau sur Pascal," *Romance Notes* 18 (1977): 272–79. Domna Stanton makes the same point in "Pascal's Fragmentary Thoughts: Dis-order and Its Overdetermination," *Semiotica* 51 (1984): 213.

Whatever Pascal's intentions were, we cannot treat the *Pensées* as a completed work, nor even as notes for a single work. Even if all fragments relating to the *Provinciales* and the *signature,* along with personal notes such as the *Mémorial* are set aside, there remains a multitude of other subjects, many of which would undoubtedly have been left out of any one completed work.[4] But this multiplicity is precisely what makes the *Pensées* unique and valuable—they are so much more than notes for one work. They are notes about things that occupied Pascal's thoughts, and they represent his thinking about a variety of subjects, including thinking. Instead of bemoaning the lack of a finished product, as so many of Pascal's friends, readers, and critics have done, we should be open to the advantages of the fragmentary nature of the *Pensées.*

One of the main advantages of having a text in fragmentary form is that, ideally, it has not been edited, cut, or rearranged. After almost three hundred years, we finally have editions which are complete and faithful to the manuscript, including paleographic (Tourneur) and photographic (Brunschvicg, Lafuma) editions as well as a concordance; Jean Mesnard's critical, chronological edition is still to come. These tools allow the reader to see exactly what Pascal wrote before subsequent deletions and changes were made by editors, many of whom thought they knew better than Pascal what he meant to say. Such an edition is perhaps unfair to Pascal, since no one would care to have scholars poring over his or her unrevised notes, but it allows us to see his thoughts on many subjects, sometimes as he first jotted them down and sometimes with the changes he made himself.

In addition, these notes, which have come to us directly as Pascal wrote them, are often brief, to the point, and on a single subject, and they thus make it easier to follow the process of his thoughts. It appears that at the moment of composition he felt no need to adapt the style or the content of such fragments to what might come before or after, to make them fit a context, to arrange them with transitions in mind; he felt no need to go through the

---

[4]Sellier believes that the early *liasses* dealing with miracles (his dossiers 30–32) would also have been left out; see his edition of the *Pensées,* p. 118, n. 7.

ordering and arranging process (referred to as *ordre,* or *méthode,* in the *Logique* and in the *De l'Esprit géométrique*), which inevitably distorts the direct expression of thought. There are many such fragments, spontaneous efforts to capture a thought in writing, that are unaffected by considerations of rhetoric, *bienséance,* or even communicability. It is these fragments, written with the first words which came to mind, which allow a reader to come in close contact with Pascal's thought, to see "a mind thinking."[5]

Pascal's efforts to arrange the fragments and to establish a detailed plan for his projected work came, for the most part, at a later stage, when he cut out individual fragments from the large sheets upon which they were written and organized them into dossiers, or *liasses* (see chapter 7 for details). His is hardly a definitive classification and it by no means includes all the fragments; Sellier sees it as "en pleine transformation" at the time of Pascal's death (see his edition of the *Pensées,* p. 18). It is impossible to know how complete these dossiers are or where the titles come from. Mesnard, in *Les* Pensées *de Pascal,*[6] and Sellier, in the introduction to his edition, make strong cases for the titles being Pascal's own, but there is still some doubt.

The dossiers are only after-the-fact arrangements and tell us little about what was in Pascal's mind as he wrote the fragments; the fragments were not revised after the classification. The reconstitution of the original sheets of the manuscript now being prepared by Pol Ernst will be much more useful in determining Pascal's train of thought, but it unfortunately will contain less than half the *Pensées.* In addition, Mesnard's efforts to establish the chronology of the individual fragments—as well as the thematic "noyaux" in which Pascal goes from a brief note to a longer, more structured development—will be of great help.[7] For the most part, however, we remain obliged to consider each individual fragment in itself and to concentrate on what Pascal actually wrote

---

[5]Morris Wm. Croll, "The Baroque Style in Prose," in J. Max Patrick, et al., eds., *Style, Rhetoric and Rhythm* (Princeton: Princeton University Press, 1966), 210.

[6]Paris: S.E.D.E.S., 1976.

[7]For more information on Mesnard's "noyaux," see his "Pourquoi les *Pensées* de Pascal se présentent-elles sous forme de fragments?" *Papers on French Seventeenth Century Literature* 19 (1983): 635–49.

rather than on what he might have written or on how he might have used what he wrote, if he had had more time.

As a result, most questions of method on a scale larger than that of the individual fragments must depend on accounts of Pascal's associates and relatives or on inference and conjecture. However, if we are concerned with the method(s) of what Pascal actually wrote, there are indications in the *Pensées* themselves, in fragments that discuss such questions as thought, language, style, knowledge, and order. These fragments can be used as a basis for a study of Pascal's thought processes and of how he expressed his thoughts, the two major aspects of what I am calling *method.* Method is defined in dictionaries of the seventeenth century as "a way of doing something,"[8] and for Pascal, in the *Pensées,* this something was the expression of his thoughts for himself and others. It necessarily includes the process through which the thoughts were developed and combined, as well as the way in which they are expressed in writing, and is precisely the relationship between thought and language mentioned at the beginning of this introduction: between thought and the language that expresses it lies a method that ties them together.

One principal goal of this study is the understanding of Pascal's style(s); just as method is a "manière pour faire quelque chose," so style is the "manière dont chacun s'exprime" (Richelet's dictionary), what Pascal calls "la manière d'écrire" (618/745). The language that expresses thought will thus be the subject of my discussions of Pascal's style, or rather of his styles, since different methods bring him to use different styles. These discussions will emphasize what Wimsatt calls "expressive forms," or devices: they "express more special forms of meaning . . . common enough to reappear frequently in certain types of thinking and hence to characterize the thinking, or the style."[9] Such forms,

[8]The main dictionaries I have used are those of Richelet (1680), Furetière (1694), and the Academy (Académie Française, 1694); see the bibliography for complete information. Richelet mentions a strict, ordered means of doing something and also a more subtle means: "Certaine maniere facile & arretée pour faire quelque chose. . . . Adresse, subtilité, moien pour faire quelque chose." These two types of methods resemble Pascal's *esprit de géométrie* and *esprit de finesse,* and his geometric and subtle styles which I will discuss in chapter 11.

[9]W. K. Wimsatt, Jr., "Style as Meaning," Chatman and Levin, eds., *Essays on the Language of Literature* (Boston: Houghton Mifflin, 1967), 372.

such stylistic features, can be seen as reflections of a writer's thought processes and are different from other stylistic features, such as rhythm, rhyme, onomatopoeia, and even metaphor, which are essential components of a writer's expressive strategy but not necessarily of his or her thought processes.

These latter stylistic features are part of the figures of traditional rhetoric, of which Pascal and Port-Royal were extremely wary, and which Pascal referred to as constituting a "tableau" rather than a portrait (481/578). They preferred logic and grammar, conception and expression, and they neglected such essential elements of traditional rhetoric as invention.[10] Logic and grammar were closely related, and there was a distinct preference for expression (style) that reflected thought as directly as possible, for style that was a "thinking out into language."[11]

To understand Pascal's methods and styles, it is necessary to understand the words he uses in discussing them in his scientific and religious writings as well as in the *Pensées.* His vocabulary often seems confusing or contradictory, but it is possible to reach a clear understanding of most words. It is true, as Hugh Davidson says, that "one of the most notable things about the *Pensées* is that the meanings and values of words shift constantly,"[12] and a word such as *sentiment* can refer to an opinion or to a mental operation. Still, the context and a comparison with similar passages usually make the meaning of a word clear. What really shifts is the *value* we attach to a word, how positive or negative a connotation we give it depending on its relation to other words in the text, and on our own associations with it. The heart may be "creux et plein d'ordure" (171/139) or an excellent means of knowledge (142/110), but this does not necessarily mean we cannot attach a clear meaning to the word in its context. Pascal

---

[10]Hugh M. Davidson, *Audience, Words and Art: Studies in Seventeenth-Century French Rhetoric* (Columbus: Ohio State University Press, 1965), 64–65.

[11]John Henry Cardinal Newman, "Literature, a Lecture in the School of Philosophy and Letters" (1858), 276–77. This is only one of many similarities between Pascal and Newman. In particular, the illative logic described in Newman's *Essay in Aid of a Grammar of Assent* (New York: Longmans, Green and Co., 1947) resembles what I call Pascal's inferential method (see Chapter 9).

[12]*Blaise Pascal,* Twayne's World Authors Series (Boston: G. K. Hall, 1983), 85.

mentions this possibility of interpreting passages differently depending on context in the third *Ecrit sur la grâce* (pp. 332B, 326A; see below, chapter 6, p. 73). There are also numerous fragments of the *Pensées,* such as 289/257, where there is a question of choosing one of several possible meanings for a word.

When searching for consistent meanings for some of these words, it is helpful to consult the logic and grammar, written by Pascal's close associates at Port-Royal, to which he contributed perhaps more than we know (especially part three of the *Logique*)[13]. Thought, language, method, and style are treated at length in these two works, and there are numerous similarities in terminology and in content, as well as some common examples and illustrations which become obvious as we compare them. I will refer to Port-Royal's terminology often in the chapters which follow. At the risk of some repetition, an overview of their position here will make these later references easier to understand.

According to Port-Royal, the art of logic consists of "les reflexions que les hommes ont faites sur les quatre principales operations de leur esprit, *concevoir, juger, raisonner,* et *ordonner*" (p. 37). Conception is defined as the formation of ideas through which we represent things that present themselves to our minds, and *jugement* is the joining together of various ideas and, at the same time, the affirmation or denial of their logical similarity. *Jugement* is the most crucial step of the mental process, since most errors come from "faux jugemens dont on tire de mauvaises consequences" (p. 21).

The example of *jugement* given in the introduction to the *Logique* suggests that forming a *jugement* is basically the same thing as defining something by attributing qualities to it: "ayant l'idée de la terre, et l'idée de rond, j'affirme qu'elle est ronde, ou je nie qu'elle soit ronde" (p. 37). The process is the same as that of forming a sentence: "Ces jugemens sont des propositions qui

[13]Arnauld and Nicole mention Pascal's contribution in the first preliminary discourse to the *Logique,* p. 21. See Louis Marin, *La Critique du discours* (Paris: Minuit, 1975), 17–24. Jan Miel, in "Pascal, Port-Royal and Cartesian Linguistics," (*Journal of the History of Ideas* 30, 1969: 267), suggests that the ideas of the *Logique* and *Grammaire,* which Chomsky called "Cartesian linguistics," are more Pascalian than Cartesian.

sont composées de diverses parties: il faut commencer par l'explication de ces parties, qui sont principalement les Noms, les Pronoms, et les Verbes. Il est peu important d'examiner si c'est à la Grammaire ou à la Logique d'en traiter" (p. 103). *Jugement* and language are thus very similar, since both consist of joining together different elements (ideas, words) in order to attain and to express a more complete understanding.

The other two mental operations are, for Port-Royal, much less important. *Raisonnement* is the forming of a *jugement* out of several other *jugements,* that is, the forming of a syllogism by adding a third term—"La necessité du raisonnement n'est fondée que sur les bornes étroites de l'esprit humain, qui, ayant à juger de la verité ou de la fausseté d'une proposition, . . . ne le peut pas toujours faire par la consideration des idées qui la composent. . . . Il a besoin de recourir à une troisième idée" (p. 178). Port-Royal considers this easy, since most people notice any false consequences that result from faulty *raisonnements;* if the *jugement* has formed correct principles, the *raisonnement* is likely to come to the correct conclusion (pp. 177–78).

The last part of the *Logique* discusses "ordonner"—that is, the disposition of a person's thoughts on a subject in the most appropriate manner for making this subject known (p. 38)—and much of it is taken from Pascal's *De l'Esprit géométrique* (*Logique,* p. 21). *Ordonner* is basically demonstration, a "suite de plusieurs raisonnements" (p. 291), or Pascal's "art de convaincre." Port-Royal also calls this mental operation "méthode," but it is only a small part of what I call Pascal's methods; it does not necessarily concern his thought process, at least not the formation of his thoughts.[14]

It is clear in the *Logique* that Arnauld and Nicole prefer the *jugement* over the *raisonnement,* and that this preference is linked to their view of human nature ("les bornes étroites de l'esprit humain"). Pascal shares this preference, also for reasons based on

---

[14]These last four paragraphs are taken, with slight revisions, from my article, "Logic and Anti-Rhetoric in Pascal's *Pensées,*" *French Forum* 2 (1977): 22–23. The article deals with some of the same questions as this study, but I have revised several of the conclusions, especially those concerning Pascal's use of terms relating to knowledge on pp. 26–27.

his view of the human condition as fallen from a state of grandeur and happiness to one of limited knowledge and of misery. A linear chain of *raisonnements* is doomed to be inaccurate in its referentiality and therefore incomplete. The closest one can come to a true pre-Fall knowledge, where language is truly referential, is a combination of *jugements* which leads closer and closer to certainty.[15]

In part 1 of this study (chapters 1–4), I deal in more detail with terms related to knowledge. Of all these terms, *coeur* is probably the most important and is certainly the most widely discussed and diversely interpreted. Much of the difficulty in interpreting it is due to a lack of understanding of related terms. It is with these related terms that we must begin, reserving a detailed discussion of *coeur* for chapter 3. In the first chapter, I concentrate on *sentiment,* because it is related to conception and to *jugement,* and because it is a term that is almost always misunderstood. It is so intimately related to *coeur* that they are often confused and even used indiscriminately,[16] but Pascal distinguished between them carefully. In the second chapter, I discuss the principles that are formed by *sentiment,* and the related terms *fantaisie,* instinct, nature, and model. In the final chapter in part 1, I discuss reason as a general term as well as the more limited terms *raisonnement* and *esprit.*

The second part (chapters 5–7) is devoted to the methods Pascal uses in his various writings, the formation and the expression of his thought. This subject follows naturally from the discussion of the terms in the first section. I begin with Pascal's scientific works (chapter 5), then turn to the *Ecrits sur la grâce* and the *Provinciales* (chapter 6), and finally to the *Pensées* (chapter 7).

In part 3 (chapters 8–11), I discuss Pascal's styles, using the first two parts as a guide. His views on thought and its expression

[15]These ideas are developed in more detail in chapters 8, 11, and 12. See Sara E. Melzer's *Discourses of the Fall* (Berkeley: University of California Press, 1986) for a detailed study of lapsarian knowledge and language.

[16]A good example is Jean Laporte's *Le Coeur et la raison selon Pascal* (Paris: Elzévir, 1950).

suggest a certain way of writing that is related to his preference for *sentiment*—and *jugements* based on it—over *raisonnement*; the *Pensées* in particular can be analyzed from this point of view. My analysis concentrates on stylistic features that could be expected to characterize these views, especially the use of *être*, and repeated words (chapter 9), and of conjunctions (chapter 10). In chapter 11 I look at three styles in the *Pensées* in which we find these stylistic features in different combinations, and I look at how the distribution of these styles does not always reflect progress toward a projected apology as an apology is generally conceived.

In the conclusion (chapter 12) I suggest some philosophical and theoretical reasons for the way the styles are distributed, that is, for why Pascal used language in such a way as to reveal its strengths and weaknesses as he portrayed the misery and grandeur of the human condition. An appendix describes the computer programs and statistical procedures I have used in analyzing Pascal's styles.

Part I

Thought and Knowledge

1

Sentiment

An understanding of the role of *sentiment* and of how it is different from that of the heart is essential to any interpretation of the *Pensées.* First, Pascal makes it clear that *sentiment* is the most important of all mental activities, especially for his purposes in dealing with human nature and with religion. Where reason, which constitutes human greatness (628/759), is concerned, "Tout notre raisonnement se réduit à céder au sentiment" (455/530). As we will see, *sentiment* furnishes the principles upon which the reason works and is thus indispensable to any intellectual endeavor, including science. Fragment 455/530 continues to point out the difficulty in distinguishing *sentiment* from *fantaisie,* not to limit the importance of *sentiment,* but to reveal the weaknesses in human mental powers. Fragment 142/110 makes the same point—"Plût à Dieu que nous n'en [de la raison] eussions au contraire jamais besoin, et que nous connussions toutes choses par instinct et par sentiment."

Second, as we see in the last paragraph of 142/110, *sentiment* plays an essential role in religious belief—those who are persuaded by a "sentiment de coeur" are much more "légitimement persuadés" than those who have religion only "par raisonnement," since without a "sentiment de coeur," "la foi n'est qu'humaine et inutile pour le salut." This "sentiment de coeur" is not the same as *sentiment,* as will be clear later, but they are obviously very closely related.

Third, *sentiment* is intimately related to several other key concepts in the *Pensées* in addition to that of the heart. It is associated, for example, with *instinct* in 142/110, with *jugement* in 670/512 and 671/513, with the *esprit de finesse* in 670/512, with *principes* in 142/110 and 670/512, with *raison* and *raisonnement* in 455/530 and 622/751 (and by opposition in many others), with prophecy in 360/328, and with faith and religion in general in fragments such as 142/110 and 661/821. The same associations are found in the various uses of the verb *sentir,* and some of them are found in certain uses of the noun *sens.*[1]

In spite of its importance, *sentiment* has never been the object of a rigorous study. Some critics have neglected it; others have confused it with *coeur* so that, even when passages are interpreted carefully, it is hard to know where *coeur* stops and *sentiment* begins; others have associated it with sentimentality, or relegated it to the realm of faith, thus neglecting its essential intellectual role; none has studied all the different ways the term is used in the *Pensées.*[2]

Dom Michel Jungo, for example, in his *Le Vocabulaire de Pascal,* devotes a section to *coeur* but mentions *sentiment* only in passing: "Le sentiment lui aussi connaît."[3] He does mention an "intellectualisation de *coeur,*" however, and an "appréhension immédiate, intuitive, des principes de toute connaissance," but he never specifies the role of *sentiment.*

In a similar way, J. Cruickshank mentions an "innate acquaintance with certain general principles"[4] that applies perfectly to *sentiment* (142/110, 670/512), but he says of *sentiment* only that it, along with *instinct,* is associated with *coeur.* Thomas Harrington, whose *Vérité et méthode dans les* Pensées *de Pascal* contains many insightful observations about Pascal's method and epistemology, never defines *sentiment* and confuses it with *coeur* and with *sentiment de coeur.* His "Pascal et la philosophie" describes *sentiment* as "notre seul critère de vérité," but still does not attempt to define the term carefully.[5]

A much more rigorous approach to Pascal's use of the word

---

[1]Association does not imply synonymy but rather common procedures, origins or goals. For example, *sentiment* as a mental operation can work within *coeur,* form *principes,* or reach conclusions similar to those of *instinct.* The rest of part one will make these distinctions clearer.

[2]A good indication of the difficulty of interpreting *sentiment* is the variety of ways the term has been translated. In Krailsheimer's translation (Penguin), for example, we find the following words, and other related ones, to render passages containing *sentiment:* realization; feeling; intuition; moving their hearts; persistent inward sense; sentient beings; perception; instinct; opinion; heartfelt.

[3]Paris: Editions d'Autrey, 1950, 115.

[4]"Knowledge and Belief in Pascal's Apology," in J. C. Ireson, et al., eds., *Studies . . . Presented to H. W. Lawton* (Manchester: Manchester University Press, 1968), 98.

[5]Paris: Vrin, 1972. "Pascal et la philosophie," *Méthodes chez Pascal* (Paris: P.U.F., 1979), 38.

sentiment is found in Pierre Dumonceaux's *Langue et sensibilité au XVIIe siècle.*[6] Dumonceaux analyzes carefully Pascal's use of the word in its sense of opinion ("mon sentiment," for example), with specific references to the *Provinciales,* but he never treats *sentiment* as a mental operation ("*le* sentiment"). The distinction between *sentiment* as opinion and as mental operation is essential and must be kept in mind as we compare fragments in which the word appears. It is useful to adapt the terminology of Hugh Davidson in *The Origins of Certainty,* where *coeur* is a "power," within which *le sentiment* functions as an "operation," forming *sentiments* as "products."[7]

These distinctions will be clearer in chapter 3, but for now they can help us avoid some of the confusions evident in the works mentioned above. Alberto Caturelli's simple statement in *En el corazón de Pascal* may seem self-evident, but it makes a point that many critics have neglected or failed to make explicit: "Si existe un 'sentimiento' del corazón, el sentimiento no es el corazón";[8] and I might add, if there exists a "sentiment de (du) coeur," it is not the same as *sentiment.*

Some critics have dealt with *sentiment* separately, but associated it with the modern meaning of sentimentality and emotional feeling, neglecting Pascal's insistence that it is intellectual and certain (142/110). Elizabeth Moles, in "Three Categories of Intelligence in Pascal" interprets "on les sent plutôt qu'on ne les voit" (670/512) as "emphasizing feeling as opposed to analytical power."[9] Jacques Morel, in "Réflexions sur le sentiment pascalien," describes *sentiment* as a "conscience . . . d'un contact immédiat et durable avec un objet d'affection ou de sentiment," which leaves room for an intellectual operation, but he then continues to speak of an "irruption de l'irrationnel," of "heureux mirages du sentiment."[10] Even Davidson's excellent discussions

---

[6]Geneva: Droz, 1975.

[7]Hugh M. Davidson, *The Origins of Certainty* (Chicago: University of Chicago Press, 1979), 43–45. Pierre Magnard makes a similar point in "Pascal dialecticien," in *Pascal présent* (Clermont-Ferrand: G. de Bussac, 1962), 260: "Si le mot 'coeur' désigne une faculté, le sentiment en est l'opération."

[8]Córdoba, Argentina: U. Nacional de Córdoba, 1970, 13.

[9]*Australian Journal of French Studies* 8 (1971): 264.

[10]*Revue des Sciences Humaines* 97 (1967): 24, 27.

of Pascal's "means and meanings" do not warn the modern reader sufficiently against allowing such expressions as "the sentimental origins of rational certainty" (*Origins of Certainty,* p. 10) or such words as *feel* and *feeling* to detract from Pascal's conception of *sentiment* as an intellectual operation.

Most critics, however, even if they have not undertaken an exhaustive study of Pascal's use of *sentiment,* have agreed to see in it a means of acquiring knowledge as well as faith, a means characterized by immediate perception that cannot be explained in discursive language or logic. Jeanne Russier, in *La Foi selon Pascal,* realizes that *sentiment* plays a role in our perception of facts and ideas as well as of God, and that "le savoir entier repose donc sur le sentiment."[11] Jean Laporte treats *sentiment* in a similar way, though he remains vague about the respective roles of *coeur* and *sentiment;* he describes the latter as a "connaissance très ferme encore qu'immédiate" which "ne doit rien en elle-même au discours ni à l'analyse" (p. 57), as the source of one's social, mental (moral, esthetic, scientific), and religious life (p. 67).

At about the same time as these two standard works, the lesser known works of José Perdomo García reach similar conclusions and offer many insightful views. His *La Teoría del conocimiento en Pascal* is a very useful study of Pascal's methods, of his views on knowledge and how to communicate it, as is his "El corazón como fuente de conocimiento en Pascal" concerning the heart and *sentiment.* He characterizes the latter as immediate and different from any purely rational (i.e., discursive) means of knowledge.[12]

Later scholarship has refined these general views of the role of *sentiment.* Louis Marin, in his *La Critique du discours,* discusses a "logique . . . du sentiment" which is "vécue," not "pensée," and associates it with "idée," as the term is used in the Port-Royal *Logique.*[13] From a different critical perspective, Jean

---

[11]Paris: P.U.F., 1949, 426.

[12]*La teoría del conocimiento en Pascal: Filosofía crítica Pascaliana* (Madrid: Consejo Superior de Investigaciones Científicas, 1956). "El corazón come fuente de conocimiento en Pascal," *Revista de Ideas Estéticas* 11 (1953): 260.

[13]Paris: Minuit, 1975, 367, 199.

Mesnard, in his *Les* Pensées *de Pascal* (1976), points out that *sentiment* "a un sens tout intellectuel," that it is "une sorte d'intuition immédiate opposée et préalable à un 'discours' rationnel qui se déroule dans le temps et use de médiations" (p. 88). Even here, however, the confusion between *coeur* and *sentiment* remains—*sentiment* is described as a "faculté par laquelle le coeur procède aux principes" and the coeur as "la faculté des principes" (p. 88).

Harcourt Brown brings the perspective of a historian of science to his chapter on Pascal in *Science and the Human Comedy.* In a discussion which, like that of Marin, takes into account Pascal's interest in science and in logic (the authors of the Port-Royal *Logique* associate *sentiment* with *idée* and with *conception*), Brown writes that *sentiment* refers to "the immediate perception, the image, sound, sensation, or other datum of consciousness," and that it does not indicate a feeling or emotion.[14] Domna Stanton, in *The Aristocrat as Art,* also warns against associating *sentiment* with "an emotion of the natural self," though she translates "sentiment naturel" as "natural feeling." For her, working from the perspective of the *honnête homme, sentiment naturel* refers to "the hyperacuity of superior beings."[15]

The importance of consciousness, of conception, is emphasized in Edouard Morot-Sir's *La Métaphysique de Pascal,* probably the best brief treatment of Pascal's epistemology. He describes *sentiment* as a "conscience immédiate de vérités ou de valeurs," whether they be ideas (*vérités*), sensations, passions, or imaginations (*sensations,* or *valeurs senties*). He also makes the essential point that *sentiment* is not only opposed to reason, to rational, discursive proof, but to discursive *language.* Words can be "immédiatement sentis" by *sentiment,* but they also demand "médiation" and step-by-step sequence, which is not within the domain of *sentiment.*[16]

This characteristic of human language—that individual

[14]Toronto: Toronto University Press, 1976, 65.
[15]New York: Columbia University Press, 1980, 202.
[16]Paris: P.U.F., 1973, 106, 108.

words can be understood in an immediate way, but that they also exist in combination with others—suggests an approach to understanding *sentiment* (and other words) as Pascal used it. All ideas associated with a word need to be present,[17] and we must always be aware of the context in which they are used. Dictionaries from the period provide most of these associated ideas, but it is also necessary to study words which Pascal and other writers of his time used in conjunction with the word in question, as well as the contexts in which they used them; texts written by writers known to have intellectual connections with Pascal are especially useful.

The context in which words are used in a specific text is now easy to determine, thanks to computer-generated concordances.[18] Still, we must have some framework within which to establish categories, so that we can have a meaningful way of grouping similar uses and of distinguishing them from others. This is especially important when dealing with a fragmentary work such as the *Pensées,* since the context of a word is often extremely brief, and words used in a similar way often occur in several different parts of the text.

In the case of the *Pensées,* and particularly in the case of terms dealing with knowledge and belief, at least two such frameworks are available.[19] The first is Davidson's power-operation-product terminology (mentioned above), since it is important to know whether Pascal is writing about a mental operation or its result, whether some operations and their products are associated with or opposed to others, and if a particular operation is a subdivision of a larger power. Such distinctions are particularly important for an understanding of *sentiment* in the *Pensées,* since it can refer either to a product (opinion, impression) or an operation (function, faculty).

---

[17]This is the problem Pascal mentions concerning the *esprit de finesse*—"les principes sont dans l'usage commun" but "si déliés et en si grand nombre qu'il est presque impossible qu'il n'en échappe" (670/512).

[18]Hugh M. Davidson and Pierre H. Dubé have prepared concordances to the *Pensées* (Ithaca, N.Y.: Cornell University Press, 1975) and to the *Provinciales* (New York: Garland, 1980).

[19]A chart grouping these terms within these two frameworks can be found at the end of chapter 4.

The second framework is the familiar Pascalian theory of the three orders—*corps, esprit, charité*—to which Davidson applies his terminology of power, operation, and product. *Sentiment* and other terms concerning knowledge can be used to refer to physical objects and bodily needs (I); to ideas, imaginations, passions, truths, and so on (II); or to God, revealed truth, and faith (III). Once we understand within which order, or domain, a term is being used, it is much easier to understand what sort of knowledge is involved. It is precisely the confusion between the role of *sentiment* in orders II and III that has led some critics to associate it with faith alone, or with something irrational, sentimental, or both. A passage from the Port-Royal *Logique* will illustrate how this framework of the three orders can be applied to *sentiment;* we will also see how complex the term can be. The passage will serve as an example for further distinctions that can be made and provide some preliminary definitions.

As an example of the confusion that can arise when people pay more attention to words than to the things they represent, chapter 2 of part 1 discusses several meanings of *sentiment:*

> Il y a de même beaucoup d'équivoques dans les mots de *sens* & de *sentimens,* lors même qu'on ne prend ces mots que pour quelqu'un des cinq sens corporels. Car il se passe ordinairement trois choses en nous lorsque nous usons de nos sens. . . . La 1. est qu'il se fait de certains mouvemens dans les organes corporels. . . . La 2. que ces mouvemens donnent occasion à notre ame de concevoir quelque chose. . . . La 3. est le jugement que nous faisons de ce que nous voyons. . . . La premiere de ces trois choses est uniquement dans notre corps. Les deux autres sont seulement en notre ame, quoiqu'à l'occasion de ce qui se passe dans notre corps. Et néanmoins nous comprenons toutes les trois, quoique si differentes sous le même nom de *sens* & de *sentiment.* (p. 84)

The first meaning is sense perception (*sentiment* is of course related to *sens*) and takes place in the first order, in our bodies. The second is conception, or perception, and takes place in the second order, in the mind (*âme*). The third is judgment, based on perceptions (in turn based on sense perceptions), and takes place in the second order also.

The framework of the three orders helps to distinguish the first usage from the other two, and to show that the first usage is not a mental operation although it is a necessary preliminary. To distinguish between the other two, the examples and explanations given in the *Logique* make it clear that judgment is one step beyond conception, since it is based on conceptions. Conception is a simple movement of the brain, whereas judgment is a decision made about two or more conceptions (ideas). In another passage from the *Logique,* these terms are defined more carefully—*concevoir* is "la simple vue que nous avons des choses qui se présentent à notre esprit . . . et la forme par laquelle nous nous représentons ces choses, s'appelle *idée.*" *Juger* is an action "joignant ensemble diverses idées" (p. 37).

If we consult dictionaries of the period, we find the same distinction. Furetière is the best example; aside from references to hunting and to the passions, two uses which do not occur in the *Pensées,* his two definitions of *sentiment* are "la premiere propriété de l'animal d'avoir des organes propres à recevoir les differentes impressions des objets," and "se dit figurement en choses spirituelles, des diverses veues dont l'ame considere les choses, qui luy en font concevoir de differentes idées ou opinions." In short, there are *impressions* made by the senses on the mind, and *opinions, jugements* (Furetière uses "concevoir" here, where Port-Royal would use "juger") made about these impressions; the two are obviously related, but distinct. Other dictionaries give similar definitions, with "impression" and "opinion" occurring regularly.

These three uses of *sentiment* (sense perception, impression, judgment) account for approximately half the occurrences of the word in the *Pensées;* for the other half, it is necessary to return to the first framework, that of power-operation-product. In all of these first three uses, *sentiment* refers to a *product* of some mental operation, whereas in other occurrences it refers to the operation; in such cases it is often preceded by the definite article: *le sentiment.* Richelet calls this operation the "faculté de sentir," the Academy "la fonction des sens" (we must interpret "sens" here as the *Logique* suggests, as what happens in the *âme* as well as in the *corps*).

As Pascal uses *sentiment,* there is one other distinction to make—that between operation in the sense of a mental faculty, and in the sense of functioning, of mental awareness, that is, between the faculty that allows something to happen and the something that actually happens. In the latter case, it is usually *sentiment* of something, not just *le sentiment* in the abstract.

It has taken this long to get to Pascal's use of *sentiment,* because it is important to establish an approach to the study of such a term, to look at the variety of the term's uses current in his lifetime, and to establish the existence of a well-established philosophical, logical vocabulary that included the term *sentiment.* The references to the Port-Royal *Logique* are of great importance because it was written while Pascal was writing the *Pensées* by people with whom he was in close contact and with whom he discussed certain sections. It seems hard to doubt that he had a similar understanding of the term.

There are, then, four basic ways to understand *sentiment* in the *Pensées*—as a product, (1) an impression on either the senses or the mind and (2) an opinion about the impressions one has had; as an operation, (3) the mental operation itself and (4) the functioning of that operation, that is, awareness or consciousness. To be complete, we have only to make room for the third order in this scheme, for the operation that produces faith instead of human truths, that causes belief instead of knowledge. There is now room for all three orders, as well as for both operations and products. Some examples are in order:

1a. impression on the senses—"Le sentiment du feu, cette chaleur qui nous affecte d'une manière toute autre que l'attouchement" (565/686).

1b. impression on the mind—"le sentiment intérieur qui leur reste de leur grandeur passée" (240/208); "il faut un sens bien délicat et bien net pour les sentir et juger droit et juste, selon ce sentiment" (670/512).

2. opinion—"on doit avoir ce sentiment par un principe d'intérêt humain" (681/427).

3. mental operation—"plût à Dieu . . . que nous connussions toutes choses par instinct et par sentiment" (142/110); "ceux qui sont accoutumés à juger par le sentiment ne comprennent rien aux choses de raisonnement" (622/751).
4. functioning—"le sentiment n'en [de la manière d'agir de l'esprit de finesse] appartient qu'à peu d'hommes" (670/512); "il faut avoir perdu tout sentiment pour être dans l'indifférence de savoir ce qui en est" (681/427).

It is not always possible with absolute certainty to assign an occurrence of *sentiment* in the *Pensées* to one category. Sometimes there is not enough context, as in 531/646, where the word *sentiment* appears alone at the beginning. In other instances, the difference is often slight between the operation and the awareness of its functioning, as in 689/437: "On n'est pas misérable sans sentiment." In particular, it is sometimes difficult to distinguish between the second and third orders in fragments where Pascal talks about the opinions of Christians—"Pour savoir si un sentiment est d'un père," (614/733)—or where he discusses knowledge and belief at the same time: "il faut donc mettre notre foi dans le sentiment" (661/821). Still, it is clear that Pascal is talking about a certain process (operation) and a product which involve our senses, mind, and faith. This is brought out even more clearly in the use of *sentiments* in the plural, and in the use of *sentir* and of *sens.*

As we might expect, the plural form *sentiments* is used only with the sense of impression or opinion; there is only one operation involved, and it makes no sense to refer to it in the plural. There is one example (630/764) in which *sentiments* has the meaning of "affections, passions" (Academy) rather than of more intellectual impressions, but this fragment is usually attributed to Mme de Sablé.[20] That this is the only example in the *Pensées* of *sentiments* with this meaning could be an additional reason for attributing the fragment to her.

With three exceptions, all occurrences of *sentiments* deal with the second order. In 565/686, however, it is a question of

[20]See the notes in the editions of the *Pensées* by Sellier and Le Guern.

sentiments of heat being "le mouvement de quelques globules," and in 175/142 and 759/931 it is a matter of Christian *sentiments,* such as being "pleins de sentiments" to love God (175/142).

The distinction between opinions and impressions is not always clear. There are only three fragments in which *sentiments* refers to what are obviously the considered opinions of others on specific subjects—559/680 (Montaigne), 745/915 (Jesuits), and 791/954 (Arnauld). In most of the other cases, it is definitely a matter of products of *sentiment,* but it is often hard to tell whether they are carefully considered and expounded opinions (as in 559/680, 745/915, and 791/954), or rather convictions, states of mind, or intuitive impressions. For example, 683/430 takes up the familiar theme of the misery and grandeur of man; it refers to "les sentiments bas que les hommes ont naturellement d'eux-mêmes" and "ces sentiments de grandeur, qui sont aussi naturels à l'homme." In an English translation, we might refer to "low *opinion* of themselves" and to *feelings* of grandeur," but we have to assume that Pascal used the same word in both instances for a reason. A *sentiment-opinion* is not a carefully reasoned out decision; it is a *jugement* which combines two impressions, or ideas, and is, according to the Port-Royal *Logique,* the source of most of our errors (pp. 21, 177). *Sentiments* are not verifiable through other mental processes because, as in the *esprit de finesse,* the principles involved are too numerous. We cannot prove that people retain a certain grandeur from their past condition, but the lack of proof did not keep Pascal from being certain about the existence of the remnants of this grandeur—"Quelque impuissance où nous soyons de le prouver par raison, cette impuissance ne conclut autre chose que la faiblesse de notre raison, mais non pas l'incertitude de toutes nos connaissances" (142/110).

Of the fifty-seven occurrences of the various forms of *sentir* listed in Davidson and Dubé's concordance—these include several variants, and one instance of *sent* (230/199) which is read as *sont* by Tourneur—only one does not involve the production of an impression (product) by *sentiment.* This exception is found in a fragment merely attributed to Pascal (Lafuma 1000) and is thus probably not in his own words. There are examples of all three orders—"ces divers corps que nous sentons" (164/131); "le peuple est vain, quoique ses opinions soient saines, parce qu'il n'en sent pas la vérité" (127/93); "Dieu se fera sentir à tous" (360/328). It is generally people, or their *sens, âme,* or *coeur,* who "feel" such things as truth, their condition, principles, the passage of time, or (less frequently) physical objects or God's truth. There are no examples of feeling emotions or anything sentimental.

The word *sens* is used in several ways in the *Pensées.* Of 107 occurrences, most refer either to the five senses or to the meaning of a text or author. There are eight occurrences, however, of "le sens" as a mental operation which is usually associated with *jugement* and characterized by drawing consequences. It is difficult to pin down its exact meaning, however, until it is made clear how Pascal used such terms as *jugement, raison, raisonnement, finesse, géométrie,* and *justesse.* I will return to *sens* in chapter 4, after a discussion of these other terms. After all, we cannot expect an easy definition when Richelet lists the following words in his definition of *sens—jugement; raison; esprit; intelligence; pénétration; pensée; sentiment.*

In summary, *sentiment* is used in four basic ways: two in the area of operation and two in the area of product; all three orders are involved. With the reservations expressed above, we can classify the thirty-six occurrences of *sentiment* in the following way (note that 142/110-1, for example, identifies the first occurrence of *sentiment* in fragment 142/110):

OPERATION

1. Operation

Order II: 142/110-2, 455/530-1, 455/530-2, 531/646, 622/751-1, 622/751-2, 658/814-1, 658/814-2, 658/814-3, 661/821-1, 671/513

Order III: 142/110-3, 142/110-4, 360/328, 661/821-2

PRODUCT

1. Impression

Order I: 565/686

Order II: 107/73, 142/110-1, 164/131, 240/208, 455/530-3, 455/530-4, 670/512-1

Order III: 210/179, 742/913

2. Functioning

Order II: 670/512-2, 681/427-1, 689/437

2. Opinion

Order II: 168/136 (var), 590/712, 681/427-2, 707/470, 745/915, 812/991

Order III: 614/733, 627/758

There are eighteen occurrences as operation and eighteen as product. There is only one occurrence in order I, but there are twenty-seven in order II and eight in order III. Twenty-eight of the thirty-six occurrences refer to a mental operation or to an impression on the senses or the mind, and only eight to an already formed opinion about these impressions; furthermore, none of these eight occurs in the definitive text of the preliminary dossiers which Pascal constituted.

Sentiment, then, refers to an operation and to the product of that operation. It is an operation that involves the reception of sensual stimuli and of intellectual impressions, and the formation of impressions and opinions about them. It also receives divine stimuli, and forms impressions and opinions about them. Such an operation obviously plays a crucial role in the search for knowledge. Louis Marin makes an important point in commenting on the Port-Royal *Logique* when he associates *sentiment* with *idée* (*La Critique du discours,* pp. 198–99). In the *Logique,* what I have called "impression" is basically the same as *idée:* "On appelle concevoir la simple vue que nous avons des choses qui se présentent à notre esprit. . . . Et la forme par laquelle nous nous représentons ces choses, s'appelle idée" (p. 37). What I have called "opinion" is essentially what the *Logique* calls *jugement*—"joignant ensemble diverses idées" (p. 37; see also p. 84).

Seen in this light, *sentiment* is nothing less than the way people form ideas about the physical (and spiritual) universe and the way they combine ideas to reach an immediate understanding of the combination without proceeding through discursive reasoning (what the *Logique* calls *raisonnement* and opposes directly to *sentiment*).[21] In a fragment on the *esprit de finesse,* where *sens* seems to be synonymous with *sentiment,* Pascal says that "il faut un sens bien délicat et bien net pour les [the *principes* of the *esprit de finesse*] sentir et juger droit et juste, selon ce sentiment, sans pouvoir le plus souvent le démontrer par ordre comme en géométrie" (670/512). First, we have to have a *sentiment,* or idea, of the principles involved; then, we can make a *jugement* by combining these principles. Normally, we cannot prove (*démontrer par ordre,* i.e., *raisonner*) what we have *senti.*

Sentiment acts quickly—"il agit en un instant et toujours est prêt à agir" (661/821)—and grasps concepts immediately—"Ceux qui sont accoutumés à juger par le sentiment . . . veulent d'abord pénétrer d'une vue" (622/751). *Sentiments* are natural, and we accept them without constantly questioning them—"Nous les sentons naturellement en nous" (164/131). *Sentiment* also receives religion as well as sensual stimuli. There are those "à qui Dieu donne la religion par sentiment de coeur" (142/110), and those who can prophesy, that is, speak of God through a "sentiment intérieur et immédiat" (360/328). We should note, however, that in these two fragments—the only ones in which Pascal speaks of *sentiment* as a religious operation—*sentiment* is qualified either by the addition of "de coeur" or of "intérieur."

---

[21]*Logique,* p. 37, and part III, passim.

As Maria Vamos points out, in *Pascal's* Pensées *and the Enlightenment: The Roots of a Misunderstanding* (Geneva: Studies in Voltaire and the Eighteenth Century, 1972, 95), the Port-Royal edition of the *Pensées* equated *sentiment* with "intelligence vive et lumineuse." The editors showed a poor understanding of the overall meaning of the fragment (142/110), but they did seem to understand how Pascal used *sentiment.* Their substitution of the operations *sentiment* and *raisonnement* for the powers *coeur* and *raison* shows an attempt at clarification, at more precise vocabulary, and an understanding of the differences between the two means of attaining knowledge.

Pascal's associate at Port-Royal, collaborator on the *Provinciales* and editor of the Port-Royal edition of the *Pensées,* Pierre Nicole, uses similar terminology in his Preface to the *Recueil de poésies chrétiennes et diverses* (1671): "Il faut ne concevoir pas seulement par des raisonnements abstraits et métaphysiques, en quoi consiste la beauté des vers; il la faut sentir et la comprendre tout d'un coup, et en avoir une idée si vive. . . . Cette idée et cette *impression vive* [italics mine], qui s'appelle *sentiment* ou *goût. . . .*" This preface is often attributed to La Fontaine and is quoted from the Clarac edition of his *Oeuvres diverses* [Paris: Gallimard, 1958), 782. Nicole also insists on *sentiment* as an impression—but a completely intellectual one—in his "Dissertation contre le P. Hilarion, 'Sur les pensées imperceptibles.'" See Gilbert Chinard, *En lisant Pascal* (Geneva: Droz, 1948), 127–28.

He is generally quite careful to distinguish how we know God from how we know worldly and intellectual things; the humiliation of human reason that allows us to open ourselves to the mysteries of Christianity is a constant theme in the *Pensées.*[22]

This is all one can say directly about *sentiment.* Its other characteristics can be determined only through a study of related terms. For example, there is much in 670/512 concerning the *esprit de finesse* that seems applicable to *sentiment,* but Pascal does not say so directly. To understand all the ramifications of the term, and of others, it is necessary to look at terms to which it is related—to use what one knows about *sentiment* to interpret the other terms, and then in turn use what one has learned about the other terms to arrive at a more complete understanding of *sentiment.* This process is not the circular reasoning criticized in 457/527, whereby we might use A as an example to prove B, and then later use B to "prove" A. Rather, we find out all we can about A (*sentiment*), and then use that information to understand B (other terms). The information we learn about B can then be used to find out more about A, since it is not being used to prove what one already knew about A but to go beyond that original information.

---

[22]The expression "sentiment du coeur" was common at Port-Royal, especially in the writings of Saint-Cyran and of Le Maistre de Sacy. See Didier Anzieu's note to 680/423, in the Tourneur-Anzieu edition of the *Pensées,* I, 261, n.1.

2

Principles, Instinct, Nature, Custom, and Models

Of all the terms related to *sentiment, principe* is the most fundamental, partly because of the nature of principles in general. Richelet's dictionary refers to them as "êtres simples, premiere matiere, source, cause, premiers éléments, commencements, fonds," and they always serve as points of departure, as bases, as beginnings without which there is no continuation. Everything else depends on them, and they determine one's point of view. *Principe* is also a fundamental term because of the importance Pascal accorded to principles in his scientific and mathematical writings as well as in the *Pensées.* Before looking at why they are essential to his presentations of human nature and of religion, however, it is important to see how closely he related them to *sentiment.*

I showed in the preceding chapter that *sentiment* is the operation that receives mental impressions and that it forms opinions. It is precisely the operation within the "power" of the *coeur* which furnishes our "connaissances des premiers principes"—"le coeur sent qu'il y a trois dimensions dans l'espace. . . . Les principes se sentent" (142/110). It is also the operation that makes possible the knowledge gained through the "esprit de finesse." Basing the differences between the *esprits* of *finesse* and *géométrie* on the differences between their principles, Pascal says of the principles of the former that "il faut un sens bien délicat et bien net pour les sentir et juger droit et juste, selon ce sentiment" (670/512).

Principles are thus what *sentiment* receives and forms, its impressions and its opinions. Just as *sentiment* receives individual impressions and also combines them to form opinions, so a principle can be something individual (though usually abstract and complex), such as "espace, temps, mouvement, nombres," or something combined, such as "les nombres sont infinis" (142/

110). When a principle is individual, it is similar to what the Port-Royal *Logique* calls conception, and when combined, to what the *Logique* calls *jugement* (p. 37); both conception and *jugement* are included in the *Logique*'s definitions of *sentiment* (p. 84).

In most of Pascal's discussions of principles, especially in his scientific works, they are combinations, or *jugements,* which form the basis for the drawing of consequences. In his letters to Père Noël and to Le Pailleur and in the *Esprit géométrique,* he uses *principes* interchangeably with *axiomes.* For example, "ce que nous appelons *principes* ou *axiomes*" are propositions which are such that "il paraisse si clairement et si distinctement de soi-même aux sens ou à la raison, suivant qu'il est sujet à l'un ou à l'autre, que l'esprit n'a aucun moyen de douter de sa certitude" (p. 201A). Similarly, in the *Esprit géométrique* he speaks of the necessity of proposing "des principes ou axiomes évidents pour prouver la chose dont il s'agit" (p. 356B), an activity which comes between defining and proving, as it does in the letters to Noël and Le Pailleur; he then goes on to use the term *axiomes,* which is clearly the same as *principes.*[1] In both cases, the conception of the idea and its definition (giving it a name) come first; as Pascal wrote to Le Pailleur, "d'abord nous concevons l'idée d'une chose; ensuite nous donnons un nom à cette idée, c'est-à-dire nous la définissons; et enfin nous cherchons si cette chose est véritable ou fausse" (p. 210A). It is clear that the resulting principles are combinations of (carefully defined) ideas or conceptions.

Still, we need to make a judgment about the truth or falseness of these principles. In the same paragraph of the letter to Noël quoted above, the discussion of what constitutes a principle is preceded by a warning not to "porter un jugement décisif de la négative ou de l'affirmative d'une proposition" unless the proposition is a clearly evident principle or a deduced consequence; and the discussion is followed by "nous portons un jugement décisif des choses de la première sorte" [clear principles or demonstrated consequences]. This seems to be what Pascal means

[1]This passage is the basis for the extended discussion of definitions in the *Logique,* pp. 320–23 and 333–35; see also p. 21, where this connection is made explicit.

when he says that "même les propositions géométriques deviennent sentiments, car la raison rend les sentiments naturels" (531/646). Once a *jugement* has become a *sentiment,* that is, something received by the mind immediately and without doubt (naturally), then it can become the basis for other *jugements.*

Normally, however, these principles do not become such a natural part of our minds; they remain axioms which we have made a conscious effort to remember (although memory, according to 531/646, can also become a *sentiment*) and which serve as the basis for *raisonnements,* for the drawing of consequences (the formation of propositions). Pascal distinguishes carefully between our powers of forming principles (*coeur*) and of reasoning (*raison*), and between the operations within these powers (*sentiment* and *raisonnement*)—"Nous connaissons la vérité non seulement par la raison mais encore par le coeur. C'est de cette dernière sorte que nous connaissons les premiers principes et c'est en vain que le raisonnement, qui n'y a point de part, essaie de les combattre" (142/110). I will return to *coeur* and *raison* in more detail in the next two chapters, but it is already clear in this fragment that they represent general powers involved in the search for truth, and that *sentiment* and *raisonnement* work within them, respectively, the former forming *sentiments* and *principes,* the latter *propositions* and *preuves*—"il est aussi inutile et aussi ridicule que la raison demande au coeur des preuves de ses premiers principes pour vouloir y consentir, qu'il serait ridicule que le coeur demandât à la raison un sentiment de toutes les propositions qu'elle démontre pour vouloir les recevoir" (142/110).

Raisonnement is the operation through which the mind forms logical chains leading from principles to propositions and, if necessary, to a carefully ordered series of propositions, that is, a proof (this latter is what the *Logique* calls "ordre," or "méthode"; p. 38). It is obviously the operation of the scientific method, of the *esprit de géométrie,* which is characterized by "démontrer par ordre," by "progrès de raisonnement," by "raisonner sur des principes connus" (670/512). It is infallible, once we agree on principles and are careful with definitions and with substituting definitions for words that have been defined—"les principes étant accordés, . . . la force invincible des conséquences ne peut manquer d'avoir tout son effet" (p. 356B).[2]

If the *raisonnement* leads to a false conclusion, then we must go back to the principles, which were formed by *sentiment* ("Tout notre raisonnement se réduit à céder au sentiment"; 455/530). We have either omitted a principle or used a faulty one. The problem of omitted principles is the one at which Pascal arrives at the end of his famous meditation on the two infinities (230/199)—we cannot know all the principles, nor can we know either the whole or all the parts. He goes into more detail in 670/512: "il faut avoir la vue bien nette pour voir tous les principes, et *ensuite* [italics mine] l'esprit juste pour ne pas raisonner faussement sur des principes connus" (he qualifies the use of *voir* in the following paragraph—"on les sent plutôt qu'on ne les voit"). Unfortunately, the "principes sont si déliés et en si grand nombre, qu'il est presque impossible qu'il n'en échappe. Or l'omission d'un principe mène à l'erreur." The problem of how to keep all the principles in mind, how to consider all aspects of a question, was an essential consideration for Pascal as he developed his methods and will be discussed in more detail in part 2.

If principles are found to be faulty, it is usually because they are made up of a combination of ideas (which we have defined) and are thus subject to error if we make an unjustified combination. This is especially true when we deal with principles more open to differences of opinion than the axioms of mathematics and physics. The example given by Pascal in the letter to Noël ("si à choses égales on ajoute choses égales, les touts seront égaux"; p. 201A) concerns the ideas of equality and of the addition of numbers, concepts about which there is little argument. If we try, however, to combine the ideas of earth and of roundness (the example given in the introduction to the *Logique*, p. 37), there will be considerable argument—even if we agree on definitions, how do we decide whether the combination is true or false?

However, there is another type of principle, made up of in-

---

[2]The basis of Pascal's argument with Noël is that they cannot agree on principles and definitions; see p. 203B. Pascal, like Arnauld and Nicole, thought that most faulty logic was due to the absence of good principles, not to bad combinations of them through the *raisonnement;* see part 3 of the *Logique.*

dividual ideas, independent of any combination.[3] In 142/110 Pascal gives "espace, temps, mouvement, nombres" as examples of "premiers principes," and in 182/149 he speaks of "quelque grand principe de grandeur" and of "un grand principe de misère." These principles can form the basis of *jugements,* that is, they can be combined with other ideas or principles and, in combination, be judged true or false. Once we understand what time is, we can judge how much has elapsed, regardless of whether we judge "par fantaisie" or with a watch (457/534). Similarly, for example, we can apply a knowledge of the principle of grandeur to people's actions to decide whether there is any grandeur in people, or at least in individuals. This is the same process which Pascal discusses in 486/585–86, where we have a model to which we can compare houses, songs, poetry, women, and so on. With this principle or model in mind, it should be a simple matter to compare something to it; if the "certain rapport" between model and thing is positive, then we like the thing and find the woman beautiful.

A problem exists, however, like the one I pointed out earlier concerning principles that are a combination of ideas: just as we agree on the principles (axioms) of mathematics but not always on those of other subjects, so we know the "objet" or model for geometry or medicine, but not the "modèle naturel," the "objet de la poésie" (486/586). In other words, we know what the principles of geometry and medicine are, but not those of poetry. In terms of the example concerning time in 457/534, a watch provides firm principles upon which to base *jugements,* but *fantaisie* is an opinion with no basis. It can look like a justifiable opinion (it is "semblable et contraire au sentiment"; 455/530) but will not bear scrutiny.

Pascal insists on the necessity of knowing all the principles, in 670/512, where he also makes it clear that there are some principles which precede *jugements.* These principles of the *esprit de finesse* are numerous and "déliés," and though they are "dans

[3]These principles are not made up of a combination of ideas, but neither are they necessarily simple. They can, in fact, be quite complex (time, grandeur, beauty), but they still make up fundamental, "first" principles.

l'usage commun," they are not "nets et grossiers," "ne se laissent pas ainsi [as in geometry] manier," and the result is that we cannot grasp them as we would an axiom in geometry. They are too fundamental ("les premiers principes ont trop d'évidence pour nous"; 230/199) and cannot be broken into parts that we can then arrange to form a principle. *Raisonnement* must yield to *sentiment*—the only solution is to "les sentir," and then to "juger droit et juste, selon ce sentiment, sans pouvoir le plus souvent le démontrer par ordre comme en géométrie, parce qu'on n'en possède pas ainsi les principes, et que ce serait une chose infinie de l'entreprendre."

This solution seems to have appeared to Pascal only in the midst of the composition of this fragment. The first two paragraphs, except for "sur des principes connus" at the end, are not in his hand, and the fourth paragraph ("ce qui fait donc . . . ," from which the quotation at the end of the preceding paragraph is taken) is a restatement of the first two, as if he were not satisfied with them. In the restatement, there is still a question of the difference between the two *esprits* being in their respective principles, but Pascal is more specific about how to "manier" these principles; he makes the qualification about the difference between *voir* and *sentir* mentioned above; he insists on the immediacy of "voir la chose," of "juger d'une seule vue"; and so on. Most importantly for our discussion here, he realizes that the original statement "avoir la vue bien nette pour voir tous les principes, et ensuite l'esprit juste pour ne pas raisonner faussement sur des principes connus," was not a clear description of the *esprit de finesse,* that it might be taken as applying to the workings of the *esprit de géométrie.* The first statement, "raisonner . . . sur des principes connus" is qualified in the fourth paragraph by "sans pouvoir le plus souvent le démontrer par ordre comme en géométrie," and the emphasis is placed upon forming (*sentir,* not *voir*) the principles and judging according to that *sentiment.* That is enough with this sort of principles ("tout d'un coup voir la chose, d'un seul regard et non pas par progrès de raisonnement").

Pascal refuses to establish an airtight distinction between the two *esprits,* however. The *esprit de finesse* arrives at knowledge through a "sorte de raisonnement." The mind actually passes through definitions and then through principles (here, *principes* is used in its sense of combinations of defined ideas), but it does it "tacitement, naturellement et sans art"; few people are aware of what is going on, and none can express it. As Michael Polanyi points out in *The Tacit Dimension,* the mind combines a principle, which it cannot make explicit, with an observed object, and is aware of the non-explicit principle (model) only through this process. For example, we are unable to describe all the features of someone's face, but we are able to use our tacit knowledge of these features to recognize that face.[4]

Seen in this way, then, all of what Pascal calls principles do have something in common. Most importantly, they enable us to proceed to new knowledge. Whether we combine principles with something else we come into contact with and make a judgment about the resulting combination, or whether we deal with principles which are themselves combinations of ideas and draw consequences from them, they remain the absolutely essential bases of thought. To be useful, they must be (or must become), *sentiments,* that is, impressions or opinions that have been received immediately by the mind, that have become natural. They are given ("étant donné" occurs frequently in Pascal's scientific works), and the mind receives them—in 142/110, the *coeur* wants to *recevoir* its principles; in 78/44 the wisest reason *prend* its principles; in 164/131, principles are *donnés,* be they true or false. Such direct reception—the same which characterizes the operation of *sentiment*—is obviously the only way to receive abstractions such as time and space, grandeur and misery, since we cannot prove them through the use of reason (142/110). We could say, on the other hand, that principles such as the axioms of geometry are learned, understood, penetrated, and so on (669/511, 670/512). But once they are understood, they become givens, basic data ("même les propositions géométriques deviennent sentiments"; 531/646); we cannot proceed to proofs and demonstrations unless the principles are universally accepted as something received by the mind in such a way that there can be no doubt about them. Proving propositions "par progrès de raisonnement"

[4]New York: Doubleday, 1966, 4–10.

is a different mental operation from that of receiving principles through *sentiment;* unless the latter operation has taken place, the former is impossible.

Just as *sentiment* operates in every area of the search for knowledge, so are principles to be found in all these areas. Jean Prigent sums up what Pascal has said about "la diversité des principes": "ils naissent toujours d'une expérience; épreuve intellectuelle de l'évidence en géométrie, rapport des sens en physique et dans les sciences d'observation, témoignages en histoire."[5] Thus, the senses can observe principles in the first of the three orders, the mind can receive them when it judges them to be clear or to be contained in authorized sources (history, jurisprudence, etc.),[6] and the heart can receive them (and transmit them to the mind; p. 355A) from divine sources.

It is important to note, however, that the awareness of principles always involves the mind (an awareness that Pascal and his contemporaries often call the *âme*); the mind must receive the sensual data and make sense out of it, rather than just form an impression (*sentiment*). The true principles of physics, for Pascal, are experiments ("elles sont les seuls principes de la physique"; p. 231B), and what he calls principles are hardly simple sensual observations—for example, "Je prends pour principe, que jamais un corps ne se meut par son poids, sans que son centre de gravité descende" (p. 238A). Observations of the senses are necessary in order to carry out experiments and to form principles which one's mind and other physicists can accept, but they do not constitute principles in themselves.

On the other hand, all principles are not really what we would call intellectual. The mind receives its opinions, says Pascal in the *Esprit géométrique* (pp. 355–56), through the *volonté* as well

---

[5]"La Réflexion pascalienne sur les principes," *Mélanges de littérature française offerts à monsieur René Pintard* (Strasbourg: Centre de Philologie et de Littérature Romanes de l'Université de Strasbourg, 1975), 124; see also pp. 127–28. In the same paragraph, Prigent describes principles as given and received. Davidson (*Blaise Pascal,* p. 103) also insists on the importance of principles and on their diversity.

[6]See the *Préface sur le Traité du vide,* p. 230A–B, for Pascal's distinction between disciplines based on authority and memory and those based on *raisonnement* and experiments.

as through the *entendement,* through the *coeur* as well as through the *esprit.* While the principles of the *esprit* are "vérités naturelles et connues de tout le monde," those of the *volonté* are "certains désirs naturels," and the "voie" of the *volonté* is "basse, indigne et étrangère." These desires are not simple principles, such as those of time and space or of misery and grandeur, but rather the affirmative judgment on the desirability of being happy. Once we realize that people recognize the existence of happiness and judge it desirable, then this desire can become a principle that can help us to understand them.

The principles of grandeur and of misery are also involved in a similar process, one which is at the heart of the *Pensées.* A consideration of the principles which exist in human beings (misery and grandeur, for example) leads to the formation of a principle (182/149) which can explain people's actions, a principle which is tightly related to human corruption and godliness, to needs for religion, and to the nature of Christ and of Christianity—Christ can be a principle and an object. It is here that some other related terms, especially instinct and nature, need to be studied, before we can see fully how Pascal dealt with principles. As Prigent points out at the end of the paragraph quoted above, "La recherche de la vérité nous éloigne des prestiges de la géométrie et nous conduit à une méditation sur la nature et sur l'origine de l'homme."

Instinct

Human origins are of course related to the principles which characterize human nature, since both terms suggest a beginning. How do we know anything about our beginnings, except through divine revelation? For Pascal, the answer is usually associated with the word *instinct(s),* which appears sixteen times in the *Pensées* (not counting two variants). It has been variously interpreted and has usually been identified with *principes,* with *coeur,* or with *sentiment.*[7] It is difficult to give the term a precise definition, but a thorough study of each use does lead to certain conclusions.

First of all, instinct is usually reserved for animals. Richelet's dictionary says that the word "ne se dit que des animaux," but that of the Academy, after a first definition which refers to animals, adds that "il se dit aussi de l'homme & se prend pour un premier mouvement sans réflexion." Pascal, however, only uses it once to refer to animals, in 137/105, where animal *instinct* is opposed to human *esprit.*

In all the other fragments where he uses it, *instinct* refers to a means of knowledge. In 142/110, the "connaissances des premiers principes: espace, temps, mouvement, nombres" are called "connaissances du coeur et de l'instinct," and form the basis upon which reason operates. It is hard to see here just what the differences are (if any) between *coeur* and *instinct,* especially since in the following paragraph Pascal speaks of knowing "par instinct et par sentiment," although we might expect him to use the same pair of operations in each case. It remains clear, however, that the instinct furnishes principles to the mind, and that it is thus very similar to *sentiment* as well as to the heart.

This "we might expect" is one of the (if not *the*) most important problems in interpreting an unfinished, fragmentary work such as the *Pensées.* Are *sentiment* and *coeur* the same? Is *sentiment* a subset of *coeur*? Does the meaning of *instinct* change according to the pair in which it is used? The editors of the Port-Royal edition of the *Pensées* had trouble with this fragment too—they omitted all but the last paragraph—but this solution is unacceptable. We must make the effort to understand Pascal's text,

---

[7]García, in *La Teoría del conocimiento en Pascal,* insists on its rational aspect and on its similarity to *sentiment:* a "modo de conocer intuitivo frenta a modo racional" (p. 147). On the other hand, Morot-Sir (*La Métaphysique de Pascal,* pp. 106–107), opposes it to reason and associates instincts with principles. Mesnard (*Les* Pensées *de Pascal,* p. 88) makes *instinct* "le meilleur synonyme du mot 'coeur.'" Baudin says that the heart is "notre instinct" but not "l'instinct" (*Etudes historiques et critiques sur la philosophie de Pascal,* Neuchâtel: La Baconnière, 1946–47, I, 216). Henri Petitot more or less gives up; for him, Pascal opposes to the *esprit géométrique* "cette connaissance spontanée et sans règles qu'il appelle indifféremment: bon sens, sentiment, nature, instinct, coeur"; ("La Théorie de la connaissance chez Pascal," *Revue Thomiste* 17 (1909), p. 583)!

not ignore it or interpret it according to what we expected to find. I return to some of the problems of interpreting this fragment in the discussion of instinct which follows, and again in the chapters on the heart and on reason.

In most of the other occurrences of *instinct* in the *Pensées,* Pascal is concerned with a special type of knowledge, that is, precisely the knowledge of our origins discussed briefly above. In these cases, it is a question of being aware of "la grandeur de notre première nature" (168/136), of the "bonheur de leur première nature" (182/149), or of a "bonheur hors de nous" (176/143); the word is especially frequent in the dossier "Grandeur." It is also a question of understanding our nature(s)—"Deux choses instruisent l'homme de toute sa nature: l'instinct et l'expérience" (161/128), or "Instinct et raison, marques de deux natures" (144/112).

Instincts such as these are not exactly principles that the *sentiment* has understood tacitly through a "sorte de raisonnement" (670/512); they are more a sort of memory that becomes a *sentiment:* "la mémoire, la joie, sont des sentiments" (531/646), a recollection of something that has always existed in human beings, a recognition of something lost. Once they have been recognized, however, they can easily serve as principles, as bases for *raisonnements.* This is precisely the point of fragments such as 182/149, where "quelque grand principe de grandeur" and "un grand principe de misère" are obvious to those who study people carefully. Once we think about this misery and grandeur, then we realize that humanity's current state is characterized by an "instinct impuissant du bonheur de leur première nature" and that we are plunged into the misery of our current condition which has become a second nature. Once we have understood this, it (the complexity of the human condition, including instinct of past grandeur and awareness of current misery) becomes a principle which permits us to "reconnaître la cause de tant de contrariétés qui ont étonné tous les hommes." The switch from *principe* ("de grandeur," "de misère") to *instinct* ("du bonheur de leur première nature") and back to *principe* may seem confusing, but in fact it is quite consistent. "Quelque grand principe de grandeur," for example, is still an abstract principle which the mind can grasp if it considers the human condition carefully. The instinct of lost happiness, however, is a less abstract, perhaps less intellectual awareness of something that we have always known but never verbalized (conceptualized). Finally, this instinct plus the awareness of our present condition becomes a sort of axiom, a principle which allows us to recognize the cause of the contradictions which characterize us.

Instinct, then, is like a principle, like a *sentiment,* but not exactly. This is why Pascal refers to it in 240/208 as a "sentiment intérieur qui leur reste de leur grandeur passée," which seems to be exactly the same thing as an "instinct secret qui reste de la grandeur de notre première grandeur" (168/136). It is not exactly a *sentiment,* but a "sentiment *intérieur,*" just as the "sentiment *de coeur*" (italics mine) in 142/110, which describes a way in which people receive God's religion (but not *premiers principes* such as time and space) is not the same as the *sentiment* mentioned in the first two paragraphs of the fragment.

There still remains the question of the relation of *instinct* to *coeur.* The almost cryptic 187/155 associates them with *principes,* and the arrangement of the three words suggests that *instinct* and *principes* are both related to *coeur:*

Coeur \
Instinct <
Principes /

This is in accord with the interpretation which I have just proposed in which instincts are very similar to principles but refer more to an awareness of something that remains from the past. The phrase "ces connaissances du coeur et de l'instinct" in 142/110 is best interpreted as relating, not opposing, knowledge through the instinct to that through the heart and *sentiment,* since they all furnish principles. The similarity of instinct, heart, and *sentiment* is also implied by their opposition to similar concepts—*instinct* is opposed to *raison* (144/112, 25/406) in the same way that *coeur* and *sentiment* are in 142/110, and "sentiment intérieur" (240/208) refers to the same thing as does *instinct* (168/136, 182/149). A full understanding of *instinct* is impossible without a careful consideration of still other related terms, especially *nature* and *coutume*—both of these are very similar to instinct, and also to *coeur* in the sense in which it is used in 171/139—"que le coeur de l'homme est creux et plein d'ordure."

With "creux" and "ordure," we return to instinct as it refers to animals, and the richness of Pascal's use of the term becomes more apparent. As he discusses human instincts, he can turn toward past glory or present misery, toward the "ange" side or the "bête" side, toward either of the two "principes qui partagent les volontés des hommes: la cupidité et la charité" (738/502). The definition in the Academy's dictionary seems to reflect this usage perfectly—it refers to animals but sounds like something Pascal would say about people (in their corrupt state): "Certain sentiment & mouvement que la nature a donné aux animaux pour connoistre ce qui leur est bon ou mauvais." This is the basic question which Pascal poses, and he goes about answering it, not by supplying easy solutions, but by exploring the duality at its core. Why is there good and bad? Where do they come from? How do we recognize them? This last question, since it deals more directly with human experience, is the easiest for Pascal to answer, and this is why an understanding of his epistemology is so crucial to an understanding of the *Pensées*. The duality in human nature and the Fall which explains it from a theological point of view can be seen as epistemological phenomena—direct knowledge through *sentiment* is as far from indirect knowledge through *raisonnement* as pre-Fall purity is from post-Fall corruption.

Nature, Custom

Instinct and principles, then, are both associated with finding out essential information—what is good, what is true, what are the bases upon which we should live. Principles are things that come first, and instincts inform us of what has been; it is a matter of origins and "l'incertitude de notre origine qui enferme celle de notre nature" (164/131). Human nature is ultimately involved in any consideration of knowledge, principles, and instincts, and it is especially important in the *Pensées*, whose greatness for many readers is found precisely in their analysis of human nature.

The word *nature* has three basic uses in *Pensées.* The first, that of the physical world, does not concern us directly here. The other two, an original first nature and a current, customary second nature, are closely related but are also a quantum leap apart (if we may refer to the Fall as a quantum leap). As Pascal expresses it in 160/127, "La nature de l'homme se considère en deux manières, l'une selon la fin, et alors il est grand et incomparable; l'autre selon la multitude, . . . et alors l'homme est abject et vil."

This is the familiar Pascalian distinction between *grandeur* and *misère,* between angel and beast. In other fragments in the same dossier ("Contrariétés"), Pascal expresses the same distinction in other terms—*nature* and *coutume* (or second nature; 158/125, 159/126), *instinct* and *expérience* (161/128), *un* and *divers* (162/129). On the one hand, there is a nature which is unique, oriented toward a single goal (*fin*), which is instinctive, and which is associated with grandeur, with "quelque instinct impuissant du bonheur de leur première nature" (182/149). This nature, however, is contrasted with the actuality of our present condition, with the common ("multitude"), diverse, base actions that have become habit and custom with most people. In short, there is what Pierre Magnard and others call "l'idée de nature," which challenges "la nature empirique."[8]

Magnard, in a later work, expresses the same distinction in another way: theologically, nature refers to a person's "ressemblance avec Dieu qui l'a créé à son image," while philosophically it refers to the "principe immanent des opérations de l'homme."[9] The first is the way people were created, the way they should be (or would have been without the Fall); the second is the way they are. Pascal often criticizes the latter nature—"Quelle est donc cette nature sujette à être effacée" (159/126), but he never loses his faith in the former, "notre véritable nature," revealed by "la vérité incréée et incarnée" (164/131).

---

[8]"Pascal dialecticien," *Pascal présent* (Clermont-Ferrand: G. de Bussac, 1962), 261.

[9]*Nature et histoire dans l'apologétique de Pascal* (Paris: Belles Lettres, 1975), 150.

Pascal's criticism of this second nature, that is, of custom, is well known: "la coutume est une seconde nature" (159/126); "la coutume est notre nature" (680/419). Custom seems natural, a ready source for our principles, but it is arbitrary, always changing (453/520), and unfounded. Still its existence is unavoidable, and we are reduced to following it, whether we are one of the common people who think it justified or whether we are one of the wiser people who follow it only because it is established—"La coutume ne doit être suivie que parce qu'elle est coutume, et non parce qu'elle est raisonnable ou juste" (454/525; see also the dossier "Raison des effets").

In discussing and criticizing custom, as in discussing principles and instinct, the basic question is one of origins. Where does the honor of the "personnes de grande naissance" come from (124/90)? What is the basis of true grandeur, or of just laws (115/80). The fragments of the dossier "Raison des effets" make it clear that it is a matter of judging well—in order to judge well, we must have a point of view, an orientation; in order to have a dependable point of view (perspective), we must know the origins of the nobility and of laws, not just the way they exist in the present. Pascal points out that nobility comes from an accident of birth, that laws depend on force, and that if we are aware of these origins, we can have a "pensée de derrière la tête" and judge properly, and avoid the "ignorance naturelle qui est le vrai siège de l'homme" (117/83).

This ignorance "naturelle" is nature in the sense of custom, and, if we are to judge properly, it must be replaced by a "nouvelle lumière," or a "lumière supérieure" (124/90), that is, by a new point of view. Two variants of 124/90 make it clear that this is basically the same thing as having new principles, new starting points—Pascal's original text had "principe nouveau" instead of "nouvelle lumière," and "principe plus intérieur" instead of "lumière supérieure." The change suggests that, since he had discussed each "gradation" from the *peuple, demi-habiles* and *habiles* to *dévots* and *chrétiens parfaits,* that is, from worldly judgment to judgment influenced (inspired) by faith, he wanted a term ("lumière") which had closer connections with religious inspiration. In any case, it is clear that he associated a new point of view with new principles, with a new way of seeing the basic aspects of a problem.

These basic aspects could also be called, in Pascal's vocabulary, the nature of the problem. In the case of custom, of second nature, error is usually involved. The outward opinion, such as that of the people in 124/90, for example, may be correct, but not for the right reason—the people "n'en sent pas la vérité ou elle est" (127/93). The truth is in the basis, the root of the problem, so to speak. It is fairly easy to ascertain in factual, worldly matters ("Le monde juge bien des choses, car il est dans l'ignorance naturelle, qui est le vrai siège de l'homme"; [117/83]), but this natural ignorance often covers up our true nature, our first nature. This first nature is our nature "selon la fin," our nature in what Magnard calls the theological sense.

This nature is closely related to both principles and instinct. It is the instinct that recalls this true nature in the midst of what Jansenist theology saw as our current corruption, our second nature—"Voilà l'état où les hommes sont aujourd'hui. Il leur reste quelque instinct impuissant du bonheur de leur première nature, et ils sont plongés dans les misères de leur aveuglement et de leur concupiscence qui est devenue leur seconde nature" (182/149). Once we have recognized this condition of coexisting grandeur and misery, it becomes a new principle, or a "nouvelle lumière." Fragment 182/149 goes on to say "De ce principe que je vous ouvre vous pouvez reconnaître la cause de tant de contrariétés qui ont étonné tous les hommes. . . . Voyez s'il ne faut pas que la cause en soit en une autre nature." In short, we judge one way according to our "ignorance naturelle," but another according to this new principle, which is based upon an understanding of true human nature.

This first nature is hypothetical, an "idée de nature," and depends on conclusions drawn from observation, on instinct, or on faith. The main argument Pascal makes is that humanity cannot be understood without positing this first nature, that is, without accepting it as a principle. But as with all principles, how do we know whether they are true or false:

> nous n'avons aucune certitude de la vérité de ces principes, hors

> la foi et la révélation, sinon en ce que nous les sentons naturellement en nous. Or ce sentiment naturel n'est pas une preuve convaincante de leur vérité, puisque . . . il est en doute si ces principes nous sont donnés ou véritables, ou faux, ou incertains selon notre origine (164/131).

Nature and custom become confused, and even the "premiers principes" such as number, space, and movement may not be truly natural (680/419). Again, there is the question of principles, of origins, of what seems natural but is still uncertain except when backed up by faith or revelation.

This hypothetical first nature is that of the pre-Fall state, of humanity in all its grandeur, just as the second nature is that of the post-Fall state, of humanity in all its misery. Human grandeur is also related to the quality of thought and reason, as in the famous fragment on the "roseau pensant," or in 628/759: "Pensée fait la grandeur de l'homme." Nature can be seen, philosophically, as the "principe immanent des opérations de l'homme" (Magnard, *Nature et histoire,* p. 150), and our fallen mental operations are as far from their origins (the principles upon which they are based) as our second nature is from the first. As Pascal says in 142/110, our instinct and *sentiment* are often not enough, and we need the less direct operation of the *raisonnement,* which will be discussed in the next chapter. We can at least be aware of our condition (we can be aware through instinct and draw conclusions through reason; or we can be made aware through reasonable discourse); if we cannot reason our way to ultimate knowledge, we can try to understand whence our greatness comes. It comes, according to Pascal, not only from reason but from God who gave it.

As Magnard points out in the passage cited above, nature in its theological sense refers precisely to a person's relationship with God, with a "ressemblance avec Dieu qui l'a créé à son image." However, Pascal does not need to rely on the authority of theology to convince a reader to turn toward God (back toward original nature) or toward Christ the mediator, away from *divertissement, concupiscence,* and other finite pleasures. Pascal needs only to establish a few related principles: our second nature is corrupt; mankind is corrupt; our first nature is pure; God (by definition) is pure. The conclusion is clear—the original is preferable to its representation, to its corrupt image which, like reason and nature, has its perfections and its defects (762/934).

Models

This conforming to an image, to a standard, also characterizes Pascal's idea of the natural. In the famous fragment concerning beauty (486/585–86), Pascal describes "un certain modèle d'agrément et de beauté qui consiste en un certain rapport entre notre nature faible ou forte telle qu'elle est et la chose qui nous plaît" (486/585; the problem in such areas as poetry is that we cannot specify this model). Similarly, if we wish to persuade another, "il faut avoir égard à la personne à qui on en veut, dont il faut connaître l'esprit et le coeur, quels principes il accorde . . ." (p. 356A). If anything is to please us, it must be formed on this "modèle naturel qu'il faut imiter," and if we wish to persuade another, we must please and approach this person through his or her standards, according to his or her nature. In short, as Morot-Sir puts it, "le naturel pascalien . . . est la relation de convenance entre la nature humaine et l'objet qu'elle désire" (*La Métaphysique de Pascal,* p. 27). A poem or a woman must conform to our nature if it or she is to be pleasing. All too often, according to Pascal, this nature is our second feeble corrupt nature, and we do not always have "ce bon modèle" (486/585) or "ce modèle naturel" (486/586). But if it is our first, divine nature that is involved, then we should be pleased by anything that conforms to this divine model, that is, God, or Christ, and we should try to conform ourselves to this model, to allow our first nature to overcome our second.

This idea of conforming to a model is closely related to what Pascal and Port-Royal call *jugement,* which was presented briefly in the Introduction and which has been mentioned often in conjunction with *sentiment* and principles. *Jugement* consists of combinations of ideas or of principles, and constitutes one more reason why nature (and custom) and principles are so closely related. Since the main model is a divine one, a nature that has been lost, instinct also plays a major role; it is mostly through instinct, Pascal thinks, that we become aware of our grandeur, of our first nature.

These *jugements* are also the opinions that Pascal calls *sentiments,* and we can say that the operation of *sentiment* in this sense of combining ideas is essentially the same as that of comparing something to a model. This is especially true when we compare something to a principle that is natural, a part of human nature (this is *sentiment* in its sense of impression). Thus, this model involving our nature and our principles is the basis for the essential mental operation that is *sentiment,* a type of knowledge which we must have to supplement our powers of formal reasoning. This model involving our nature is also the basis for faith, for our coming to resemble God. Finite beings cannot resemble infinite God; there is a need for a mediator to help establish the proper relationship, and Pascal saw that mediator in Christ.

As Morot-Sir points out so well in his discussion of what Pascal means by *naturel* (*La Métaphysique de Pascal,* pp. 24–28), this model involving our nature is also the basis for effective language (communication). Not only do we need to accommodate what we say to our listener's desires, to his or her nature, but even in less affective language we need to follow the model of straightforward thought ("L'éloquence est une peinture de la pensée"), to conform our words to our thoughts, and to use words in accordance with their definitions.[10] For Pascal, if language is to be effective, its words must correspond to its object, to the things, ideas, and feelings it tries to represent. To be effective in communicating with people, language must conform either to their corrupt nature ("cette voie est basse, indigne et étrangère";

[10]Pascal emphasized the importance of words in the establishment of meaning in 645/789; see Morot-Sir, *La Métaphysique de Pascal,* p. 25. The *Logique* also insists on the near inseparability of words and ideas at the end of the Introduction and at the beginning of Part II (pp. 38, 103). *Sentiment* and its principles are as integral to language as they are to thought—when the *Logique* introduces its definitions of *jugements,* it adds, "Il est peu important d'examiner si c'est à la Grammaire ou à la Logique d'en traiter" (p. 103).

p. 355A) or to their more divinely related, reasonable nature; in either case there is a natural model to which it must adhere.

The notion of models is essential for a thorough understanding of Pascal's methods, as is the closely related question of language, of how Pascal put his method into practice. A detailed discussion of these questions, however, is impossible without an understanding of Pascal's use of *coeur* (chapter 3), since it encompasses all the terms discussed in this chapter as well as *sentiment*. We must also look at Pascal's views on less natural, more discursive, and logically rigorous means of attaining knowledge (chapter 4), which are based on the terms discussed in the first two chapters.

3

The Heart

One important question about Pascal's use of the term *coeur* has been raised in the previous chapter—is knowledge through the instinct separate from that through the heart? A first step in answering this question is found in 527/634; the fragment adds to the distinction between nature and custom a further distinction between custom and instinct—"C'est la coutume qui fait donc cela, car elle contraint la nature, et quelquefois la nature la surmonte et retient l'homme dans son instinct malgré toute coutume bonne ou mauvaise."

Just as in fragments such as 168/136 and 171/139, where instinct is associated with a sort of memory of our former grandeur, here it is associated with our first nature and opposed to our second (to custom). Instinct is not so much a means of attaining knowledge as it is of retaining it; instinct is opposed to that which is corrupt and artificial, that which is separated from true (i.e., first) nature. The heart, on the other hand, is much less passive. Pascal never used *instinct* in passages such as that in 142/110 where it is the heart which "sent qu'il y a trois dimensions dans l'espace" or asks of "la raison un sentiment de toutes les propositions qu'elle démontre." The heart is an active faculty[1] which asks, feels (142/110, 680/424), names (258/225), sees (339/308), and so on, whereas the instinct is normally only vaguely aware of something in the remote past.

The heart is also often associated precisely with that which is corrupt and artificial, that which is separated from our true nature, from former grandeur. "Que le coeur de l'homme est creux et plein d'ordure," exclaims Pascal, in 171/139, and elsewhere he speaks of "la concupiscence et la malice du coeur" (423/835), or of "la malignité qui est cachée et empreinte dans le coeur de l'homme" (309/278). Pascal does not always associate the heart with the corrupt side of human nature, and 309/278 makes it clear that this corruption is not the only thing in the human

---

[1]See Mesnard, *Les* Pensées *de Pascal,* p. 166.

heart. There is a good side, which is tempted by the "malignité," the "mauvais levain"; if there is a "coeur de pierre," it is different from the *coeur* in general which seeks truth actively rather than let itself be corrupted by falsehood. Pascal thus returns to the distinction between our two natures—"Dieu délivrera la bonne nature de l'homme de la mauvaise." Just as there are two natures in us, so are there two aspects of our heart.

The presence of these two aspects is not surprising, since Pascal closely associates the heart with the natural.[2] Fragment 309/278 refers to the "malignité" in the human heart as "naturelle," and 168/136 and 743/978 refer to *ennui, mensonge, hypocrisie,* and so on, as having "une racine naturelle" in the heart. The principles that the heart knows are often referred to as natural (158/125, 164/131, and 454/525, for example), and the ability to know things through the heart (as through instinct and *sentiment*) is a "bien" given by nature (142/110). The heart is also the part of us which loves, and it does this naturally—"le coeur aime l'être universel naturellement et soi-même naturellement" (680/423). This, again, is the same distinction that Pascal makes concerning nature—there is a first nature related to the divine ("l'être universel") and a second nature related to the corrupt present condition ("soi-même").

We can thus specify two principal uses of the word *coeur* in the *Pensées.* Laporte calls them (1) "faculté de connaissance" and (2) "volonté" (*Le Coeur et la raison selon Pascal,* pp. 100–101); similarly, Henri Petitot calls them (1) "connaissance naturelle et spontanée" and (2) "sensibilité et volonté ("La Théorie de la connaissance chez Pascal," p. 586; see also pp. 577, 583–84). The first is related to our first nature, to our capacity for understanding truth; the second is related to our second nature, which is corrupt, and although it should (and can) seek God, it seeks instead pleasures that are neither reasonable nor moral nor religious, such as *divertissement, gloire,* earthly goods, and human love.

---

[2]This relationship between the heart and human nature is pointed out by Magnard ("Pascal dialecticien," p. 260), where the heart is a faculty, *sentiment* its operation, and nature its "fondement." Magnard goes on to specify instinct as its "principe d'activité," but, for reasons given above, I find this impossible to accept.

Whatever terms we use to characterize these two aspects of *coeur* as Pascal uses it, it is clear that one is a kind of intellectual *operation*, involving *sentiment* and principles, and related to instinct (142/110), and that the other is an *attraction* to various objects, persons, pleasures, and so on. Used in these two ways, the heart is involved in all three of the Pascalian orders, as they are described in 339/308—*corps, esprits, charité (Dieu, sagesse)*. If we use this framework to divide the various things which Pascal says are in the heart, we find the following:

FIRST ORDER	SECOND ORDER	THIRD ORDER
Biens temporels	Connaissances	Biens spirituels
Objet	Raisons	Dieu (loi, crainte)
Gloire	Pensées	Inclination
Ordure	Passions: vanité	Pénitence
Créatures	joie	Foi
Concupiscence	tendresse	Jésus-Christ
	Ennui	
	Malignité, malice	

The heart is thus the seat of earthly pleasures (first order), of knowledge and of passion (second order), and of divine revelation (third order). Jeanne Russier describes the heart in much the same way in *La Foi selon Pascal* (p. 156), referring to the Biblical notion of the heart as "le fond de l'être." However, she and other critics who take this position sometimes give the impression that the heart is the seat of everything, even of reason which Pascal carefully opposes to the heart (329/298, 680/423, 680/424, 142/110, etc.). Russier describes the heart as "le siège de la pensée" (p. 156), and Jan Miel describes it as the "seat of all the faculties of the soul, whether discursive volitional, affective, or intellectual."[3] Human powers of rational thought certainly do not have their seat in the *coeur,* though they often must turn there for their principles. In this sense, the heart *is* the basis for all human intellectual endeavors, for *sentiment* as well as *raisonnement,* for *esprit de finesse* as well as *esprit de géométrie,* and it is in part,

[3]*Pascal and Theology* (Baltimore: Johns Hopkins University Press, 1969), 158.

at least, definitely an intellectual faculty. Still, we must remember that as much as Pascal emphasized knowledge acquired through the heart, through its operations of instinct and *sentiment,* he realized that "la nature . . . ne . . . nous a donné que très peu de connaissances de cette sorte; toutes les autres ne peuvent être acquises que par raisonnement" (142/110).

Before going on to look at the other side of Pascal's intellectual coin—reason and in particular *raisonnement*—it is important to see just how the terms already discussed, especially *sentiment, principes* and *instinct,* relate to his notion of the heart. All of these terms are present in 142/110, though in various combinations, and a coherent interpretation of this fragment can put all these terms into perspective.

First of all, *coeur* and *sentiment* are very closely associated. The heart *sent,* the principles which it knows *se sentent,* and the equivalent of the proofs which reason would futilely ask of the heart's principles is a *sentiment* of its propositions. This is very much in accord with the interpretation of *sentiment* proposed at the end of chapter 1, where *sentiment* is an operation within the power of the heart. With the exception of the one occurrence of *sentiment* as a first order sensual impression (565/686), all the occurrences of *sentiment* in the *Pensées* are operations or products taking place or being formed within the power of the heart. The heart is a vastly larger concept than *sentiment,* but the mental operation which Pascal calls *sentiment* is definitely the way the heart operates as it attains knowledge of its principles.

These principles form the basis upon which "la raison s'appuie," but the instinct is involved also—"c'est sur ces connaissances du coeur et de l'instinct. . . ." As I pointed out at the beginning of this chapter, we cannot equate heart and instinct totally, although many critics have tried to do this—the heart is associated with concepts such as time, space, and movement, whereas the instinct retains a notion of past grandeur. The next sentence of 142/110 definitely associates the heart with space and numbers; but perhaps time, for example, is more in the domain of the instinct (especially since memory is involved). In any case, there is a distinction between heart and instinct.

Thus, in the second paragraph, when Pascal opposes reason to the other way in which we attain knowledge, we expect the same breakdown, that is, "plût à Dieu . . . que nous connussions toutes choses par instinct et par [coeur]." The text reads "par instinct et par sentiment," however, which implies that *sentiment* is to be equated with *coeur.* This substitution makes sense when, in paragraph 3, Pascal opposes "sentiment de coeur" to *raisonnement,* in the same way he had earlier separately opposed *coeur* and *sentiment* to it. He is speaking here of faith, not of knowledge of the principles of worldly existence, and he needs a different term. What he seems to be doing here is to qualify the intellectual implications of *sentiment* using *coeur* in its other sense (that is, he is not referring to *coeur* as a mode of human knowledge—second order—within which the *sentiment* operates), so that *coeur* now refers to *volonté* (third order), to an attraction for God which is inspired by Him. *Raisonnement* is thus opposed to *sentiment* and to *coeur* in its intellectual sense where human knowledge is involved and to *sentiment de coeur* where faith is involved. Just as *coeur* is used in a different way, so is *sentiment.* In the first two paragraphs, concerning human knowledge, *sentiment* was an operation, but here in the third paragraph, concerning faith, it is an opinion which is in the heart, not through the operation of *sentiment* or of *jugement,* but through divine intervention.

Sentiment, then, is the operation through which the heart functions, and principles are the results of this operation. Instinct can also furnish principles, but it is not through the intellectual process of *sentiment,* that is, through the formation of impressions and the combination of these impressions into principles, or *jugements.* In this sense, instinct is more like *sentiment* than like the heart, since it also forms impressions though in a non-intellectual way. This non-intellectual aspect of instinct is precisely why it is associated with animal instinct, while *sentiment* is a very human mental operation.

The heart is opposed to reason in two ways. The first way is mentioned in 142/110—the heart furnishes principles, and then the reason acts on them.[4] Heart and reason cannot explain their operations to each other, and neither is self-sufficient—the heart cannot know "toutes choses," and the reason cannot function without the principles which the heart furnishes it. This distinction is one between two mental operations, and when Pascal uses *coeur* in this way, we must be extremely careful not to think of it as something mystical, instinctive (i.e., non-human, non-mental), or supernatural (the heart can be open to God, though this is a different usage); and it is especially not irrational—"le coeur a ses raisons" (680/423) whether the reason is aware of them or not, just as the *esprit de finesse* does not ignore definitions and principles, but operates tacitly, naturally (670/512).

The second distinction between heart and reason involves the second meaning of *coeur,* that is *volonté.* Pascal opposes *volonté* to *esprit* and to *raison* in the *Pensées* (266/234, 680/418, 458/539) and to *entendement* in the *Esprit géométrique* (355A). Here the heart is not at all intellectual; on the contrary, it prohibits the mind's functioning (judging) well (458/539). When the heart finds something pleasing, that is, when it is attracted to something agreeable with which it has "un certain rapport" (486/585), it causes the mind to look at things as it does.

Pascal was reluctant to try to give any rules for persuading through the volonté ("the art d'agréer"; p. 356A), but he realized that it was an important means of communicating knowledge, even if it was a "voie . . . basse, indigne et étrangère" (355A). He had this low opinion for the same reason that he had a low opinion of custom, of second nature—it is not natural. The "entrée . . . la plus naturelle est celle de l'entendement" (355A), since it corresponds to our first nature. Pascal also says, however, that the "volonté aime naturellement" just as "l'esprit croit naturellement" (524/631). "Naturellement" must be taken in two ways here, according to our two natures—the *volonté* can love corrupt things naturally, through our second nature, or pure godlike

[4]To be more precise, it is the *raisonnement* which acts on principles and which operates so differently from the heart. These distinctions will be made in more detail in the next chapter.

things through our first nature. This is why Pascal can also use *volonté* in two ways, depending on whether he is referring to the second or the third order, that of divine wisdom: "Il y a trois ordres de choses. La chair, l'esprit, la volonté" (761/933). The fragment does not mention *volonté* again, and speaks very little of the third order, but the sense seems to be that those who are in the order of *volonté* follow God's will, for "Dieu seul donne la sagesse." Human wisdom is no matter for pride, and the only true glory is to follow God's will—"qui gloriatur, in Domino glorietur."

It is important to note how many of Pascal's terms concerning knowledge—especially this sort of immediate, non-discursive type of knowledge which is characterized by *sentiment*—have at least two uses; the terms include *sentiment* (opinion and operation), *nature* (first and second), *coeur* (operation and attraction), *volonté* (loving the corrupt and the divine). This duality is obviously due to Pascal's view of the human condition as lost between the two infinites; human beings are so complex (see the concluding paragraphs of 230/199) that nothing is simple for us, and any terms used to describe how we attain knowledge are also likely to have multiple uses, depending on whether we are dealing with our corrupt state or with what is left of our divine nature. A similar duality exists concerning our means of attaining knowledge—through the heart and through reason. To understand this last duality, it is necessary to look at terms such as *raison, raisonnement*, and *esprit*.

4

Reason

The discussion of the heart in the preceding chapter shows how different the heart is from discursive reason. If Pascal, in fragments such as 142/110, wishes that we could obtain all our knowledge through the heart, he nonetheless recognizes that this is impossible. There are many aspects of truth which cannot be known through immediate, natural understanding—that is, within the *coeur* (a "power") using the *sentiment* (an "operation") to form *principes* (a "product"); a more discursive process is necessary when we must combine and arrange a wide range of information and come to a conclusion—within the *raison* (a "power") using the *raisonnement* (an "operation") to form *raisonnements* (a "product"). As Pascal says in 142/110, the heart "sent . . . que les nombres sont infinis," but it is *raison* which "démontre ensuite qu'il n'y a point deux nombres carrés dont l'un soit double de l'autre." The first type of knowledge can be grasped but not demonstrated, whereas the second type goes beyond our powers of immediate, natural comprehension and must be demonstrated through a logical, linear process. The activities of the *raisonnement* and the *sentiment* correspond very closely to the functions of the left and right hemispheres of the brain, respectively. The left hemisphere is analytic, verbal, and sequential; the right is synthetic, simultaneous, and intuitive.[1] Still, we arrive at both types of knowledge "avec certitude, quoique par différentes voies." In discussing these two types of knowledge, Pascal uses the terms *sentiment, principe,* and *raisonnement* with remarkable consistency, given that the *Pensées* are a collection of fairly disparate notes taken over a period of several years.

I have described in the first three chapters how *sentiments* and principles are formed and how they relate to the heart. The

[1]To take an example close to Pascal's interests, Carl Sagan (*The Dragons of Eden,* New York: Random House, 1977, 183), suggests that the right hemisphere recognizes the notions (principles) of geometry and of space—as does the Pascalian *sentiment*—whereas the left carries out the demonstrations of geometry—as does the Pascalian *raisonnement.*

raisonnement was mentioned briefly in the Introduction and will be discussed in detail in this chapter (we will look especially at how it differs from *raison*). First, however, it is important to look briefly at some definitions in order to support the distinctions made in the preceding paragraph. Furetière defines *raisonnement* as "action de l'entendement," and then adds "se dit aussi de l'argumentation formée par la puissance qui raisonne," that is, the product formed by the *raisonnement* as an operation. *Raison* is defined as "entendement," clearly the power within which the operation works to form its products. The dictionaries of Richelet and of the Academy make similar distinctions, defining *raisonnement* both as "faculté" and as "discours raisonné" (Richelet) or "argument, syllogisme" (Academy); *raison* is defined in a more general way, as "puissance de l'âme." These dictionaries also give a definition of *raison* that is similar to the second definition of *raisonnement;* I will return to this in the detailed discussion of *raison*.

La Fontaine makes a similar distinction in the "Discours à Mme de la Sablière" (*Fables*, IX), although he is distinguishing between animals and people, not between two types of human knowledge. If he were the creator, says La Fontaine, "Je rendrais mon ouvrage / Capable de sentir, juger, rien davantage / . . . Sans qu'un Singe jamais fît le moindre argument" (214–17). By "argument" he means, as does Pascal in 661/821, "un raisonnement qu'on fait en posant certains principes dont on tire des consequences" (Furetière), the ability to reason, the second type of knowledge mentioned above, while "sentir, juger" represents the first.

Pascal preferred the first type of knowledge (that of the heart and the *sentiment*) to the second (that of the *raisonnement*). Although it is precisely the ability to reason that sets humans apart from animals (143/111, 617/741; *Préface sur le Traité du vide*, p. 231B), in the Augustinian view shared by Pascal and Port-Royal, reason can also lead us away from God and can go beyond its bounds.[2] On the one hand, each person is a "roseau pensant,"

[2]See the dossier "Soumission et usage de la raison," and Mesnard's commentary in *Les* Pensées *de Pascal*, pp. 160–61.

and all his or her dignity "consiste donc en la pensée" (232/200); on the other, reason is "corrumpue" (498/601) and "impuissante" (164/131); it needs the support of nature or of God. We do not need reason to attain knowledge of God, and since for Pascal this is our chief end, the ability to reason well is not absolutely necessary, useful as it may be (142/110, 203/172).

This view of our ability to reason as non-essential is presented clearly in the Port-Royal *Logique,* using the same terms that Pascal does in the same ways. In the first place, the *raisonnement* is only a crutch to fall back on when we cannot understand something directly, that is, by judging through *sentiment:*

> La necessité du raisonnement n'est fondée que sur les bornes étroites de l'esprit humain, qui ayant à juger de la verité ou de la fausseté d'une proposition, . . . ne le peut pas toujours faire par la consideration des deux idées qui la composent. . . . Lors donc que la seule consideration de ces deux idées ne suffit pas pour faire juger si l'on doit affirmer ou nier l'une de l'autre, il a besoin de recourir à une troisième idée. (p. 178)

In the second place, using *raisonnement* well or badly is not a major problem; most difficulties lie earlier in the reasoning process—"La plûpart des erreurs des hommes . . . viennent bien plus de ce qu'ils raisonnent sur de faux principes, que non pas de ce qu'ils raisonnent mal suivant leurs principes" (p. 177). Or, as Nicole expressed it in the first preliminary discourse, "la plûpart des erreurs des hommes ne consist[e]nt pas à se laisser tromper par de mauvaises consequences, mais à se laisser aller à de faux jugements dont on tire de mauvaises consequences" (p. 21). If we have good principles, and if we can make good judgments based on them, then reasoning from that point is easy.[3]

The authors of the *Logique* refer to the formation of *idées* (individual, simple principles) as conception and to the formation of *jugements* (combined, complex principles) as *jugement* (p. 37).

---

[3]Pascal makes a similar point about the importance of principles in the *Préface sur le Traité du vide,* p. 232A. The ancients lacked the principles, the experiments that seventeenth-century scientists had, but not the "force du raisonnement."

The three preceding chapters have shown how these two terms are closely related to Pascal's conception of *sentiment* as an operation which forms impressions (ideas, simple principles) and then combines them into *jugements,* or opinions (complex principles, also called *sentiments*). In making a *jugement* we make a decision about the truth or falsity of an opinion by deciding whether the two ideas being combined form an acceptable combination; the decision often involves comparing something to a model. For example, we make a decision about roundness and the earth (*Logique,* p. 37), about a particular poem and a model of a good poem (486/585–86, 503/611), about a description of a miracle and an event (425/840, 429/846, and 437/858), about a prophecy and its accomplishment (414/382), or about the actions and motives of others (124/90, 125/91) and of the church (473/567). Ultimately, in a work like the *Pensées,* there is a question of judging whether a religion is true or false by comparing it to a model of what the true religion should be.

Ideally, we can make these judgments directly and with certainty. In practice, however, as the quotations above from the *Logique* point out, we cannot always form an opinion, a *jugement,* through a simple comparison of two ideas. Rather we must resort to a third term—and therefore to two or more *jugements* which can then be combined to form a *raisonnement,* or *argument* (syllogism). The process is basically a logical, discursive one in which we draw consequences from given principles. We are now two steps removed from direct knowledge of principles through the heart or *sentiment* and one step from combining them into affirmable or deniable *jugements;* we are also, according to Pascal and Port-Royal, further from basic truths.

There is one other major mental operation mentioned in the *Logique,* one for which the authors owe a considerable debt to Pascal, as they acknowledge in the first preliminary discourse (p. 21). This operation is the disposition of "diverses idées, divers jugements & divers raisonnements . . . en la maniere la plus propre pour faire connoître" a certain subject (p. 38). It is called *ordonner,* or *méthode,* though Pascal refers to it more frequently as *disposition* (575/696), *démonstration* (201/170, 222/190, 329/298; *L'Esprit géométrique*), or *ordre* (329/298, 457/532, 38/2, 39/

5, 42/8, etc.). Once *jugements* and *raisonnements* have been formed, it is necessary to arrange them in order to communicate them to others; this is obviously a crucial question for the *Pensées,* whose "proper" organization has been debated for three hundred years.[4] Much of this debate revolves around the distinction which Pascal makes between different types of orders ("Le coeur a son ordre. L'esprit a le sien"; 329/298) or of *esprits (justesse, géométrie, finesse).* It is essential to understand all these terms in order to understand Pascal's view of knowledge that is not attained through the heart.

First, however, we must consider the word "raison," since it is intimately associated with all these terms, including *coeur.* Laporte (p. 101, n. 1) and others suggest that, as with so many other Pascalian terms dealing with knowledge, *raison* has two important and different usages—that it sometimes refers to thought, to intelligence in general, and that at other times it refers to *raisonnement.* (There are of course other usages, such as "rendre raison," "la raison de toutes choses," "avoir raison," etc., but they do not refer directly to types of knowledge and thus are not of immediate concern here.) The same distinction is made in the dictionaries of Richelet, Furetière, and the Academy—*raison* is defined in all three as "puissance de l'âme" and also as "preuve par discours, par argument" (Academy), "argumentation, preuve" (Furetière), and "ce qu'on alégue, qu'on dit & qu'on aporte pour prouver" (Richelet).

It is difficult to justify this distinction in the text of the *Pensées.*[5] The meaning of intelligence in general, of our ability to think, is clear, for example, in 78/45 ("Ces deux principes de vérités, la raison et les sens"), 736/491 ("L'homme n'agit point par la raison, qui fait son être") and 536/651 ("La mémoire est nécessaire pour toutes les opérations de la raison"). However the

---

[4]Most of the debate over the organization of the *Pensées* has been over the apologetic method of a non-existent apology, rather than over Pascal's arrangement of thoughts, or *jugements* and *raisonnements,* in his effort to communicate. This communication-oriented arrangement will be one of the main subjects of part 2 of this study.

[5]Laporte gives no examples of *raisonnement,* and never follows up his distinctions.

meaning of *raisonnement,* of *argument,* in the seventeenth-century sense of the term, is suggested only in 661/821 ("La raison agit avec lenteur et avec tant de vues sur tant de principes") and 142/110 ("prouver par raison"), and, as I shall show, there are other ways of interpreting these passages.

Such a distinction between these two usages of *raison* is especially hard to justify in fragments such as 455/530, where, after opposing *sentiment* and *raisonnement,* as we would expect (since the opposition is between two means of acquiring truth—direct combination of ideas, or through the introduction of third terms), Pascal mentions *raison* as a possible rule to settle arguments about whose opinion is *sentiment* (i.e., true), and whose is *fantaisie* (i.e., false). Why did he change terms, if he didn't intend for *raison* to mean more than *raisonnement*?

Fragment 142/110 is the ultimate test for such a distinction. There are nine occurrences of *raison,* and three of *raisonnement* (including one in the second sentence, written by his scribe, where Pascal changed *raison* to *raisonnement;* only the passage from "et c'est sur ces connaissances" to "quoique par différentes voies" is in Pascal's hand, except for the change mentioned above and the "la foi" added to the last sentence). The reason for the change from *raison* to *raisonnement* seems clear—Pascal did not want to exclude all of human reason from the knowledge of first principles, only the part that forms formal arguments based upon these principles. Similarly, in the other two uses of *raisonnement,* there is a clear distinction between a formal reasoning process—the step-by-step acquisition of knowledge—and direct knowledge.

But what of the other occurrences of *raison*? "Prouver par raison," as mentioned above, definitely seems to refer to *raisonnements,* and therefore so would the "notre raison" which follows. Most of the other occurrences of *raison* do seem to refer to a faculty, to a general operation, and this would be why Pascal did not use *raisonnement* in these instances. The possibility remains that he did not correct his scribe's copy carefully, but there is no need to assume an error if we can interpret the text as it stands.

This generality seems to be the clue to an understanding of Pascal's vocabulary here. The first occurrence of *raisonnement* is definitely opposed to the formation of principles, a specific mental activity; the other two occurrences refer specifically to the acquisition of knowledge through formal reasoning. All the occurrences of *raison,* then, could be considered more general, including "prouver par raison," since proving would have to include the formation of principles (axioms) and their arrangement (*ordre*).

Indeed, the basic question that must be answered in distinguishing between *raison* as thought or intelligence in general and as *raisonnement* in particular is: what else does *raison* include when it refers to more than just *raisonnement*? The "principes de la raison" (230/199, 682/428, variant of 181/148) are not *principes* in the specific sense of combinations of ideas or of bases for further reasoning, but *principes* in the more general sense of rules, that is, guidelines that we must follow to reason properly. They go far beyond the rules for forming correct syllogisms and include—indeed, emphasize—sense perception, conception of ideas and the formation of *jugements (sentiments)* as well as the arranging of *jugements* and *raisonnements.* Or, to borrow the terms of the Port-Royal *Logique* again, *raison* includes conception, judgment, and order (method) as well as *raisonnement,* and the first two are the most important. Before the *raisonnement* can operate, especially in activities such as mathematical proofs, we must have definitions that must be conceived and combined into principles (axioms) through some mental process. If the *raison* "démontre . . . qu'il n'y a point deux nombres carrés dont l'un soit double de l'autre" (142/110), it must define number, square, double, and so on, and use these to form principles upon which to form *raisonnements.* It must also arrange these *raisonnements* to form a proof, or demonstration.

Seen in this way, *raison* definitely refers to something larger than *raisonnement.* Even the passage in 661/821, ("La raison agit avec lenteur"), mentioned above as seeming to contain *raison* in the sense of *raisonnement,* could refer to *raisonnement* and *ordre,* to the formation of arguments, and to their arrangement. There are no passages in the *Pensées* in which we cannot satisfactorily interpret *raison* as referring to the ability to think in general, and *raisonnement* as one aspect of this ability to think, that of forming syllogisms, of arriving at a decision concerning the truth or falsity of a proposition by forming a *jugement* out of several others.[6] Thus, to return to 455/530, *raisonnement* is related but opposed to *sentiment,* since both operations involve forming *jugements,* making decisions; like *sentiment, raisonnement* can be either an operation, as here, or a product, as in 704/467, but in either case it refers to this specific mental activity. *Raison* is suggested as a means of deciding whether a proposed *sentiment* is a *fantaisie* or not, since it might be a question of principles, of their combination, or of their arrangement (*ordre*), that is, of any of the operations of reason (536/651).

When *raison* is seen in this way, its relationship to the heart is easier to understand. Both deal with principles, both try to combine ideas in an effort to discover what is true and what is false, that is, to form *jugements;* it is just that *raison* does more.[7] The heart never goes beyond conception and judgment, beyond the immediate perception of truth through direct combinations of ideas. Reason, on the other hand, goes beyond these two steps when necessary and includes *raisonnement* and *ordre.*[8] While Pascal, like Arnauld and Nicole, preferred the more direct knowledge of the heart or of *sentiment* and disliked the idea of having to take these extra steps (142/110; *Logique,* p. 178), he recognized their necessity and their usefulness.

Heart and reason, then, are not completely different types of mental operations. Pascal only opposed them directly in 142/110 and 680/424. I have shown how the real opposition in 142/110 is between *coeur* and *raisonnement,* not *raison* more generally, and 680/424 deals with knowing God—reason obviously has no place in the third order, but this does not mean that it is incompatible with the heart in the second. In this intellectual realm of the

---

[6]Most of the dictionary entries mentioned earlier in this chapter, especially those from Furetière, note that both *raison* and *raisonnement* serve to distinguish between the true and the false.

[7]According to the *Logique,* p. 37, *raisonnements* are *jugements* formed from other *jugements.* In the *De l'Esprit géométrique,* Pascal deals only with method (*ordre*) but mentions another object of the search for truth, "la découvrir" (p. 348A). This step, which comes before arrangement (disposition, demonstration), is precisely the formation of *jugements* and *raisonnements.*

[8]It is important to remember that "le coeur a son ordre" (329/298), although its order is different from that of the *esprit,* of formal reasoning, and it is not the *ordre* discussed in the *Logique.*

second order—we must not forget that the heart also functions in the first and third where it is by necessity opposed to reason—heart and reason share a common goal, the search for truth. Reason is more varied, but not better—its very variety, its characteristic of being "ployable à tous sens" (455/530), makes Pascal prefer the more direct knowledge of the heart.

The best example of how reason can go beyond the heart is in Pascal's description of the *esprit de finesse,* to which I will return in more detail shortly. In brief, however, the *esprit de finesse* functions very much like the heart, and its principles are similar—"il faut un sens bien délicat et bien net pour les sentir et juger droit et juste, selon ce sentiment. . . . Il faut tout d'un coup voir la chose, d'un seul regard et non pas par progrès de raisonnement" (670/512).[9] Until this point in the fragment, we may be tempted to equate the *esprit de finesse* with the heart, but Pascal goes on to point out that the *esprit de finesse* is a sort of *raisonnement,* that it begins with definitions and principles and then goes on to form *raisonnements,* even if it does it tacitly, naturally. The *esprit de finesse* thus goes beyond the heart and is like the *esprit de géométrie* (and the *esprit de justesse*) in that it is involved with drawing conclusions, something the heart does not do.[10]

The differences between heart and *esprit* are clearest in the essential 329/298, where Pascal opposes the heart not to *raison* but to *esprit* whose order is "par principe et démonstration"; it is ridiculous to confuse them, just as it is to do so in 142/110. This opposition between *coeur* and *esprit* is more fundamental than that between *coeur* and *raison* both because, as I have pointed out, the latter two are not really that different, and because *esprit* in the *Pensées* is normally used in association with *raisonnement* and with *démonstration,* making it the precise opposite of the heart.[11] In 414/382, for example, those who "jugent

[9]See Davidson, *The Origins of Certainty,* p. 44, for example. Jean-Jacques Demorest (*Dans Pascal,* Paris: Minuit, 1953, 45) refers to the heart as "l'esprit de finesse enflammé par la foi." For Petitot ("La Théorie de la connaissance chez Pascal," p. 583), the heart can be understood only "par opposition à l'esprit géométrique."

[10]See Mesnard, *Les* Pensées *de Pascal,* p. 90.

[11]This is not the only way *esprit* is used in the *Pensées,* but it is the way it is

par le coeur" are different from those who "jugent par l'esprit," that is, from those who through the *raisonnement* form *jugements* out of other *jugements,* whereas those who judge by the heart operate more directly. In 203/172, religion enters into the "esprit par des raisons" but into the "coeur par la grâce," more directly. *Esprit* is also opposed to *sentiment* (658/814), and it alone sees hidden causes (480/577)—the heart can understand without delving into causes.

It is also in this way that Pascal uses *esprit* in discussing the three *esprits* of *finesse, géométrie* and *justesse.* In spite of the notoriety of the former two, as described in 670/512, the distinction between the *esprits* of *justesse* and *géométrie* is more fundamental—these are really two different types of mental activity, whereas the *esprits* of *géométrie* and *finesse* differ more in the nature of their principles than in their operation. It is as if Pascal first described the "deux sortes d'esprit" (669/511; i.e., *justesse* and *géométrie*), and then made a secondary distinction between *géométrie* and *finesse,* since the latter two deal with numerous principles; otherwise a reader might infer that, since both deal with numerous principles and are thus different from the *esprit de justesse,* they are more similar than they actually are.

Of the two main types of *esprit* described in 669/511, that of *justesse* is able to "pénétrer vivement et profondément les conséquences des principes," whereas that of *géométrie* is able to "comprendre un grand nombre de principes sans les confondre." These two *esprits* are precisely what Arnauld and Nicole call *raisonnement (esprit de justesse)* and *ordre (esprit de géométrie)*—penetrating principles is the act of forming proper *raisonnements,* and understanding a larger number of principles is arranging them in a convincing demonstration (following the rules that Pascal gives in the *Esprit géométrique* and that Arnauld and Nicole adapted in part IV of the *Logique*). Pascal makes the connection between the *esprit de justesse* and *raisonnement* ex-

---

normally used when dealing with intellectual operations, with the search for knowledge. It is also used in such ways as the Holy Spirit, the spirit of the letter, wit or mental quickness, esprit de corps, "dans cet esprit."

plicit in 670/512—"il faut avoir la vue bien nette pour voir tous les principes, et ensuite l'esprit *juste* pour ne pas raisonner faussement sur des principes connus" [italics mine].[12] Similarly, in the same fragment, he associates the *esprit de géométrie* with "démontrer par ordre," which is itself opposed to "les [principes] sentir et juger droit et juste, selon ce sentiment, sans pouvoir le plus souvent le démontrer par ordre comme en géométrie."

Given this fundamental distinction between the two mental operations that characterize the discursive operations of the mind (*justesse-raisonnement* and *géométrie-ordre,* both of which are opposed to the operations of the heart, of *sentiment*), it only remains to distinguish between two *esprits* which deal with a large number of principles and which draw consequences from them. The difference lies in their principles—those of the *esprit de finesse* are "dans l'usage commun et devant les yeux de tout le monde," and those of the *esprit de géométrie* are "éloignés de l'usage commun." Both are a "sorte de raisonnement" and begin with definitions and principles (note that definitions are never mentioned in discussions of the heart), but the *esprit de finesse* operates "tacitement, naturellement et sans art." This does not make its operations different from that of the *esprit de géométrie,* however—"les géométres seraient donc fins s'ils avaient la vue bonne."

It is obvious that the *esprit de finesse* operates very much like the heart, since Pascal insists on *sentir* and *juger,* on "tout d'un coup voir la chose," on "voir tous les principes," and since he later says that *sentir* is a better verb than *voir,* which is traditionally associated with more formal reasoning. Still, it remains a type of *raisonnement,* and it draws conclusions from definitions and principles, whereas the heart does not.

The presence of definitions is a major difference between *coeur* and *esprit,* between *sentiment* and *ordre (démonstration, méthode).* Pascal never speaks of the heart as having to define its terms, but he insists on it constantly where proofs (*ordre*) are concerned (see his letter to Noël and the *Esprit géométrique,*

---

[12]This seeing is the action of the *sentiment*—"on les sent plutôt qu'on ne les voit."

pp. 356–57, for example). The heart does not need to define its terms; its understanding is direct and immediate, and it deals with things that are natural. The *esprit de finesse* includes definitions, but they are rarely apparent, since its principles are "devant les yeux de tout le monde" and since it operates naturally; the *esprit de géométrie,* however, deals with principles which are so far from common usage that it must define the terms used in forming these principles before it can operate.

Although Pascal never says so outright, it seems clear that the heart could never operate on such uncommon, unnatural principles, even though it deals naturally with the infinity of numbers and the three-dimensionality of space (142/110). Such principles, although they are concerned with science, are also essential to an understanding of human nature, as is everything with which the heart deals. Pascal came to consider geometry as "le plus haut exercice de l'esprit" but he also considered it useless (letter to Fermat, 1660, p. 282B); it is not the sort of thing with which the heart is concerned. Geometry is not natural in the sense that it does not involve human nature or human needs, and it is precisely these needs of which the heart and the instinct are especially aware. Here, Pascal's notion of the heart, as many critics have pointed out, is close to the Biblical notion of "le fond de l'être," of one's innermost needs.[13] Reason, on the other hand—and not only in the realm of geometry—often deals with principles that are less essential to basic human needs. Its principles may come from anywhere, as long as they are clear and evident. They may be definitions or axioms, or already established propositions: "même les propositions géométriques deviennent sentiments, car la raison rend les sentiments naturels" (531/646). With these principles established, we can go on to *raisonnement* and to *ordre,* to proofs.[14] Obviously, not all of the activities of reason are based

---

[13]See Russier, p. 156, and García, "El Corazón como fuente de conocimiento en Pascal," p. 259. According to Miel and Laporte, the heart is the seat of all our faculties: *Pascal and Theology,* p. 158; *Le Coeur et la raison selon Pascal,* p. 101.
[14]The Port-Royal *Logique* includes definitions ("de nom"), axioms, and propositions which have already been proved as principles that we can safely use in proofs (pp.88, 323).

on such principles. The *esprit de finesse* deals with precisely the opposite kind of principles, much more like those of the heart, though the fact remains that, as part of reason, it goes on to draw consequences and is thus different from the heart.[15]

In 671/513 Pascal equates *jugement* with *sentiment* and *sciences* with *esprit.* Then, in a similar sentence, he equates *finesse* with *jugement,* and *géométrie* with *esprit.* It is obvious, as in his comments on *coeur, sentiment,* and *raisonnement* in 142/110, that he would prefer *finesse–jugement–sentiment* to be enough and not have to involve *géométrie–sciences–esprit* (i.e., *raisonnement* and *ordre.* It is also obvious that he cannot bring himself to deny that the *esprit de finesse* is really a type of *raisonnement,* more closely related to geometry than to heart, at least in its mode of operation. *Coeur* remains separate from *raison,* even if its principles are comparable and preferable. Not only is *coeur* more direct and spontaneous, and thus less open to distorting influences, it also deals with useful principles—especially the "morale du jugement" of 671/513, though the *esprit de finesse* could do this also—in all three orders. Ultimately the major advantage of the heart is that it can operate not only in the realm of human knowledge but also in that of the senses, of the body, and of God. *Sentiment* can also operate in all three realms (see chapter 1), it can "feel" sense impressions, ideas, and God. The *sentiment,* however, is not just the operation through which the heart acquires knowledge; it is also the operation which forms the principles and *jugements* upon which the more formal reasoning processes, *raisonnement* and *ordre,* are based. *Sentiment* is thus associated with *coeur* and with *esprit–raison* and is the fundamental operation of the former and the basis of further operations of the latter.

---

[15]We can see Pascal's hesitations about the nature of the *esprit de finesse,* which he calls a type of *raisonnement* without equating the two. He qualifies its capacity to "tout d'un coup voir la chose" with "au moins jusqu'à un certain degré" (just as he qualified "sans . . . pouvoir le démontrer par ordre" with "le plus souvent"). I have already discussed how he qualifies the use of *voir* with "on les sent plutôt qu'on ne les voit."

As I pointed out at the end of chapter 1, the association of *sentiment* with *coeur* and with *esprit–raison* explains why Pascal's use of the term *sens* as mental operation is so hard to define. (Arnauld and Nicole's choice of *sens* and *sentiment* as examples of words with multiple meanings is another indication of the complexity of these terms; see p. 84 of the *Logique.*) The "sens bien délicat" of 670/512 which is necessary to *sentir* and to *juger* is obviously the same as *sentiment,* and the "sens droit" and "droiture de sens" of 669/511 are equally obviously examples of *raisonnement.* In the last paragraph of the fragment, Pascal uses "droiture d'esprit" instead of "droiture de sens" and makes the association even clearer.

The other uses of *sens* as mental operation fall into two categories—448/894 and 449/902, in which we would have to lose our *sens* to draw certain conclusions, and 78/44, 681/427, and 682/428, in which *sens* is linked to *jugement* by *et,* making it hard to decide whether *sens* means something similar to *jugement* or something different. The first category is best interpreted as referring to reason in general, but with emphasis on the *raisonnement,* since in both fragments there are conclusions to be drawn. In the second category, *sens* in 78/44 seems to refer to *raisonnement,* but in 681/427 and 682/428 we could interpret *sens* either as referring to *raisonnement* or as being a synonym for *jugement* (and thus opposed to *raisonnement*). It is also possible that *sens* refers to common sense ("le bon sens") in both these fragments, as it does earlier in 682/428; in this case the meaning of *sens* would be similar to the one it has in "perdre le sens" in 448/894 and 449/902. (The passage in 681/427 that is similar to 682/428 does not mention "sens commun" and "sentiments de la nature," but simply "tout sentiment.")

The last two passages from 681/427 and 682/428, one a rewriting of the other, show Pascal searching for the best terminology. They are a perfect example of the complexity of his view of mental capacities, of how it can be difficult to interpret the terms that refer to them. It is sometimes especially difficult to separate *sentiment* and *raisonnement,* since, despite their differences, the latter depends on the former and its products can themselves become *jugements* or *sentiments* (more complex ones formed from simpler ones). The human mind operates in various ways, and terms which refer to it in general must necessarily remain somewhat vague, so that they can be adapted to the particular type of reasoning in question. This is especially true of *raison* and of *sens,* and to a lesser extent of *sentiment* and of *coeur.* Still, as I have shown, these latter two terms can be interpreted much more precisely than is usually done, and terms such as *raisonnement, principes, esprit, instinct,* can be interpreted quite precisely. In short, it is possible to be quite clear about what Pascal meant when he referred to specific mental operations, but when he referred to our reasoning powers in general, we cannot expect him—especially in a collection of notes—to be quite so precise.

The complexity of human nature as Pascal saw it is reflected in the complexity of his discussion of the search for knowledge. Not only do people function in three different orders, but they are also caught between states of former grandeur and present misery, between the angels and the animals, with a hope of something to come. Pascal's preferences obviously go to the third order and to our former nature; he prefers that we know "toutes choses par instinct et par sentiment," not "par raisonnement" (142/110). His preferences for a method of communicating the truths that he knew (felt) also go in this direction, but he was perfectly aware that most methods, like most knowledge, derive from the *raisonnement* and from *ordre.* These methods will be the subject of the next part.

Before going on to the next section, however, it is helpful to see Pascal's terms together, organized according to the terminology of the Port-Royal *Logique* (in capital letters across the top). Operations are identified with 'O' and products with 'P.'

CONCEVOIR	**JUGER**	**RAISONNER**	**ORDONNER**
raison (a power)			
	finesse (O)	justesse (O)	géométrie (O)
définition (P)	principe (P)	démonstration (P) proposition (P)	ordre (P) preuve (P)
idée (P) sentiment (OP) principe (P)	jugement (OP) sentiment (OP) principe (P) sens (O)	raisonnement (OP) sens (O)	disposition (P)
	instinct (OP)		
coeur (a power)			

Part II

Methods

5

Methods in the Scientific Works

The most general sense of the word method, in the seventeenth century and today, is that of a way of doing something.[1] It is a term which refers to a combination of individual mental operations (such as conception of ideas plus the formation of principles) and almost always supposes the existence of some other method, of some other way of doing the same thing. In many cases, a person will defend his or her method against that of another person, but it often happens that someone who is acutely aware of the complexity of human nature is also aware of a variety of ways of doing the same thing. We find both cases in Pascal, depending on whether he is in what Robert Nelson calls an adversarial or an advocative relationship.[2] In the first instance, when he is trying to point out errors to a correspondent or to a reader, he is usually adamant about the existence of a single method which alone is applicable to the case in question. When he is in an advocative relationship, however, trying to help bring someone around to a certain point of view, he is more likely to acknowledge the existence of different methods of arriving at a given goal.

The something that Pascal is doing in almost all his writings is communicating truths he has found. There are various kinds of truths, from simple physical phenomena (first order) to divinely revealed truths (third order) including scientific theories and human psychology. Some are subject to authority (theology, history), others to observation (physics), still others to demonstration (mathematics), but in all these cases there is a basis for determining the truth and for convincing a reader of that truth. In areas such as philosophy and human psychology, however, whether we have a persuasive text such as the *Pensées* or a lyrical one such as the *Mémorial* or the *Mystère de Jésus*, there is no objective, universally accepted basis.

---

[1]See the dictionaries of Richelet, Furetière, and the Académie Française.
[2]*Pascal: Adversary and Advocate* (Cambridge: Harvard University Press, 1981).

One way we may distinguish among different types of truth is by a careful application of the terms we discussed in part 1. Some truths, for example, are accessible through the heart, others through reason; some are in the first or second order, others in the third; some have more everyday ("dans l'usage commun"; 670/512) principles than others. It is also useful to look at texts such as the *Préface sur le Traité du vide,* in which Pascal distinguishes among various disciplines concerned with the search for truth. Differences among ways of determining and communicating truth will become clearer after discussions of Pascal's methods in each of these areas. In general, however, his statement at the beginning of *De l'Esprit géométrique*—a work whose subject is method—applies equally well to his scientific, religious, philosophical or psychological texts:

> On peut avoir trois principaux objets dans l'étude de la vérité; l'un, de la découvrir quand on la cherche; l'autre, de la démontrer quand on la possède; le dernier, de la discerner d'avec le faux quand on l'examine.

He goes on to say that the demonstration of truth already possessed includes the distinguishing of it from falsehood, and we can conclude that the search for and the demonstration of truth constitute Pascal's primary goals in his writing. Or rather, since demonstration involves demonstrating a truth to someone, we can conclude that these goals are the search for and the communication of truth.

It is precisely within this context of the communication of demonstrable truth that Pascal uses the word *méthode* most often, both in the *De l'Esprit géométrique* and in his mathematical works such as the *Traité des ordres numériques, Des Caractères de divisibilité des nombres,* or the *Sommation des puissances numériques* (see pp. 68B, 84A, and 93B, for example). He uses it only once in the *Pensées,* and rarely in his works on physics, preferring words such as *ordre* or *règle,* to which I will return later. In physics, "la preuve consiste en expériences et non en démonstrations" (p. 232B); in the *Pensées* Pascal is obviously concerned with less scientific methods. In discussing his methods, it is important to follow the same procedure as in discussing individual mental operations—we must discuss what he says about method in general and about certain individual methods, before going on to a more general discussion of how he wrote and what methods he used. Pascal is one of the rare writers who affords us access to at least three levels of discourse: what he said, the methods he used to say it, and what he thought about these methods. The second is necessary to understand a fragmentary text like the *Pensées* in which context is so often lacking, and the third is necessary to understand the second.

His most complete discussion of method is in *De l'Esprit géométrique,* the beginning of which I have already quoted. Regardless of which title we prefer to use, it is essential to consider the works commonly known as "De l'Esprit géométrique" and "De l'Art de persuader" as a single work.[3] I will follow the precedent of Arnauld and Nicole, in the *Logique;* they refer to "un petit écrit non imprimé" which contains the discussion of *définitions de nom* and of five rules for "la méthode des sciences" (*Logique,* pp. 21, 333). Since the second of these two subjects is treated by Pascal in what is known as "De l'Art de persuader," it is obvious that Arnauld and Nicole—who had access to Pascal's manuscript and who knew him while he wrote it—considered it as part of what they call "De l'esprit Géométrique" (p. 21).

The most important reason for considering these two supposedly separate works as one is that there is no break between them. The subtitles which Lafuma and other editors give to the two sections of the work are completely misleading. The text identifies a first section, "De la méthode des démonstrations géométriques, c'est-à-dire méthodiques et parfaites," which Pascal opposes in the preceding paragraph to the "ordre géométrique, c'est-à-dire méthodique et accompli" (p. 349A). In other words, Pascal had two subjects to discuss—the method of demonstrating truths in geometry and the way of ordering, or organizing them. (These are other words for the distinction that he makes in the first paragraph, between demonstrating and distinguishing it

[3]I will use the standard title *De l'Esprit géométrique* to refer to both parts of the work, though "Réflexions sur la géométrie en général" is perhaps more accurate.

from the false—"les deux ensemble enfermeront tout ce qui sera nécessaire pour la conduite du raisonnement à prouver et discerner les vérités"; p. 349A.) He never takes up the second subject, however, except in a paragraph (p. 357A) that he never developed: "Je passe maintenant à celle [règle] de l'ordre dans lequel on doit disposer les propositions, pour être dans une suite excellente et géométrique. . . . Après avoir établi. . . ." [Pascal's ellipses]. Thus, if there is a "Section II" at all, it begins with this paragraph; the discussion of the "art de persuader" that begins on p. 355A is certainly not a second section opposed to the first.

A discussion of the *art de persuader,* in fact, follows quite logically from the discussion concerning demonstration. Pascal's discussions of his two main points (define everything—paragraphs 9–36; prove everything—paragraphs 37–44) lead him to the same examples (time, space, number, etc.), and then to the "plus grandes merveilles de la nature." A long discussion follows of the same "double infinité," the subject of the famous fragment of the *Pensées* on "la disproportion de l'homme" (230/199). The last paragraph of this discussion uses much of the same vocabulary as 230/199 and concludes with an explanation of why he felt it necessary to write this long digression (p. 355A).

This paragraph also explains the necessity for my "digression" into the form of *De l'Esprit géométrique:* what one demonstrates is inseparable from how one demonstrates it and from how one talks about how to demonstrate it. Pascal's efforts to convince his prospective readers of the truth of this difficult key concept of double infinity, along with his more general discussion of the means of demonstrating truth, are inseparable from the *art de persuader,* just as demonstration is inseparable from communication. He states in the second sentence that a discussion of demonstration includes a discussion of discerning the true from the false; he identifies discernment with the arranging of demonstrations, with the "ordre géométrique," as opposed to the "conduite des démonstrations géométriques" (p. 349A). In this way, we persuade someone of a truth we have already found. Before going on to the specific rules for demonstrations, pp. 356B–357A (he intended to "donner entières" both subjects), he pauses to point out that the *art de persuader* includes both *agréer* and *con-*

vaincre and that he feels capable of discussing only the latter. Thus, there is no complete discussion of the *art de persuader* but only of half of it; this half of the discussion is the *art de convaincre* which, like the entire *De l'Esprit géométrique,* consists of demonstration and ordering (arranging). This "véritable méthode qui formerait les démonstrations . . . consisterait . . . à définir tous les termes et à prouver toutes les propositions" (p. 349A), while "ordre" consists of "disposer les propositions [which have already been proved] . . . dans une suite excellente et géométrique" (p. 357A).

Thus, Pascal can write at this point "Voilà en quoi consiste cet art de persuader, qui se renferme dans ces deux règles: Définir tous les noms qu'on impose; prouver tout, en substituant mentalement les définitions à la place des définis." This specific "cet art" is obviously not the entire *art de persuader*—Pascal has already said that he is not going to discuss the *art d'agréer,* and he has not. What he discusses is "la méthode entière *des preuves géométriques* de l'art de persuader" (p. 356A; italics mine). He has completed his discussion of how to demonstrate truth (the first of his two points), but to introduce the missing second point, there is only the truncated paragraph "Je passe maintenant à . . . l'ordre." Still, as he said at the beginning, "si l'on sait la méthode de prouver la vérité, on aura en même temps celle de la discerner." ("Discerner" is the same as to establish the "ordre géométrique," i.e., to arrange the demonstrations formed previously.) Pascal was obviously more concerned with the demonstration of truth than with arranging his demonstrations. This concern may be partly responsible for his not having completed an apology, for his not having laid his ideas out in an easy-to-follow order, and it is consistent with his preference for simpler mental operations (*jugement* rather than *raisonnement,* for example).

These simpler mental operations, which have been discussed in previous chapters, correspond exactly to the eight rules that Pascal gives for the *convaincre* (as opposed to *agréer*) part of the *art de persuader,* "la méthode entière des preuves géométriques de l'art de persuader." Definitions, which are the subject of the first three rules, correspond to the first mental operation, conception. As one of the operations of the heart, conception can be physical (stimuli that the senses receive) or intellectual (ideas that the mind receives). In order to use these ideas anywhere except in our own minds, we are obliged to give them names ("nous ne pouvons faire entendre nos pensées les uns aux autres, qu'en les accompagnant de signes extérieurs"; *Logique,* p. 38), that is, to define them, so that they can then be combined to form principles, or axioms. The next two rules concern these axioms that are formed by the judgment, that is by the second mental operation whose function is to combine ideas. Since we are dealing with language, these ideas are replaced by words whose definitions have been carefully determined. The judgment is also an operation of the heart. The last three rules concern demonstrations or, more precisely, the use of definitions (rule 8) and proofs (rule 7) in demonstrations. Definitions obviously refer back to conception, but creating proofs involves the third mental operation, *raisonnement,* or the combining of *jugements* into discursive, logical chains (syllogisms). These proofs can then be combined to form demonstrations.

It is important to note that the first and third of these three categories of rules, which correspond to three mental operations (definitions, axioms, and demonstrations), begin with a reference to an earlier step which can obviate the need for the step in question. Pascal warns against the creation of unnecessary definitions and demonstrations and, since demonstration involves proofs, he includes a warning against unnecessary proofs as well. Pascal says later that we can ignore these warnings (a step in a demonstration is not invalid just because it is unnecessary), but his inclusion of such warnings indicates his desire to keep things as simple as possible. If an idea is clear, it does not need to be defined, just as an obvious proposition does not have to be proved. He makes the same point in the *Pensées* where, echoing the authors of the *Logique* (see the beginning of part 3, for example), he says "plût à Dieu . . . que nous connussions toutes choses par instinct et par sentiment" (142/110) rather than through *raisonnement.* This point is brought home more strongly when we realize that, in the *De l'Esprit géométrique,* Pascal never discusses the final step in the process, the fourth mental operation—*ordre* (which Arnauld and Nicole also call *méthode*). In spite of the fact that the entire work deals with demonstration, there are no rules given for the actual establishment of a complete demonstration ("l'ordre dans lequel on doit disposer les propositions"), but only for forming its parts (definitions, axioms, and proofs).

Now, in the fourth part of the *Logique* ("De la Méthode"), Arnauld and Nicole include demonstration, since it normally consists of several *raisonnements*, but they are careful to distinguish it from what they call *méthode*, which is "bien arranger ses pensées" (p. 291; see also p. 299). They go on to add two rules for method, for arrangement, to the ones they have already established for definitions, axioms, and demonstrations. Pascal never does this. We could attribute his omission to a lack of time, but it could easily be due to a lack of interest or to an uncertainty on his part about how to do it. Indeed, Arnauld and Nicole admit the difficulty of following their two rules, "soit à cause des bornes de l'esprit humain, soit à cause de celles qu'on a été obligé de donner à chaque science" (p. 334). We cannot always apply what we say about a specific case to the entire genre, nor can we always say everything.

Pascal probably became aware of these problems for the first time in his mathematical research. He uses the word *méthode* there fairly often, almost always in association with generalizing a particular rule or approach. The first instance that can be dated accurately is from 1654, in his correspondence with Fermat about the "règle des partis." It is followed by numerous others in his mathematical works from that time on.[4] Pascal wrote to Fermat on July 29, 1654, "Votre méthode est très sûre et est celle qui m'est la première venue à la pensée dans cette recherche; mais . . . j'en ai trouvé un abrégé et proprement une autre méthode bien plus courte et plus nette." On August 24, he added, "la méthode que je vous ai ouverte et dont je me sers partout est commune à toutes les conditions imaginables" (pp. 43A, 46B).

[4]"Méthode" appears in the *Traité du triangle arithmétique*, which is mentioned as finished in 1654, and in the two treatises published with it in 1665, *De numeris multiplicibus* and *Potestatum numericarum summa*, which were probably written in or before 1654. See Lafuma, *O.C.*, p. 50A.

One sees here two of the most important characteristics of Pascal's work in mathematics—the search for a simple, concise approach, and the search for an approach that would apply generally to all related possibilities.

It is this second characteristic that is of special interest here, since this desire for a universally applicable method informs not only the *De l'Esprit géométrique* but also the *Pensées,* where Pascal was looking for a means of convincing any reader of the truth of his (Pascal's) view of human nature and religion. In his letters to Fermat as well as in his treatise on the arithmetic triangle written at about this same time (see especially the "conséquence douzième," p. 53A), Pascal develops what is commonly referred to as the "méthode de récurrence."[5] Mesnard and Prigent compare it to induction, but we must be careful not to confuse it with induction in the sense of reasoning from the particular to the general through a logical chain (as Prigent seems to do on page 123, where he refers to a chain beginning with "une première vérité incontestable"). This is one meaning of induction in mathematics, but there is another: proving that if something holds for one integer, it also holds for all others. It is obviously impossible to make a case for each individual integer, since there is an infinite number of them, so such a method is necessary if one is ever to proceed beyond isolated cases. The whole point of a *méthode de récurrence,* then, is to avoid the necessity of chains of inductive reasoning simply by replacing one half of a *jugement* (A = B) with a related concept (C = A), so that a simple *raisonnement* (A = B and C = A) can be formed. This method is thus not only widely applicable but also concise and simple.

An excellent example of Pascal's concern with this universality of method is the final paragraph of his *Traité des ordres numériques,* written in conjunction with the treatise on the arithmetical triangle. Using the imperfect tense, he describes the beginning of his research and defends his early findings in which he reached his results "non pas suivant une règle générale mais

---

[5]Mesnard, *Les* Pensées *de Pascal,* p. 62; Prigent, "La Réflexion pascalienne sur les principes," pp. 119, 123. See also Brunschvicg, *Blaise Pascal* (Paris: Vrin, 1953), 133–35 and Lafuma, *O.C.,* p. 43A.

suivant une règle appropriée à chaque ordre particulier" (p. 68B). He was consoled in this lack of a more general method by the fact that other methods were no better, and he had little hope of finding a general method applicable to each order. But—and here he passes to the *passé composé*—he had better results than he had hoped for, and he can announce that the method he has already described is "tout à fait générale." He continues by saying that this general method was

> fort goûtée de mes savants amis, amateurs de solutions universelles. Ce sont eux qui m'ont conseillé de tenter une résolution générale des puissances numériques à l'instar de la résolution générale des ordres. J'ai suivi leur avis, et je n'ai pas trop mal réussi, ainsi qu'on pourra s'en rendre compte plus bas. (p. 69A–B)

Along with the obvious desire to show the full generality of his method, we see here the future author of the *Provinciales*, manipulating his verb tenses to create a brief narrative in the midst of a serious treatise, criticizing his competitors indirectly, showing the approbation of other experts, resorting to understatement to praise himself, and finally presenting his evidence.

There are numerous other passages in which Pascal insists on the generality of his method (pp. 73A, 84A, 90A, 91B, 93B, 102A, and 131A, for example), but it is not necessary to quote them all to make it clear that Pascal was constantly concerned with developing a method that was as general as possible. This is the same concern we find in *De l'Esprit géométrique*, where the method of geometry represents the "véritable méthode." It is the rigorous nature of a geometric proof, or demonstration, that allows us to establish a truth beyond doubt, and Pascal uses it not only to prove individual cases but also to prove the applicability of what he has just shown to all related cases. For example, in the "conséquence douzième" (pp. 52B–53A) of the treatise on the arithmetical triangle, Pascal first states the problem and establishes his definitions; he then proposes two propositions, the first of which is clear and evident and does not require proof (see rule 1 for demonstrations, p. 357A) and the second of which (i.e., that the proportion in question is the same in all similar cases) is not. He thus proves the second proposition, using the proposition already accepted as evident (rule 2 for demonstrations) and substituting definitions for less precise terms, such as "en une base quelconque, comme en la quatrième Dλ, c'est-à-dire si D est à B comme 1 à 3 . . ." (rule 3). As he said in *Des Combinaisons,* "je pourrais dire d'un mot que. . . . Mais voici comment je le démontre" (p. 53B).

Pascal had to make this same point (we must show how we arrive at an opinion, rather than just stating the opinion) to Père Noël; he insists on the importance of demonstrations in most of his writings about physics. Noël's methodology was extremely suspect, and his definitions were especially vague. Pascal took him to task in a magisterial exposition of the scientific method, in which he states a "règle universelle" for the recognition of truth: to make a definitive judgment about the truth or falseness of a proposition, one of two conditions must exist:

> (1) Qu'il paraisse si clairement et si distinctement de soi-même aux sens ou à la raison, suivant qu'il est sujet à l'un ou à l'autre, que l'esprit n'ait aucun moyen de douter de sa certitude, et c'est ce que nous appelons *principes* ou *axiomes.*
> (2) Qu'il se déduise par des conséquences infaillibles et nécessaires de tels principes ou axiomes, de la certitude desquels dépend toute celle des conséquences qui en sont bien tirées. (p. 201A)

This is essentially a summary of the eight rules in *De l'Esprit géométrique.* Pascal insisted on the proper way to demonstrate truth in this letter to Noël because his argument with Noël concerned conclusions drawn from certain principles, or definitions. He makes a similar argument in his letter to Le Pailleur about Noël, stating that "les degrés qui nous mènent à la connaissance des vérités sont la définition, l'axiome et la preuve" (p. 210A). Obviously, Pascal insisted on demonstrations in physics that were as rigorous as those in mathematics, and especially on the importance of principles (axioms, a term which Pascal does not use in the *Pensées*).

There is a major difference, however—the principles of physics are experiments. Pascal spends most of his second letter to Noël discussing experiments that provide principles from which to deduce the hypotheses he is supporting. He discusses the importance of experiments in more detail in the *Préface sur le Traité du vide,* in which he describes experiments as "les seuls principes de la physique" (p. 231B). In a mathematical demonstration, consequences are deduced from principles based on definitions that may be arbitrary, but in physics these principles must be drawn from observation and experimentation. While some subjects, such as history and theology, obtain their principles from some authority, physics falls solely within the domains of *expériences* and *raisonnement* (pp. 230–31). We notice here Pascal's familiar theme of the three orders in which senses and reasoning are opposed to authority, be it human or divine. The senses form the basis of experiments, and reason the basis of demonstrations (*raisonnements*), and we must use both carefully in order to arrive at the truth about physical phenomena.

In the *Préface sur le Traité du vide* Pascal also points out that the reliance on experiments causes a problem which cannot be solved as easily as it was in mathematics: "dans toutes les matières dont la preuve consiste en expériences et non en démonstrations, on ne peut faire aucune assertion universelle que par la générale énumération de toutes les parties ou de tous les cas différents" (p. 232B). The "méthode de récurrence" is not applicable here, since we cannot prove something about a particular phenomenon without looking at it individually. In mathematics, where all definitions are arbitrary, the "vérités sont étroitement enchaînées les unes aux autres" (p. 70A) and what is true about one can be shown to be true about all.[6] There is no such link among phenomena of the physical world, however, and we must look at every case, that is, define every term.

---

[6]Pascal often insists on the arbitrariness of definitions. See *De l'Esprit géométrique:* "Rien n'est plus libre que les définitions" (p. 350B) and the first *Provinciale:* "Je ne dispute jamais du nom, pourvu qu'on m'avertisse du sens qu'on lui donne" (p. 374A).

Pascal was aware of the problem of defining terms in mathematics also but felt that it was surmountable. He admits in *De l'Esprit géométrique* that his "véritable méthode" is impossible, since "les premiers termes qu'on voudrait définir, en supposeraient de précédents . . . et . . . il est clair qu'on n'arriverait jamais aux premières" (p. 349B). The example of geometry shows, however, that there are certain words which "désignent si naturellement les choses qu'ils signifient, à ceux qui entendent la langue, que l'éclaircissement qu'on en voudrait faire aporterait plus d'obscurité que d'instruction" (p. 350A). In fact, there are certain words "incapables d'être définis," of which nature has given everyone "une idée pareille," "sans paroles" (p. 350B). We can thus begin from these terms, define all others, and thus use successfully the rules for demonstrations which Pascal gives later. As examples of words everyone understands, he gives *temps, espace, mouvement, égalité, majorité, diminution,* and *tout.* Although he has problems with Père Noël, to whom he has to explain a sentence which he thought "évident et convaincante d'elle-même" ("tout ce qui est espace est corps"; p. 204B), he finds a way of rewording his sentence and remains convinced that there are terms upon which to base a demonstration.

Pascal is acutely aware here of the importance of language, and of its failings. It is through language that we define terms, combine them to form principles, and combine these principles to form propositions and proofs (i.e., sentences and paragraphs). The success of geometry depends on nature, which sustains our "lumière naturelle . . . au défaut du discours" (p. 350A). Similarly, Pascal falls back on something like nature in fragments of the *Pensées* such as 670/512, in which a "sorte de raisonnement" is carried out "tacitement, naturellement et sans art," and 142/110 ("plût à Dieu . . . que nous connussions toutes choses par instinct et par sentiment, mais la nature nous a refusé ce bien"). I will return to Pascal's views on language in more detail later, especially in chapters 11 and 12, but it is important now to look at what happens when we deal with terms about which there is no agreement, no natural, shared common definition.

In all of the above texts, Pascal is concerned with demonstration, with the *raisonnement,* and is acting on the assumption that "on ne devrait jamais consentir qu'aux vérités démontrées," which would be based on shared definitions. This process is what he calls the "art de convaincre," but he was well aware of its opposite, the "art d'agréer." The principles of "l'esprit sont des vérités naturelles et connues à tout le monde," but those of the *volonté* are "certains désirs naturels et communs à tous les hommes" (p. 355B). These desires cause us to accept ideas, or opinions, with as much certitude as we do ideas that are demonstrated through reason—after all, they are natural and shared by all, just as are the undefinable terms mentioned above which go to make up the principles of the *art de convaincre* (outside artificial realms such as geometry). Problems thus arise not when we are concerned with the certainty of these opinions but when they conflict with opinions received through reason (*entendement,* demonstration, *art de convaincre*). The result is a "balancement douteux entre la vérité et la volupté" (p. 356A); if we wish to be persuasive, we must address the *volupté* through the *art d'agréer* as well as the *vérité* through the *art de convaincre;* the two together make up the *art de persuader.*

Pascal goes on to explain the principal difficulty: while our desires are natural and common to all people, "les principes du plaisir ne sont pas fermes et stables." He can present a way to form convincing demonstrations, but only if "les principes qu'on a une fois avoués demeurent fermes et sans être jamais démentis" (p. 356A–B). The problem is that there are very few of these undisputed principles outside of geometry, so the method that he presents is not applicable to all subjects. It would be if all subjects had firm principles, which is why he can begin his discussion of his method immediately after a discussion of why it would not work—there is nothing wrong with his method, and anyone could use it if all the principles were well-formed and agreed on.

We find here the same assessment of the capacities of the human mind that we find in the *Logique*—"la plupart des erreurs des hommes . . . viennent bien plus de ce qu'ils raisonnent sur de faux principes, que non pas de ce qu'ils raisonnent mal suivant leurs principes" (p. 177). It is also the same assessment that Pascal makes in the *Pensées,* such as in 670/512—once we recognize the principles in a science such as geometry, "il faudrait avoir tout à fait l'esprit faux pour mal raisonner sur des principes si gros qu'il est presque impossible qu'ils échappent." Given the proper principles, Pascal felt he could prove anything.

6

Methods in the *Ecrits sur la grâce* and the *Provinciales*

Pascal felt that he could prove anything, given the proper principles, because he had confidence in human reason and in the senses within their proper domains. As he said near the end of the last complete *Provinciale,* "le rapport des sens et de la raison agissant dans leur étendue [est] certain" (p. 467A).[1] The human brain can form an idea of concrete physical objects or of abstractions (ideas); it can then create combinations of these conceptions (concrete or abstract) and form an opinion as to the validity of the combinations. It can also create more complex combinations by adding third terms and it can even arrange these more complex combinations in order.

These mental operations are those discussed in part 1—conception, judgment (combining conceptions), *raisonnement* (the more complex combinations), and *ordre,* or *méthode.* They also form the elements of the geometric method Pascal discusses in *De l'Esprit géométrique* (see the preceding chapter) in which he expresses his preference for the simpler ones (principles, or axioms, rather than *raisonnements*) and his special concern for the proper definition of terms and establishment of principles. This method is not the "véritable ordre, qui consiste . . . à tout définir et à tout prouver" (p. 349B), since there will always be terms too simple to be defined and principles too clear to be proven, but it is the one that Pascal thought was the best available. He uses it to some extent in all his writings that are intended to communicate knowledge; though he does not say much in *De l'Esprit*

[1]The idea of domains, of limits to the applications of reason and the senses, will become clearer as this chapter progresses. One of Pascal's earliest statements of this idea is in the *Préface sur le Traité du vide* in which he differentiates among disciplines by the nature of their principles (authority versus experience, for example). He says there that the principles of theology are "au-dessus de la nature et de la raison" (p. 230B). Still, reason can work with these principles.

géométrique about its applications to subjects other than geometry, he does so in several other places.[2]

The most important applications for the present study, which is concerned ultimately with Pascal's methods in the *Pensées,* are those which deal with religion. As early as January 1648, less than two years after the beginning of the Pascal family's association with Jansenism, Pascal wrote to his sister Gilberte of his discussion with M. Rebours (confessor of the nuns at Port-Royal):

> Je lui dis ensuite que je pensais que l'on pouvait, suivant les principes même du sens commun, démontrer beaucoup de choses que les adversaires disent lui être contraires, et que le raisonnement bien conduit portait à les croire, quoiqu'il les faille croire sans l'aide du raisonnement. (p. 272A)

It is clear that Pascal is thinking of using the geometric method, especially since he mentions that M. Rebours' reaction to this statement was influenced by his knowledge of Pascal's experience in geometry.

We find numerous examples of "le raisonnement bien conduit" in the *Ecrits sur la grâce,* some of which possibly date from this same period in Pascal's life.[3] The first *Ecrit* begins with "il est constant que" as Pascal establishes his principles, and draws what conclusions he can from them ("Il est donc évident que . . ."). He then defines the problem ("Il est question de savoir si . . .") and clears up some terms ("celle qui sera dominante et maîtresse de l'autre sera considérée comme unique en quelque sorte"). Only after these preliminary considerations does he go into specific cases, beginning with phrases such as "c'est ainsi que" (p. 311A–B).

These opening paragraphs of the first *Ecrit sur la grâce* are

---

[2]Pascal discusses applications of the geometric method to physics in the letters to Noël discussed in the previous chapter. In the *Provinciales,* see letter 18, pp. 466B–467A. In the *Pensées* there is of course the discussion of the three *esprits* in 669/511 and 670/512, as well as discussions of proofs of Scripture (305/274), of beauty and taste (486/586), and of his approach to the subject (454/527, 457/532, and 661/821, for example).

[3]See Miel, *Pascal and Theology,* pp. 195–201, and Nelson, *Pascal: Adversary and Advocate,* pp. 53–56 and 272, n. 3.

an excellent lesson in the geometric method described by Pascal in *De l'Esprit géométrique.* Though he does not comment much on method per se, the vocabulary ("il est constant que," "il est question de savoir si," "sera considérée comme," etc.) is a lesson in itself and makes clear to the reader not only what Pascal is saying but also how he is approaching the problem and how the reader should approach this and similar problems. There are similar expressions throughout the *Ecrits,* all of them efforts by Pascal to use reason to justify Augustinian theology, just as he used reason to justify his findings in his scientific work. We also find references to other aspects of Pascal's geometric method, such as his preference for avoiding proofs (*raisonnements*) wherever possible ("ne démontrer aucune des choses très connues d'elles-mêmes"; p. 357A). Why go to the trouble of demonstrating something when "la simple intelligence de la langue le témoigne" (fourth *Ecrit,* p. 336A)? Similarly, the third *Ecrit* contains expressions such as "n'est-il pas visible que," "qui ne voit que," and "qui ne sait que" (pp. 327B–328B).

Another important characteristic of Pascal's application of the geometric method, which he mentions in the *Ecrits sur la grâce,* is the "enchaînement admirable" between propositions that seem contradictory (p. 322A). This phrase recalls his statement in *Des Produits de nombres consécutifs:* "tant les vérités sont étroitement enchaînées les unes aux autres" (p. 69B–70A). In the latter work, Pascal describes his approach to a problem as applicable to all related cases—a "résolution générale." Just as scientific problems that seem quite different can be solved with one well-constructed approach, so statements that seem to be contradictory can be shown to be true when seen in the context of the right approach (the right theology). The "right approach" allows us to make the necessary distinctions, to know how to look at things that at first seem contradictory. We must have careful definitions, so that we know exactly what a term means—in a specific context—before we interpret a proposition that includes that term. In the case in question, there are two ways of searching for God, two ways of abandoning Him, and so on, and "des deux propositions qui semblent opposées, l'une appartient à l'une de ces manières, et l'autre à l'autre" (p. 322B). Similarly,

St. Augustine's expressions are not contradictory "parce qu'elles regardent des choses différentes" (p. 326A).

There are important differences, however, between mathematics and theology. In the mathematical example quoted in the preceding paragraph, Pascal was dealing with numbers in different orders (squares, cubes), but still with numbers to which he could apply his reason. In the theological example, however, the two different orders are the human and the divine; seen in the particular, the effects of the two different *manières* have definite causes, but seen in common, "ils n'ont aucune cause que la volonté divine" (p. 323A). Similarly, in dealing with seemingly contradictory statements concerning human and divine wills, "la véritable cause de toutes ces différentes expressions est que toutes nos bonnes actions ont deux sources: l'une, notre volonté, l'autre, la volonté de Dieu" (p. 323B). For Pascal, we must be aware of the difference between the human and the divine, but we cannot apply our reason to the latter.

In short, when Pascal applied his geometric method to theology, he had to deal with several new dimensions: (1) language as data, not just as the expression of observations or ideas; (2) the authority of previous work on the same subject; (3) the divine. In the first case, Pascal was dealing with statements by other people, rather than with mathematical propositions or physical phenomena. The meaning of a mathematical proposition is clear, and we have only to show that it is true or false. With a linguistic proposition, however, we must often explain it before showing it to be true or false. (If the proposition is a statement by Church fathers, as in the fourth *Ecrit*, explanation is sufficient, since their authority assures the truth of the statement, once it is understood.) This process is similar to that of explaining why a certain physical phenomenon exists—except that we are dealing with definitions and principles (words and combinations of words), as in mathematics, rather than with experimental data, as in physics. For example, as mercury in a tube is at a certain level because of the effects of atmospheric pressure, so a statement by Church authorities is phrased in a certain way because they were fighting the effects of certain heresies (fourth *Ecrit*, pp. 336B–337B).

In the case under discussion in the fourth *Ecrit*, we have to choose between two possible meanings of a linguistic proposition ("Les commandements ne sont pas impossibles aux justes"); this is rarely the case with a proposition in mathematics, which is usually quite referential, due to the care taken with definitions. Pascal says that we have to examine not only the terms of the proposition but also the objective of its writer(s) and its context (p. 336A). His experience in science stood him in good stead here. He was used to examining phenomena (*esprit de justesse*), to taking care with definitions and with considerations of other phenomena that could affect the one in question (*esprit de géométrie*); and his experience in projective geometry had taught him to look at things from more than one point of view.[4] It was thus not difficult for him to apply his scientific methodology to language.

It was more difficult for him, however, to become accustomed to taking into account what earlier writers had said about a subject, although he was well aware that it was essential in certain disciplines. He begins the *Préface sur le Traité du vide* with this distinction: while some disciplines "dépendent seulement du raisonnement," others "dépendent seulement de la mémoire et sont purement historiques, n'ayant pour objet que de savoir ce que les auteurs ont écrit" (p. 230A). He includes knowing what they wrote and the meaning of what they wrote; Pascal used his scientific methodology to ascertain the latter, but that was as far as he needed to, or could, go. All that remained was to judge whether the meaning matched the meaning of previous authors. It often took a *raisonnement* to determine this meaning (again, Pascal preferred not to have to take this step, if the meaning was clear), but the meaning then became an idea to be compared to another in a *jugement* (the second mental operation).

---

[4]On Pascal's work in projective geometry, see René Taton, "L'Oeuvre de Pascal en géométrie projective," *Revue d'histoire des sciences* 15 (1962): 197–252; the article is also published in Taton, ed., *L'Oeuvre scientifique de Pascal* (Paris: P.U.F., 1964), 17–72. The importance of Pascal's work in projective geometry is also emphasized by Pierre Humbert in *L'Oeuvre scientifique de Blaise Pascal* (Paris: Albin Michel, 1947); see the quotation in the Lafuma edition of Pascal's *Oeuvres complètes*, p. 35B. J. H. Broome, whose *Pascal* (London: Edward Arnold, 1965) contains an excellent chapter on Pascal's work in mathematics and science, insists on the importance of the notion of perspective in the scientific work and in the *Pensées*; see pp. 48–49.

There is a special type of authority involved in religious subjects, that of God. A statement from the scriptures or Church fathers might not seem true, but its divine origin guarantees that it is, so we have only to interpret it properly. Furthermore, Pascal accepted as axiomatic that these divinely inspired writings could not contradict themselves: "la contrariété des propositions est dans le sens et non pas dans les paroles, autrement l'Ecriture serait pleine de contradictions" (third *Ecrit*, p. 326A; see also 289/257). Still, this was not difficult for a physicist like Pascal to accept—the experimental data with which he worked might seem strange (the existence of a vacuum, for example), but he was convinced that his sense perceptions were correct and that he had only to look at the data in a different way to make sense of them, to find causes for the effects he perceived.

In the *Ecrits sur la grâce*, then, Pascal was concerned primarily with explaining and justifying the Augustinian point of view by comparing it to accepted doctrine. He paid only secondary attention to discrediting Molinist-Pelagian and Calvinist views, assuming them to be false because they lacked authority. In the *Lettres provinciales*, however, Pascal was dealing not only with doctrines known to be true or false but also with doctrines that he considered false but which the Jesuits and many of his readers considered true—there was an authority to be accepted, but another, spurious one to be discredited. He was thus faced with the same situation that he described at the beginning of *De l'Esprit géométrique:* "On peut avoir trois principaux objets dans l'étude de la vérité: l'un, de la découvrir quand on la cherche; l'autre, de la démontrer quand on la possède; le dernier, de la discerner d'avec le faux quand on l'examine." To find the truth, he had only to read the proper authorities (scripture, councils, fathers, etc.). As in the *Ecrits sur la grâce*, he did not have to prove this truth, but he did have to explain the Jansenist position, so his readers could understand it and see it was the same as accepted doctrine. Perhaps more importantly, he had to explain the Jesuit doctrines so that the difference between theirs and accepted doctrines would be clear.

The geometric method is admirably suited to such a task,

but it is not the only method at work in the *Provinciales*. Dialogue, dramatization, irony, hyperbole, pun, variety of tone, and many other effects are at work; since they are ways of doing something, they could be considered methods. Still, these latter are ways of approaching, of preparing, the reader more than of interpreting and communicating truth, more "art d'agréer" than "art de convaincre."[5] When it came to the primary task of justifying Jansenist doctrines, Pascal used the geometric method, and often gave his Jesuit opponents lessons in its use. This is especially true in letters 11–18, though the earlier letters make a more effective use of it in a more subtle (*fin*) way and without commenting on it.[6] This more effective use is one of the best examples in Pascal's works of why he preferred the simpler mental operations (*concevoir, juger*, as opposed to *raisonner* and *ordonner*). When we can be convincing without using formal proofs, and especially without using chains of such proofs, readers will be more receptive than when we have to resort to demonstrations. This point is made repeatedly in the *Logique* and in the *Pensées* in fragments such as 142/110 and 670/512, and in his description of the geometric method in the *Esprit géométrique* (these texts were discussed in part 1). He preferred not to define terms that were "parfaitement connus," not to examine possible axioms that were "parfaitement évidents et simples," and not to prove things "très connues d'elles-mêmes" (p. 357A).

We can see Pascal aiming at such simplicity in the *Provinciales*, at a new type of "étude de la vérité" (p. 348A) intended for the non-specialist reader. He felt that the geometric method was the best for communicating (*démontrer*) truth, but he needed

---

[5]I am concerned primarily with Pascal's search for and communication of knowledge and what he said about it, rather than with how he prepared his readers to receive this knowledge. As he said in the *Esprit géométrique* (p. 356A), this latter subject, the "art d'agréer," is by no means less important, but most of it is outside the scope of this book, as it is of that of the *Esprit géométrique*.

[6]Marsha Reisler, in "Persuasion through Antithesis, an Analysis of the Dominant Rhetorical Structure of Pascal's *Lettres provinciales*" (*Romanic Review* 69 (1978): 172–85), points out that Pascal's "seeming 'dialogues' conceal a rigorously controlled persuasive process" (p. 172) and the reader is not really invited to make his or her own judgments (p. 182). Using Stanley Fish's terminology (*Self-Consuming Artifacts*, Berkeley: University of California Press, 1972, 1–2), she says that Pascal's discourse in the *Provinciales* is more rhetorical than dialectical, more satisfying to the reader's needs than disturbing.

to avoid formal proofs (which would alienate the general reader), to keep things simple, and to allow the reader to come to his or her own conclusions. Accordingly, he concentrated on definitions in the first four letters, and on principles in letters 5–10; it was only in the last eight letters, when he was responding directly to the Jesuits, that he resorted more to *raisonnements;* he was less concerned with interesting his readers and in keeping things simple than in refuting Jesuit accusations point by point. Is it any surprise that most readers, especially today, find these last eight letters the least interesting, while they still enjoy reading the earlier ones, especially the first four? It is not just that readers enjoy the irony, hyperbole, puns, and other effects that are more evident in these earlier letters; Pascal's reliance on simpler mental operations makes them easier and more enjoyable to read, and admirably effective.

Pascal begins the first letter by defining the subject of the debate at the Sorbonne in its simplest terms and by breaking it down into questions of *fait* and of *droit.* The rest of the letter revolves around the interpretation of the word *prochain* and criticizes the Jesuits less for their ideas than for their use of words. Pascal insisted on definitions before discussing the geometric method in *De l'Esprit géométrique* (p. 349A–B), and he begins the campaign of the *Provinciales* in the same way—"il n'y a rien de plus permis que de donner à une chose qu'on a clairement désignée un nom tel qu'on voudra" (*De l'Esprit géométrique,* p. 349B), and "je ne dispute jamais du nom, pourvu qu'on m'avertisse du sens qu'on lui donne" (first *Provinciale,* p. 374A). There is very little demonstration in this first letter; the truth is known (Church doctrine), and the positions of the various protagonists are known. Or rather they are known once Pascal has uncovered the true meanings behind their words. There is little else to do, and the reader does not need further convincing. Definitions are the first step, and if they are clear, a good geometrician (or theologian, or layman) does not have to go any further. It is badly used words that cause the problems, not the reasoning that comes later. In the case of *prochain,* "Heureux les peuples qui l'ignorent!" (p. 375B); if *prochain* could be banished from the Sorbonne, the dispute would be over in an instant.

The second, third, and fourth letters are written in a similar way. The second discusses the Jesuit view of grace which is "suffisante sans l'être" (p. 375B). "Les mots sont inséparables des choses," and once a term has been defined, its definition cannot be changed. The fourth letter begins with a definition of *grâce actuelle,* since the supposedly naive author insists on knowing "ce que ce terme signifiait" (p. 382A). Once the Jesuit has been forced to substitute the "définition à la place du défini" (p. 382A), the pernicious nature of his view is clear. It is clear not because Pascal proves that the Jesuits' view is pernicious, but because he reminds the reader of the accepted view of the Church, and the reader can see that the two views are not the same; the Jesuit view is thus false. This point is made most clearly in the third letter, in which Pascal explains to his provincial readers that the Jesuits mentioned no specific heretical view in their censure of Arnauld. They could not, because Arnauld was careful to show how each of his views conformed to a passage from the Church fathers (p. 380A).

In each case Pascal makes his point by clarifying a definition, or by establishing a comparison between two opinions, or doctrines. The first two mental operations (conception, judgment) are all that is needed—"ce n'est pas ici un point de foi, ni même de raisonnement; c'est une chose de fait: nous le voyons, nous le savons, nous le sentons" (p. 384B). We see something and we can know something about it, because the *sentiment* ("nous le sentons") enables us to compare it to something else that we know to be true. For Pascal, we as Christians know it to be true because there exists a body of writings whose authority is undoubted. Pascal can say, in the fourth letter, "je me moque des ces auteurs-là, s'ils sont contraires à la tradition" (p. 383A), and he continues to use this standard throughout the *Provinciales.* In letters 5–10, he deals with Jesuit moral standards rather than with their views on grace, but he still makes his points by insisting on definitions and on comparisons with Church tradition. As a seemingly objective observer, he presents the Jesuit views, Nicole says, "par le récit de quelques entretiens entre lui et l'un de leurs casuistes."[7]

[7]Nicole, *Avertissement sur les dix-huit lettres,* in the Cognet edition of the *Provinciales,* p. 471.

Again, he does not try to prove anything about the Jesuit views; he tries simply to expose them to comparison with tradition, using irony and other means to drive the point home. When the Jesuit says, in the ninth letter, "on ne peut nier que cette méthode de traiter de la dévotion n'agrée tout autrement au monde que celle dont on se servait avant nous" (p. 409B), Pascal has only to add, "Il n'y a point de comparaison," or, in the tenth letter, "Etrange théologie de nos jours!" (p. 418B).

In many cases, Pascal points out that the comparison between Jesuit maxims and Church tradition is unfavorable to the former because they mix the three orders of facts, reason, and faith. "L'esprit de l'homme se joue si insolemment de l'amour de Dieu" (p. 417B), and the Jesuits mix human lives and money (p. 401A), state and church (p. 400B), human and divine laws (p. 398A), society and morality (p. 390A). He was careful at the beginning of the fifth letter to have his Jansenist friend explain that the Jesuits' main principle is to accommodate "des personnes de toutes sortes de conditions et des nations si différentes," even those who "cherchent le relâchement" (p. 388A). This is one of the rare passages in the first ten letters where Pascal includes fairly full explanations of Jesuit doctrines, except those from the mouths of the Jesuits. Once the Jesuits' basic principle (axiom) has been established (since it is contrary to Church tradition, it is certainly not too obvious to obviate the need for explanation), Pascal can rely on the simpler mental operations.

In addition to exposing the Jesuit position to unfavorable comparison with accepted tradition, Pascal exposes the Jesuits' faulty definitions. Whereas the definitions of types of grace in the first four letters are often "définitions de nom," in which we can assign any word to something everyone understands, most of the definitions in letters 5–10 are "définitions de chose" that depend on "ce qui est enfermé dans la veritable idée d'une chose."[8] For example, the Jesuit explains in the tenth letter, "comme il y a peu d'âmes qui veuillent quitter les occasions prochaines, on a été obligé de définir ce que c'est qu'occasion prochaine"

[8]*Logique,* p. 164; these ideas are attributed to Pascal in the first preliminary discourse, p. 21. See also *De l'Esprit géométrique,* p. 349.

(p. 416A). The Jesuits change what all speakers of the language recognize as the true meaning of a term ("la veritable idée d'une chose"), and when this term is part of an expression of accepted Church doctrine, they are guilty—by comparison—of establishing new and false doctrines.

We must not confuse the Jesuits' interpreting Church doctrine in order to accommodate their supporters, with Pascal's interpreting Church doctrine (in the *Ecrits sur la grâce,* p. 336A, for example) in order to clarify its meaning or to show that it is in accord with the "sens commun" (letter to Mme Périer, 26 January 1648, p. 272A). He is careful never to change the meaning of the traditional authors and careful to define all his terms according to their normal meanings ("la simple intelligence de la langue"; p. 336A). Furthermore, following the principles of his geometric method, he explains only terms and expressions for which the meaning is not clear, such as "les commandements ne sont pas impossibles aux justes"; he does not have to explain why a statement such as "ils sont ensemble probables, et sûrs par conséquent" (p. 393A) is unacceptable.

Pascal is much more involved in explaining terms and expressions in the last eight *Provinciales.* In letter 11, when he stops presenting Jesuit doctrines and begins defending himself against their accusations, his problem is no longer a simple question of being careful with definitions and of comparing doctrines to accepted standards, but a question of explaining where his accusers have gone wrong. In the first ten letters, the Jesuits' errors, and how they arrived at them, were so clear as to need no demonstration, and Pascal was thus able to address himself to the general public. By the eleventh letter, however, he is addressing the Jesuits themselves, and he has to reason with them, much as he did with Noël concerning physics.

It is clear from the beginning of letter 11 that something is different, and it is not just the ad hominem arguments.[9] The style of the fourth paragraph, for example, is unlike anything in the first ten letters:

---

[9]Mme de Sévigné noticed the difference: "quelle solidité, quelle force . . . sur un ton tout différent" (21 December, 1689).

> Car, mes Pères, puisque vous m'obligez d'entrer en ce discours, je vous prie de considérer que, comme les vérités chrétiennes sont dignes d'amour et de respect, les erreurs qui leur sont contraires sont dignes de mépris et de haine, parce qu'il y a deux choses dans les vérités de notre religion: une beauté divine qui les rend aimables, et une sainte majesté qui les rend vénérables; et qu'il y a aussi deux choses dans les erreurs: l'impiété qui les rend horribles, et l'impertinence qui les rend ridicules. (pp. 419A–B)

The very length of the sentence, the two subordinate clauses at the beginning, and especially the numerous parallel clauses after *parce que*, give the sentence a formal, rhetorical character, rarely found in the earlier letters, which simply presents definitions and ideas to the mind without supplying all the connectives and explanations. The concentration of conjunctions in this sentence is twice that of the average letter, and that of logical conjunctions (*car, puisque,* and two *parce que*) is four times the average. Pascal is perhaps sincere when he says he is forced to enter into such a discourse, but once he does, he employs a very formal, rhetorical style with almost every element doubled so that the connections of all the parts of the complex sentence will be as clear as possible. And this sentence is only a prelude to the "C'est pourquoi" which follows!

In contrast, consider a passage from the third letter:

> Voilà de quelle sorte ils s'emportent; mais ce sont des gens trop pénétrants. Pour nous, qui n'approfondissons pas tant les choses, tenons-nous en repos sur le tout. Voulons-nous être plus savants que nos maîtres? N'entreprenons pas plus qu'eux. Nous nous égarerions dans cette recherche. Il ne faudrait rien pour rendre cette censure hérétique. Il n'y a qu'un point imperceptible entre cette proposition et la foi. (p. 380B)

There is only one conjunction (*mais*) for seven sentences. Pascal's irony builds as the implications between each sentence become stronger, as the reader supplies the missing connectives. There is nothing wrong with Arnauld's "proposition," and we do not have to be "pénétrant" to see this. Rather than argue about nothing, Pascal restates the obvious, which his reader can see even if the

Jesuits cannot. Arnauld's statement is identical to the doctrines of the Church, and nothing the Jesuits can do can change this comparison.

Robert Nelson has made similar comments about the style of letters 11–16, pointing out that the imperative and the horatory subjunctive are more characteristic than the declarative sentences of the first ten letters and that there is more of a concern for logic than for esthetics (*Adversary and Advocate,* 201–204). Most of the effects mentioned earlier (drama, hyperbole, puns, etc.) are rarely used in these last letters, as Pascal explains step by step what should have been clear after the first ten letters. He has to make explicit such things as "N'est-ce pas mot à mot le contraire de votre discours?" (p. 431A), or "Il y avait une distance infinie entre la défense que Dieu a faite de tuer, et la permission spéculative que vos auteurs en ont donnée" (pp. 432A). He has to teach them "les principes les plus simples de la religion et du sens commun," how to know when something is naturally obvious and thus does not need proving, and especially not manipulation by Jesuit casuists (p. 435A).

He also has to give lessons in proving (p. 430A–B), beginning by ascertaining what the pronoun in the statement in question refers to. It is the same problem as in so many other cases, that of reasoning from faulty principles (here, inaccurate quotations): "de sorte qu'au lieu que vous concluiez, de votre passage supposé, que Lessius n'était pas de ce sentiment, il se conclut fort bien, *de son véritable passage,* qu'il est de ce même sentiment" (p. 431A; italics mine). These lessons are meant to be insulting to the Jesuits and were obviously not included in the letters to Pascal's provincial friend.

It is not that Pascal has suddenly started using the geometric method, but that he is using *raisonnements* as well as definitions and comparisons and that he makes explicit references to his method. Many of his readers got the point in the first ten letters, but the Jesuits refused to recognize the truth, as Pascal saw it. He preferred to present it so that a reader could see it and accept it directly; when that did not work, he resorted to a stricter, more linear presentation. He preferred the operations of *sentiment* but could use *raisonnement* when he had to.

Pascal makes a similar, explicit use of the geometric method in the last two complete letters (17 and 18), addressed to Père Annat rather than to all the Jesuits. The letters are full of "pour vous le montrer clairement," "il est donc sûr," "de là vient que" (pp. 457A–458B), and so on, and the seventeenth begins with a discussion of how we should try to prove the author's heresy. Although in some passages Pascal is trying to show the Jesuits that "vous n'avez plus rien à reprendre en vos adversaires, parce qu'ils détestent assurément ce que vous détestez" (p. 462A), he demonstrates less an attitude of conciliation than the familiar tactic of comparing Jansenist doctrines to orthodox ones. Pascal is not insisting on the Jesuits' errors (he is writing to only one person), but he does accuse Annat repeatedly of stirring up unnecessary trouble. He concludes with a lesson on the three orders and the proper use of reason (p. 466B),[10] and though he offers to stop writing if Annat will, his is hardly a friendly gesture of peace. His criticism of Annat for stirring up unnecessary trouble within the Church is as condescending and harsh as was his criticism of the Jesuits as a whole for their errors of doctrine and for its malicious intents. Most importantly, Pascal does not have enough faith in Annat's integrity to present him with definitions and comparisons from which Annat could draw his own conclusions (as Pascal did for his provincial friend in the first ten letters). Annat was too predisposed to make Jesuit errors to come to the proper conclusions by himself, and Pascal had to lead him by the logical hand.

If Pascal had written all the *Provinciales*, especially the first few letters, in the style of the sentence from letter 11, it is very doubtful the letters would still be read—any more than we read Arnauld's and Nicole's treatises, for example. Whether Pascal developed his stylistic skill in spite of or because of his lack of

[10]As Duchêne points out in "D'Arnauld à Pascal: ou l'art de faire 'plus court': l'exemple de la dix-septième *Provinciale*," in *Méthodes chez Pascal* (Paris: P.U.F., 1979), p. 262, Pascal avoided the question of whether the five propositions were contained word for word in Jansenius in the first letter, but he returned to it in the eighteenth when he was refuting and arguing with Annat rather than conversing with his provincial friend.

formal education, that skill is admirably suited to his purpose.[11] Perhaps even more important, it would prove to be even better suited to his purpose in the *Pensées.* There these same stylistic features are considerably more prominent and characterize a series of "digressions sur chaque point qui a rapport à la fin" (329/298), an "art de persuader" that contains even less of a geometric "art de convaincre" than do the *Provinciales* yet retains its rigor and its power.

[11]It is interesting to note that the first letter has the highest percentage of conjunctions of any of the letters, equaled only by letter 17. The percentage drops drastically in the next two letters and does not approach the same level until letter 11. It is as if Pascal were still feeling his way in the first letter; if so, he certainly found it quickly.

7

Methods in the *Pensées*

In the two preceding chapters, I discussed Pascal's preferred method of geometry and his applications of it in science and in theology. He used this method in physics as well as in mathematics, although he had to replace the arbitrary definitions of geometry with data from experiments. In theology, he was able to use it with only minor adaptations in the *Ecrits sur la grâce* and in *Provinciales* 11–18. These adaptations were necessary because of the existence of an authority outside the realm of reason and because of the need to interpret the statements of some of these authorities. The first ten *Provinciales* are different in still other ways, since Pascal avoided the use of demonstrations and proofs, that is, of the third and fourth mental operations, *raisonnement* and *ordre.*[1]

In discussing the *Ecrits sur la grâce* and the *Provinciales* it is not always possible to quote passages where Pascal talks about method and about what he was doing. These works contain occasional references to his method, such as his comments to the Jesuits on how to proceed in certain areas (pp. 430A–B, 466B, for example), but most of the preceding chapter had to be based on suggestions in Pascal's vocabulary (the presence of words such as *définir* and *prouver*) and on an interpretation of the texts. With the *Pensées,* however, it is possible to return to the approach used in chapter 5—that of discussing what Pascal said about his method—before going on to a discussion of what he actually did. This chapter will thus be devoted to a discussion of what Pascal says about method in the *Pensées;* it will be followed by a section on the styles he uses in the *Pensées* and by conclusions about his methods.

First, it is necessary to describe the *Pensées* briefly. In doing

[1]See Davidson (*Blaise Pascal,* p. 97): "The striking diversity of contours and structures that we meet in these works causes us to suspect at once that Pascal's approach—mode of thought and discourse—must vary according to the problems encountered in the subject matters he is treating." Davidson is keenly aware of the relations between thought, methods, and styles, and I will refer to his distinctions more fully in the concluding chapters.

so, I follow to a large extent the conclusions of Philippe Sellier in his edition of the *Pensées*. He bases his description of the *Pensées* and his text on the second copy, which, he argues convincingly, reflects the state of the manuscript of the *Pensées* at the time of Pascal's death in 1662.

Although there is no finished apology, the basis of a possible plan for a possible apology can be found in the content of many of the fragments and in Pascal's preliminary classification.[2] He arranged about one third of the fragments of the *Pensées* into titled *liasses*, or dossiers of notes, grouped into two major sections (mentioned in 40/6, 644/780, and 644/781, for example)—the human condition with and without God. The first part (dossiers 3–12) deals with the human condition and human needs; he saves a discussion of Christianity and of various ways of proving its excellence for the second part (dossiers 13–28).[3] It seems clear that Pascal had in mind comparing his view of humanity and its needs with his presentation of Christianity and how it responds to these needs, so that a reader could judge for himself or herself the wisdom of embracing Christianity.

The fragments that are not included in the first twenty-eight dossiers are also divided into dossiers; they deal mostly with these same themes, though some of the fragments are obviously notes which reflect his concerns while he was writing the *Ecrits sur la grâce* and the *Provinciales*. Many fragments are amplifications, workings out of ideas only sketched briefly in the preliminary classification, or they are documentation about prophecies, miracles, the history of the Jews, and other subjects (Sellier edition, p. 18). There is also considerable discussion of ways to interpret figuratively the Bible and other related texts. In general, there is a lot of historical evidence, which can be contrasted to the psychological and philosophical evidence in the first twenty-eight dossiers, and especially in dossiers 3–11.

---

[2]It must be understood that whenever I mention a plan for the *Pensées*, I mean a possible, provisional one. The evidence for such a plan is there, and we can use it as an example of Pascal's thought process, as an aid in understanding his method(s), without assuming that it is a definitive plan.

[3]The first dossier is what Sellier calls a fleshed-out table of contents, and the second deals with *ordre*.

This psychological and philosophical evidence is based on no quotable authority and relies for its effect mainly on Pascal's skill as a convincing writer, as someone who knows how to *agréer* and to *convaincre.* For the first time, he is writing for non-believers; he thus cannot begin with an explanation of Christian doctrines (as in the *Ecrits sur la grâce*), or contrast accepted ones to spurious ones (as in the *Provinciales*), or even assume their existence, since it is the very existence and excellence of these doctrines which is in question. Nor can he use traditional proofs, such as the one which proves God's existence from nature:

> J'admire avec quelle hardiesse ces personnes entreprennent de parler de Dieu.
>
> En adressant leurs discours aux impies leur premier chapitre est de prouver la divinité par les ouvrages de la nature. Je ne m'étonnerais pas de leur entreprise s'ils adressaient leurs discours aux fidèles, car il est certain que ceux qui ont la foi vive dedans le coeur voient incontinent que tout ce qui est n'est autre chose que l'ouvrage du Dieu qu'ils adorent, mais pour ceux en qui cette lumière est éteinte et dans lesquels on a dessein de la faire revivre, . . . c'est leur donner sujet de croire que les preuves de notre religion sont bien faibles. (644/781)

Trying to use such a proof not only would not work, but it would lessen the admiration of a reader for other, more valid proofs. Pascal was convinced that his task in an apology would not be to pose a hypothesis and to prove it, but to revive ("faire revivre") something that is already there, left over from a first nature (see chapter 2). It is a matter of pointing out comparisons between existing needs and answers to those needs, that is, of proposing principles and *jugements,* not of creating strings of *raisonnements.* He could still use something like his preferred geometric method, though it would have to be adapted to the subject matter. But rather than suggest what he could, or would have done, it is preferable to look at what he says himself about method in the *Pensées.*

Much of what Pascal said about method has already been

discussed in the first four chapters, where most of the examples were drawn from the *Pensées.* These chapters dealt with his views on human mental operations, on how one acquires knowledge. These are a necessary preliminary to a discussion of Pascal's methods, of how he communicates knowledge, since he was trying to adapt his method of communicating truth to the way in which a reader would receive it. In particular, he had to be careful with definitions and establish with certainty all the necessary principles. These were the crucial steps, since he remained confident that a reader could draw the proper conclusions from these principles. Pascal also considered it crucial to maintain the distinctions between the three orders, those of facts, reason, and revelation (see chapters 1 and 4); it was important for a reader to use reason, but only in its proper realm. The contents of the Bible and other divinely inspired texts were not subject to debate, nor were obvious facts. It was also important that he maintain these distinctions himself as he wrote—a non-believer was obviously not going to accept the authority of divinely inspired texts, so principles had to be drawn from things common to all readers, that is, from what is natural.

The proper use of reason is one of the main premises upon which the *Pensées* rest, since it is the only way in which Pascal can communicate with his readers. If a person has not received religion in the heart, through God's grace, then the only other way is to receive it in the mind through reason. Force is not an effective means:

> La conduite de Dieu, qui dispose toutes choses avec douceur, est de mettre la religion dans l'esprit par les raisons et dans le coeur par la grâce, mais de la vouloir mettre dans l'esprit et dans le coeur par la force et par les menaces, ce n'est pas y mettre la religion mais la terreur. (203/172)

More specifically, as the passages from the *Pensées* quoted in chapter 4 make clear, reason is a powerful tool in the search for truth. Indeed, reason is humanity's most important characteristic and, if used correctly, can lead to God:

> L'homme est visiblement fait pour penser. C'est toute sa dignité et tout son mérite; et tout son devoir est de penser comme il faut. Or l'ordre de la pensée est de commencer par soi, et par son auteur et sa fin.
>
> Or à quoi pense le monde? Jamais à cela, mais à danser, à jouer du luth, à chanter, à faire des vers, à courir la bague etc. et à se battre, à se faire roi, sans penser à ce que c'est qu'être roi et qu'être homme. (513/620)

People should think about themselves and about God (their "auteur"), about what it means to be a person or a king, but instead they often remain mired in the pleasures of the first order. They rarely use the reason of the second order, much less think about what goes beyond it.

When Pascal talks about method in the *Pensées,* he often uses the word *ordre,* not in the sense of the three orders, but in that used in 513/620: that of arrangement, the order in which things should be treated.[4] This is precisely what he had to be concerned with as he thought about a possible apology: what to include and what order to follow. Some of the fragments mention letters, dialogues, discussions, and so on, which could be included and suggest where they might go (dossier 2, for example), while others are concerned more with the question of which approach to follow (329/298, 562/683, 563/684, and 573/694, for example). It is this choice of approach which is of special relevance to a discussion of Pascal's methods. He expressed doubts about the applicability of the geometric method to his subject:

> J'aurais bien pris ce discours d'ordre comme celui-ci: pour montrer la vanité de toutes sortes de conditions, montrer la vanité des vies communes, et puis la vanité des vies philosophiques, pyrrhoniennes, stoïques; mais l'ordre n'y serait pas gardé. Je sais un peu ce que c'est, et combien peu de gens l'entendent. Nulle science humaine ne le peut garder. Saint Thomas ne l'a pas gardé. La mathématique le garde, mais elle est inutile en sa profondeur. (573/694)

[4] *Ordre* is one of the most frequently occurring nouns in the *Pensées,* and approximately 40 percent of these occurrences have the meaning of arrangement.

Pascal could show the vanity of all types of lives by showing the vanity of each one, but the proper order would not be followed. He does not explain why, but his statement that mathematics follows the proper order although it is useless in its depth (thoroughness) suggests that it is because it would be impossible to look at every type of life. Or, it could be because one could never agree on definitions of all the terms needed to describe the vanity of a type of life; in particular, those who preferred a certain type of life would not agree that it was vain. Whatever the reason, Pascal obviously felt that he could not use exactly the same method in discussing ways of living that he used in solving problems in geometry.

Other fragments of the *Pensées* which deal with order in the sense of arrangement mention other problems with applying the geometric method directly to anthropological subjects. Our efforts to establish subdivisions, and other distinctions, in order to understand what we observe around us are doomed to fail, because these distinctions cannot reflect the complexity of nature. Human systems attempt to enclose natural truths in categories, "les unes dans les autres, mais cela n'est pas naturel. Chacune tient sa place" (563/684). It is the constant problem of definitions. Human languages and other systems of classification are incapable of dealing with nature directly, of putting it in human terms: "Mais voilà, direz-vous, tout renfermé en un mot: oui mais cela est inutile si on ne l'explique. Et quand on vient à l'expliquer, dès qu'on ouvre ce précepte qui contient tous les autres ils en sortent en la première confusion que vous vouliez éviter" (562/683).

In short, our efforts to understand the world and our place in it can have at best limited success. Therefore, a writer (unless he or she represents the authority of the Church) who deals with the human condition is confronted with the twofold problem of (1) not having the mental powers necessary for a complete understanding of the subject and (2) dealing with a subject which presents an almost infinite disorder. As Pascal says, his subject in the *Pensées* is so characterized by disorder that "je ferais trop d'honneur à mon sujet si je le traitais avec ordre puisque je veux montrer qu'il en est incapable." As a result, he intends to write "sans ordre et non pas peut-être dans une confusion sans dessein" (457/532). There will be apparent confusion, but only because he is adapting his method to his subject.

He makes a similar point in 329/298, where he compares an order characterized by digression to that of "l'esprit," which is "par principe et démonstration." In other instances in which Pascal opposes a method characterized by principles and demonstrations to another method, this alternative method is one that operates immediately on natural principles and without conscious intervention of the *raisonnement* (142/110, 670/512, for example). It is a method which relies on the *sentiment* and the heart, and it is this second term which Pascal uses in 329/298. He also refers to this method as the order of charity, however, since it is the method used by writers such as Paul, Augustine, and the authors of the gospels who are concerned uniquely with charity, that is, with God's love and with the third order. It remains a method which uses the powers of the second order (otherwise it could not be used by writers to communicate), but it always aims to show the existence of charity, "l'unique objet de l'Ecriture" (301/270). This is why Pascal speaks of digressing from the discussion of one point to a discussion of each related point, "chaque point qui a rapport à la fin, pour la montrer toujours." It is not so much the relationship between points as their common relationship to an ultimate goal which, obviously for Pascal, is God and religion, man's chief end, the "unique bien," or "unique objet."[5]

This "unique bien" is the ultimate goal mentioned in one of the most important fragments about order, 46/12. Here Pascal describes part of a possible strategy: "il faut commencer par montrer que la religion n'est point contraire à la raison." If he has doubts about following the order of geometry and keeping everything in an order acceptable to normal human logic, he still has an idea of where to start and of where he wants to go, and he is confident he can "montrer" that reason and religion are compat-

[5]It becomes clear that the "unique bien" is the same as charity, which is also the "la fin" that we have to show constantly (329/298). The importance of showing, of the verb *montrer*, will be discussed later in this chapter.

ible. This confidence suggests that he intended to use something like the geometric method, to go from point to point and establish comparisons between them, much as he did in the *Ecrits sur la grâce* or in *Provinciales* 5–10. Such an approach would be similar to the one Pascal used in the *Provinciales,* where he avoided as far as possible the more complex mental operations, especially *ordre* (in the sense of an arrangement of *raisonnements*). In doing so he would still need to establish some definitions and principles to replace accepted authority, and this is the role of the psychological and philosophical evidence mentioned earlier in this chapter. It is data that is drawn neither from authority nor from observation of natural phenomena but from Pascal's own observations of himself and others.

The possibility of Pascal's reliance on such psychological and philosophical evidence is supported by the numerous fragments in the *Pensées* where he presents such evidence or discusses its importance. Dossiers 3–16 contain numerous examples, leading up to the famous fragment "Disproportion de l'homme" (230/199) which prepares the "transition de la connaissance de l'homme à Dieu": "Voilà où nous mènent nos connaissances naturelles." Numerous paragraphs begin with phrases such as "Que l'homme contemple donc la nature" or "Que l'homme étant revenu à soi considère ce qu'il est," as Pascal tries to convince his readers to think about their condition rather than avoid it through *divertissement* (dossier 9). As Pascal makes these observations, he is pointing things out rather than proving them. A proof might come later, after all the principles are in place, but the discussion of human nature can only show readers a way of looking at their condition. Pascal's discourse does not have the authority of that of traditional Church writings, for example, and he has to depend on his readers' making a positive comparison between the way they look at themselves and the way he has described the human condition. This example of the *jugement* at work, of the operation of *sentiment* which sees things "d'un seul regard et non pas par progrès de raisonnement" (670/512).

This process of comparison is clearer when one looks at the vocabulary Pascal uses for establishing elements to be compared.

First, he does not use the word *méthode* in the *Pensées* to refer to his own work. *Méthode* occurs only once, in reference to Montaigne, who, according to Pascal, felt "le défaut d'une droite méthode" and who avoided this lack by "sautant de sujet en sujet" (644/780). The comment on Montaigne's lack of method is not necessarily negative, since Pascal himself did not claim to follow the ideal method, but the *Entretien avec M. de Sacy* suggests that he is critical of Montaigne's solution. Pascal uses an *ordre* characterized by digression, but not "de peur d'y enfoncer en appuyant" (p. 295B), out of skepticism about his ability to know, but because it is necessary to consider everything "qui a rapport à la fin" (329/298). He refers everything to "le vrai bien," while Montaigne does not even try (p. 295B). Perhaps Pascal does not use the term *ordre* here because he wants to emphasize that Montaigne realized the lack of a perfect method but could not come up with an alternative *ordre*.

Be that as it may, the preponderance of *ordre* over *méthode* in the *Pensées* is similar to that of *montrer* over *démontrer*. *Montrer* is used ninety-seven times, as opposed to nine for *démontrer*, and it almost always means "point out, show evidence." *Démontrer*, on the other hand, is always used in the sense of proving something logically, that is, of using the *raisonnement* as opposed to setting up principles for the judgment to compare.[6] It is associated with discussions of epistemology or of science, or with the methods of others (Epictetus, for example, in 133/100); it is rarely used when Pascal is making a point about human nature or about religion. A notable exception is in 425/840, where he says that

> les preuves que J.-C. et les apôtres tirent de l'Ecriture ne sont pas *démonstratives*, car ils *disent* seulement que Moïse a dit qu'un prophète viendrait, mais ils ne *prouvent* pas par là que ce soit celui-là, et c'était toute le question. Ces passages ne servent donc qu'à *montrer* qu'on n'est pas contraire à l'Ecriture. [italics mine]

---

[6]Only eight of the ninety-seven occurrences of *montrer* have a meaning similar to that of *démontrer*, and only two of these eight occur in the first twenty-eight preliminary dossiers.

The proofs that Christ and the apostles used are not precise enough to do anything except say something, to show something preliminary ("on n'est pas contraire . . ."); they cannot be demonstrative, they cannot prove. It is also significant that this passage is found in the part of the *Pensées* that deals with proofs of Christianity, a subject that Pascal excluded from the discussions of humanity and its needs. Only after the comparison has been established between these needs and what Christianity can offer does Pascal discuss proofs, either in the dossiers of the preliminary classification which follow the "transition de la connaissance de l'homme à Dieu," or in later dossiers which develop these points in more detail.[7]

In general, Pascal uses *prouver* (60 occurrences) and *preuve* (78 occurrences, singular and plural) in a way closer to that in which he uses *montrer* than to that in which he uses *démontrer.* That is, *prouver* refers to pointing out evidence, to setting up comparisons, to making simple points rather than to making formal demonstrations. Pascal is proving the excellence of Christianity, or the special nature of Christ, and he rejects the traditional metaphysical proofs, especially proofs which take the works of nature as a starting point (223/190, 644/781, 702/463, and 703/466, for example). These are too complex for the average reader and are convincing only to people who are already convinced (250/217). They probably would not convince "des athées endurcis" anyway, and Pascal considers them useless unless the person convinced by them also has a knowledge of Christ (690/449).

The proofs that he does talk about using concern the doctrine, moral laws, miracles, prophecies, and figurative texts of the Church, as well as historical evidence—in particular that drawn from the history of the Jews (21/402, 717/482). These proofs would make up the second part of the possible plan mentioned in 40/6, for example, and would be used only after the proposed first part had established Pascal's view of the nature of humanity and

---

[7]Some of the fragments that discuss proofs are notes for the *Provinciales* (788/952 and 795/960, for example) and do not directly concern the method of the *Pensées.*

its needs. The proofs are quite simple, once the evidence (principles) has been established. For example, proofs of Christianity using Church doctrine or moral laws, such as those found in dossiers 19 ("Fondements de la religion") and 27 ("Morale chrétienne"), compare the Christian view of human nature to that established by Pascal in the first part. If Pascal could show (*montrer*, not *démontrer*) them to be the same, it would require only the simplest *raisonnement* to arrive at a conclusion: I (convinced by Pascal) hold this view; the Church holds this view; therefore the view of the Church is correct (meets my needs). Similarly, if Pascal could establish the existence of a miracle or the accomplishment of a prophecy, a reader could easily conclude that some supernatural power, that is, the God of Christianity, is at work. Or, if the history of the Jewish people, who historically were enemies of Christ, can be shown to corroborate Church doctrines, these doctrines seem more plausible. The same principle applies to what Pascal calls "figures": if a Christian text taken literally seems to contradict either common sense or the views that Pascal has expounded, a figurative interpretation can resolve the seeming contradiction and thus illustrate the doctrine of the "Dieu caché" who does not make everything clear to those who do not believe (275/242).

In all these examples, Pascal is doing little more than establishing ideas or principles which the reader can compare to draw conclusions—his or her view of humanity and that of the Church; what the Jews did and what Scripture says; what Scripture predicted and what happened; ordinary events and those that show evidence of Divine intervention. He uses many of the techniques he used in the *Ecrits sur la grâce* and in the *Provinciales*, such as interpreting texts and comparing Church doctrines to other ideas, but he has to go at least one step farther. There is no accepted authority to which we can compare ideas and principles, so he has to establish the other side of the comparison, a Christian principle or doctrine. If he can do this, the conclusion is almost automatic, but it still requires some reasoning.

This necessity for reasoning to a conclusion is one reason why Pascal mentioned using these proofs only in the second half of his preliminary classification. His view of the God of Christianity is of a God who acts on both the mind and heart of people, "qui remplit l'âme et le coeur de ceux qu'il possède" (690/449). Pascal made it clear that the best way to believe was through *sentiment*—he uses the special term "sentiment de coeur" to distinguish it from *sentiment* as a purely human mental operation—rather than through *raisonnement,* since the latter "démontre" rather than "sent." "Les principes se sentent, les propositions se concluent," and *raisonnement* cannot challenge the principles accepted through *sentiment* (142/110). Pascal thus mentions using proofs only as a prelude to faith, as a means to "préparer la Machine" (45/11). "La foi est différente de la preuve. L'une est humaine et l'autre est un don de Dieu" (41/7). Faith is the goal that Pascal has set for his readers as he considers a plan, and proofs are only a means to this goal. The role of proofs is to convince the reader that Christianity is not unreasonable (46/12), to "le porter à chercher" (39/5). Once readers search for faith, and act and live like Christians, the Christian life becomes a habit, becomes custom, and they can be Christian "mechanically" while waiting for God's gift of faith. Pascal compares custom to the pomp that surrounds kings: "toutes les choses qui ploient la machine vers le respect et la terreur" (59/25) lead subjects to behave as their king would like; similarly, living in respect (Pascal rejects terror in 203/172, quoted above) of God leads people to behave as Christians, a preliminary step to being true Christians.[8]

If proofs play, at best, only an intermediary role, it is partly because, as we have seen, Pascal did not consider them absolutely convincing, especially for nonbelievers who had no inclination to believe them and who were often inclined not to believe. The weakness of proofs stems primarily from the weakness of the principles upon which they are based: "Il n'y a principe, quelque naturel qu'il puisse être, qu'on ne, même depuis l'enfance, fasse

[8]See 661/821, and Hugh Davidson's excellent discussion of "fixation of belief" in chapter 3 of *The Origins of Certainty,* especially pp. 87–89. It is important to note that 661/821 opposes *sentiment* to *raison (raisonnement)* and *argument,* and it mentions the problems caused by the multiplicity of principles. Again, Pascal prefers a simple, direct means of knowledge to the formal process of *raisonnement.*

passer pour une fausse impression soit de l'instruction, soit des sens" (78/44). When we try to decide (make a *jugement*) between two *sentiments* (principles), "il faudrait avoir une règle." However, not even reason can serve as a steadfast rule, just as we cannot prove the "premiers principes" (142/110), and Pascal concludes that there is no such rule and that "tout notre raisonnement se réduit à céder au sentiment" (455/530). If we cannot be sure about many principles, then it is evident we cannot rely on any conclusions drawn from these principles through *raisonnements.* The best we can do is rely on principles, or *sentiments,* of which we are convinced even if we cannot prove why.[9]

The absence of suitable, firm rules is a subject to which Pascal returns often in the *Pensées.* I have mentioned the lack of an accepted authority on which Pascal could base his arguments in the *Pensées,* and authority is one sense of the word *règle.* More commonly, Pascal uses *règle* in the sense of model, as in 455/530 where we need a standard of comparison in order to decide between two principles. Rather than give rules that a reader may find arbitrary (Pascal insists that "il n'y a pas de règle générale"; 452/515, 424/837), he prefers to suggest standards, or principles, from which the reader can draw his or her own conclusions.[10]

The problem here, of course, is that there is no "règle générale," no unique model or point of view (unless, of course, we already accept Christianity). Pascal discusses this problem in some detail in 486/585–86 ("beauté poétique"), where the "modèle d'agrément" depends on a "rapport" between our nature and that of the thing we are considering. Our nature, of course, is something we cannot determine through proofs, just as Pascal could not prove his conception of the human condition in an absolutely convincing way for every reader. The acceptance of such a conception depends on *sentiment,* on principles we have accepted, and the next step is to compare them to the thing in question and to judge whether they match. Similarly, we can judge songs, sonnets, women, and so on, by comparing an accepted

---

[9]See 142/110, quoted above, and Mesnard, *Les* Pensées *de Pascal,* p. 88.

[10]I have treated rules in more detail in my article "L'Idée de règle chez Pascal," in *Méthodes chez Pascal* (Paris: P.U.F., 1979), 87–99.

model to the thing in question. This works fine in geometry, for example, since "on sait bien quel est l'objet de la géométrie et qu'il consiste en preuve." However, we do not know the object of poetry, and a multitude of possible models or points of view leads to a multitude of opinions, the same situation that Pascal discusses in 530/645, and for which there is no rule that permits us to determine the best model.

The notion of *rapport* suggests a return to 329/298 (discussed earlier in this chapter), where Pascal comes as close as he comes anywhere in the *Pensées* to describing his method (*ordre*): "la digression sur chaque point qui a rapport à la fin." The "fin" here, the model to which the thing in question must be compared, is in the order of faith, whether one defines it as charity, God, Christ, the teachings of the Church, or "le vrai bien" (see 301/270, for example, or 690/449: "toutes choses concourent à l'établissement de ce point").[11] Because of the innumerable principles, digression is necessary; we cannot keep the true mathematical order in dealing with a subject as complex as the human condition. We must consider each point, because "l'omission d'un principe mène à l'erreur" (see 670/512 on the *esprit de finesse*).

The consideration of numerous principles involves one of the most important aspects of Pascal's methods in the *Pensées*, the "renversement du pour au contre" and the "pensée de derrière la tête." It is a matter of looking at all sides of a question, of a "renversement continuel" (127/93), of "opinions succédant du pour au contre" (124/90) as we move from one idea to a related, and usually opposite, one. The "pensée de derrière" allows us to hold one idea (opinion) in the back of our minds even while acting as if we held another, to consider the merits of one without forgetting the other. This means of considering principles is described in the dossier "Raisons des effets," which is oriented toward reasoning and proof more than any other in the first section of the classified dossiers (3–12). Even when trying to establish reasons (causes) for effects. Pascal proceeds as much by digression as he does linearly, such as in 135/103, where he establishes nu-

[11]In dossiers 3–12, the model is the view of human nature; that view points toward the 3rd order.

merous and often conflicting principles before arriving at a paradoxical conclusion. I will return to this fragment in chapter 9, where there will be many examples of how this notion of *renversement* leads Pascal to use binary, antithetical structures and to repeat many words. Similarly, there will be many examples in chapter 10 of fragments that use simple linking and opposing conjunctions to create similar structures.

In summary, Pascal's comments on method in the *Pensées* suggest that he wanted to rely as little as possible on the more complex mental operations of *raisonnement* and their arrangement into logical chains (*ordre*), especially in the first part of his preliminary classification. He preferred to cover as many related points as possible, establishing ideas and principles from which his readers could draw conclusions. Ideally, this would be enough. Practically, however, he considered simple proofs which would follow up on these conclusions, thus convincing the reader to live an appropriate life in preparation for the reception of faith. These simple proofs would be based on the historical evidence presented in the second half of this possible plan.

In attempting to employ such a method in the *Pensées*, varying it from part to part, from subject to subject, Pascal needed to employ at least two styles. One style would allow the expression of simple mental operations and leave the conclusions open to the reader, and the second would allow the clear presentation of historical evidence and proofs which would progress logically to a convincing conclusion. This second style is not unusual and is seen in the *Provinciales* and in Pascal's scientific works; the first, in its purest form, is largely special to the *Pensées*. In part 3 I will discuss what Pascal says about style and then analyze various styles in the *Pensées*.

Part III

Styles

8

Methods and Styles in the *Pensées*

In the strictest sense, the *Pensées* are a collection of brief texts in which we find, as the editors of the first edition put it, the thoughts of Pascal on religion and on several other subjects. The relevance of these other subjects to religion can be determined to some extent from the arrangement of the fragments into dossiers and from the content of certain fragments (those of the first two dossiers, for example), so that it is possible to speak with some certainty of Pascal's intentions, of what his thoughts were, of what he was trying to say. We can speak with greater certainty, however, of what Pascal thought about knowledge and the human communication of it and of how he wrote in the *Pensées* and in other texts. For this reason I have been careful to establish in the preceding chapters what Pascal said about the various mental operations and the methods of communicating what we have discovered (see the beginning of *De l'Esprit géométrique*). Armed with an understanding of how Pascal would be likely to approach a discussion of the ability of Christianity to explain the human condition as he saw it, we are in a better position to judge what remains of that discussion. In particular, we are in a better position to approach a study of Pascal's style in the *Pensées* and to understand how one of the monuments of French prose was created. The ultimate goal of this study of the *Pensées* is to see how Pascal constructs his portraits of thought (481/578), a goal Nathan Edelman held to be the goal of any critic: "how intimately expression captures and renders its object."[1]

As John Porter Houston put it, the power of the writings of Pascal (and of Descartes) lies more in "the correspondence to prose style of the thought process and the attitude accompanying

[1]*The Eye of the Beholder,* p. 164. See also Davidson (*Blaise Pascal,* p. 107): "If we start, therefore, with questions of method, we see that Pascal's works oblige us to make distinctions and that the distinctions give us modes of discourse."

it" than in their conventional beauty.[2] Pascal had a definite attitude about the thought processes involved in understanding human nature and religion and wanted to lead his readers to employ similar processes. It was one thing to discuss these thought processes in fragments such as those on the *esprit de géométrie* and the *esprit de finesse,* but quite another to bring a reader to use them. To accomplish this, he would need a method that would present everything—from the most general principles (misery and grandeur of humanity, for example) to the individual fragments and sentences—in a way that reflected the thought processes he believed were most applicable to his subject.

Pascal knew that the thought process he used as a geometrician, proceeding step by step from definitions to a series of proofs, was not applicable to much of the persuasive discourse he had in mind. In dealing with the human condition, for example, we cannot always define terms precisely enough, or in a way acceptable to all readers. At another level, in dealing with religion, there are precepts that depend on a supernatural authority and that are not subject to experimentation or to reason. We cannot create convincing proofs of the existence of God, of the fall from grace, or of God's incarnation, for example; even if we could, there are many readers who would not take the trouble to read through such complex demonstrations.[3]

Pascal's attitude about method, about the relationship between thought and style, must have been based mostly on his understanding of his own thought processes—his discussions of the *esprit de finesse,* of the role of *sentiment* and of *jugement,* are too finely drawn to be merely accounts of something described to him by someone like Méré, or to be borrowed from Arnauld and Nicole. He was aware not only that faith is received through

---

[2]*The Traditions of French Prose Style* (Baton Rouge: L.S.U. Press, 1981), 75. This correspondence of style to thought process is what I refer to when I describe method as putting thought into words, the relationship between thought and language. See the Introduction, and the beginning of chapter 5. The "attitude accompanying it" is something like Lanham's "style of life" which I discuss in chapter 11.

[3]See 222/190. See also Mesnard, "Pourquoi les *Pensées* de Pascal se présentent-elles sous forme de fragments?," *Papers on French Seventeenth Century Literature* 10 (1983): 645.

the heart more directly than through the mind (142/110, 203/172) but, on a more human level, that much of what we know is the result of immediate, tacit understanding rather than of a logical process each step of which can be identified (670/512). He would thus need to modify the basic geometric method with its reliance on chains of *raisonnements*—much as he did in the *Ecrits sur la grâce* and in the *Provinciales*—to create a style which would put such a modified method into practice.

This modified method would have to allow for a discussion of a large number of related subjects, a discussion that would often involve digressions and suggest confusion (562/683, 563/684, and 457/532). The method would use as subject matter topics accessible to the average reader and treat them in a way that would hold the reader's interest. It would favor the simpler mental operations of conception and judgment—the numerous digressions would make it impossible to establish a continuous series of *raisonnements*—and it would often leave the drawing of conclusions to the reader.

This method would also have to avoid the weaknesses of the methods of his adversaries such as Noël and the Jesuits. The three orders would have to remain distinct, with reason to be used in its proper realm but to give way to historical evidence or divine authority where appropriate. Words would have to be used with great care, with the accepted meaning of the word always in mind—ideas are more important than words here. No principles could be accepted unless they were perfectly clear or could be shown to be true, and no conclusions could be drawn unless they followed obviously from accepted principles.

The mention of principles and conclusions is a reminder that Pascal was following the basic premises of the geometric method in spite of having to adapt it to a discussion of human nature and religion.[4] He did not have accepted definitions and principles such as those of geometry, nor experimental data such as that of physics, but he had psychological and philosophical evidence, data drawn not from observation of natural phenomena but from his

---

[4]They are mentioned often in the *Pensées*, especially *principe* and *principes*, which occur 108 times.

own observations of himself and others. He did not have an audience trained in scientific and logical rigor, but he did have an audience that could read and use reason. He also had an audience that was attentive to style, as the success of the *Provinciales,* and the even greater, if posthumous, success of the *Pensées,* has shown.[5]

We could perhaps object that many fragments of the *Pensées* are only rough notes, written with no audience in mind. Although this may be strictly true, we cannot deny that Pascal was writing to express his ideas, and that these fragments exist as texts. They thus have an audience—even if some of them are difficult to interpret precisely because they were perhaps not intended for publication as they stand—and the best tools we have for interpreting them are a knowledge of Pascal's thought processes and of his style. Many of the difficult fragments are like notes, closer to direct expressions of thought than are the more polished, completed fragments. Normally we have little context to use as a guide for interpretation; we are thus forced to rely largely on a knowledge of how Pascal thought and expressed himself. I refer back to the three rules given in the fourth *Ecrit sur la grâce* (p. 336A) for determining the true meaning of a passage: if the "termes de la proposition" are not clear (first rule), and if there is no "suite du discours" to serve as a guide (third rule), often the only way to know the "objet" Pascal had in mind (second rule) is to know how his mind worked and how he tried to put his thoughts into words.[6]

I am particularly concerned in this chapter with a special "subtle" style that Pascal developed in the *Pensées,* a style which reflects the "modified" method mentioned earlier in this chapter and which is often found in the less polished, note-like fragments mentioned above. This style would appear to have been designed most particularly for the discussions of human nature and needs

---

[5]Roger Duchêne's *L'Imposture littéraire dans les* Provinciales *de Pascal* (Aix-en-Provence: Université de Provence, 1984; 2nd ed., enlarged, 1985) goes as far as to attribute the success of the *Provinciales* not only to Pascal's style but to his literary skills that border on "imposture."

[6]We can of course try to use related texts, or a general idea of Pascal's intentions, as a guide, but we can never be sure that these texts or intentions are indeed related to the text we are trying to interpret.

that dominate dossiers 3–12 of Pascal's preliminary classification, and designed less for the discussions of historical proofs, prophecies, and other more formally reasoned subjects which would follow. There are definitely other styles in the *Pensées* that would be more appropriate for these latter subjects, and I will discuss them in the following chapters in relation to this special style—and the method behind it—that is particular to the *Pensées.*

Our most direct contact with these note-like fragments (and with the more polished ones, but to a lesser extent) is precisely through their style, a style that Pascal thought should be an accurate portrayal of thought and nothing more: "l'éloquence est une peinture de la pensée, et ainsi ceux qui après avoir peint ajoutent encore font un tableau au lieu d'un portrait" (481/578). To extend the portrait metaphor, we must represent the original object–thought as accurately as possible; it is obviously impossible to create a perfect resemblance, but the means at our disposal (paint or words) can be made to create in the mind of the observer–reader a "portrait," that is, a good idea of what the original was like.[7] Once we have created this portrait, that is, expressed a thought directly and accurately, it is not necessary to add anything, to make a "tableau"—the observer-reader can make the image his or her own, combine it with others, and make *jugements* about it.

Pascal also uses a painting metaphor to insist the original thought be worthy of representation: "Quelle vanité que la peinture qui attire l'admiration par la ressemblance des choses, dont on n'admire point les originaux" (74/40). The idea is important in painting but even more so in language, since our ultimate worth is in our thought: "toute notre dignité consiste donc en la pensée" (231/200; see also 143/111, 513/620, 626/756, and 628/759). Thought creates a person's worth, or grandeur, and it is as

[7]See Foucault's discussion of representation and resemblance in *Les Mots et les choses,* and the awareness of the arbitrary nature of language in the *Logique.* Pascal knew he could not create a perfect resemblance, and thus he was especially concerned to keep representation as accurate as possible, despite the arbitrariness of the available means of expression.

useless to communicate thoughts that do not reflect this worth as it is to create portraits of unworthy objects. It is not so much that Pascal has no concern for beauty in language or in painting, but that he objects to the admiration of things that are not worthy of it. If we are going to offer something to another person and expect admiration, we should offer something worthy of admiration.

For similar reasons, Pascal was concerned with the effect of words on the thoughts they express: "Un même sens change selon les paroles qui l'expriment. Les sens reçoivent des paroles leur dignité au lieu de la leur donner" (645/789). There is still a question of dignity (worth) and of reversed values—just as we should not let a painting affect our judgment of the original object, so we should not let the words which express a thought distort its meaning, that is, affect whether we think it is worthy of credence. The original, be it the object of painting or of discourse, is paramount—worth and truth are in the object or thought, not in our conception or expression of it.

Again, we should not suspect Pascal of having been unaware of the importance of words, just as we should not suspect him of having been uninterested in beauty. He prided himself on the skillful arrangement of words as well as of thoughts: "Qu'on ne dise pas que je n'ai rien dit de nouveau, la disposition des matières est nouvelle. . . . Comme si les mêmes pensées ne formaient pas un autre corps de discours par une disposition différente, aussi bien que les mêmes mots forment d'autres pensées par leur différente disposition" (575/696; see also 645/784). He did put thoughts (or meanings, in 645/784) first, however. He was interested in the communication of thoughts through the careful use of the means at his disposal, not in arranging words in such a way as to attract the admiration of his readers (466/559); he was certainly interested in being admired, but more for the content than for his style.

Pascal's concern with the direct and accurate representation of thought is also apparent in fragments in which he discusses the importance of a natural style, such as 554/675. Authors who try to win admiration for their works by adding superfluous details (481/578), or by arranging words in such a way as to distort the thought behind them (645/789), write unnaturally and thus surprise (disappoint, leave less than "ravi") those of their readers who have good taste; authors who use "le style naturel" are able to talk about anything in a way anyone can understand.

Communicating in a natural way is not without its dangers, however. We may be tempted to establish clear divisions and subdivisions, and to find terms which sum up an issue, but this is not natural: "Mais voilà, direz-vous, tout renfermé en un mot: oui, mais cela est inutile, si on ne l'explique. Et quand on vient à l'expliquer, dès qu'on ouvre ce précepte qui contient tous les autres, ils en sortent en la première confusion que vous vouliez éviter" (562/683; see also 563/684). There are certain subjects in nature, and especially in human nature, that cannot be treated in simple order. Each truth has its individual place (563/684) and must be discussed in its place:

> J'écrirai ici mes pensées sans ordre et non pas peut-être dans une confusion sans dessein. C'est le véritable ordre et qui marquera toujours mon objet par le désordre même.
>
> Je ferais trop d'honneur à mon sujet si je le traitais avec ordre puisque je veux montrer qu'il en est incapable. (457/532)

We see here the concern with the dignity (*honneur*) of the subject (the *originaux* that paintings resemble), with the close relationship between words and ideas that was apparent in Pascal's comments on painting and style. If the subject to be described is characterized by disorder and is not especially worthy of admiration, then the style used to express the subject should have similar characteristics if it is to represent this disorder accurately and call attention to the subject rather than to itself.

It follows from Pascal's reluctance to establish artificial categories or to impose an artificial order on his subject that there are very few, if any, universal rules for writing. He compares judgments about language to judgment by people in a boat leaving shore who think the port is receding—they need a fixed point of view; the port is sufficiently fixed to determine the relative location of the boat, but "où prendrons-nous un port dans la morale" (576/697) or, by extension, in language? Pascal uses painting again to make a similar point in 55/21; in 452/515 he returns to the missing fixed point of view in the particular case of repeated words. There are times when we should go against the precept of avoiding repetition, since "il n'y a pas de règle générale," but only an awareness that "[on] gâterait le discours" by going out of the way to find different words. How do we know when the discourse is about to be ruined? We do not know, since there is no general rule, but if we follow Pascal's principles of being natural and of representing thought accurately, we may perhaps find the simplest and best means of expression.

We find the notion of a missing rule often in Pascal's comments on style. It appears in 466/559, where artificial rules lead to false symmetry, since there is more concern with figures of rhetoric than with "parler juste," that is, with representing ideas accurately and naturally. The notion of a rule is more difficult to understand in 671/513, where most editors and commentators have interpreted Pascal's text to mean it is the "morale du jugement" that is without rules. This interpretation seems to stem from a nineteenth-century notion that something opposed to the *esprit* must be less rigorous than this supposedly all-powerful faculty, and the same notion has kept many readers of the *Pensées* from realizing that *sentiment* can refer to a mental operation.[8] This fragment is written in a way to suggest that *jugement, sentiment, finesse, vraie morale* and *vraie éloquence* have related functions; other fragments which make the same associations make it clear that the mind is involved and that there are definitions and principles involved, even if we are often unaware of them—these operations are performed "tacitement et sans art" (670/512). In the particular case of morality, Pascal believed in the existence of clear definitions and principles, since they are handed down through the authority of the Church. There are thus rules for true morality, and the statement that "la morale de l'esprit . . . est sans règles" must be interpreted to mean that it lacks such authority even though it may have made up rules based on

---

[8]See chapter 1 for a fuller discussion of *sentiment.* See notes in the Havet and Brunschvicg editions for examples of editors who cannot accept Pascal's text as it is.

human authority (generally reason and custom, two of the principle "moyens de croire"; 655/808).

Pascal does not mention whether "la vraie éloquence" has rules, but the parallel construction suggests that it does. If it does, they are obviously not the rules of traditional rhetoric but come from a more dependable source. For Pascal, this source could only be divinely inspired writings; indeed, he does find the same characteristics in the language of Christ that he has suggested for good, direct, natural style (just as he found a source for "la digression sur chaque point qui a rapport à la fin" in Christ, Paul and Augustine; 329/298): "J.-C. a dit les choses grandes si simplement qu'il semble qu'il ne les a pas pensées, et si nettement néanmoins qu'on voit bien ce qu'il en pensait. Cette clarté jointe à cette naïveté est admirable" (340/309). "Clarté" and "naïveté" are basically the same as the direct and natural representation of thought recommended by Pascal, and the "il semble qu'il ne les a pas pensées" suggests the "tacitement et sans art" of the *esprit de finesse,* of *sentiment.* The *naïveté* also suggests Pascal's opinion that good writing consists of "pensées nées sur les entretiens ordinaires de la vie" (618/745).

If Pascal found the point of departure for his style in scripture (and in Montaigne and Epictetus), the end result had to be found in the reader. The reader had to feel he or she had come to his or her own conclusions: "on se persuade mieux pour l'ordinaire par les raisons qu'on a soi-même trouvées que par celles qui sont venues dans l'esprit des autres" (617/737; see also 536/652). To encourage the reader's own conclusions is the ultimate reason for Pascal's insistence on direct, accurate representation of thought—these thoughts should enter the reader directly, with as little interference (opinions of the author, unnecessary stylistic effects, etc.) as possible, and serve as the basis for the conclusions. Pascal was certainly not above using stylistic effects, such as the literal and figurative use of "port" in 576/697 (quoted above), but it is mostly in the way he puts fragments together (*mots, pensées, corps de discours;* 575/696) that he is able to give a reader thoughts which the reader can then put together.

In order to understand how Pascal put the fragments of the

Pensées together, it is necessary to look at his language. The fragments quoted above in which he discusses style and language are the obvious beginning, but they are far from giving a complete understanding of his view of language. Before looking at exactly what Pascal did with language, a look at the *Grammaire générale et raisonnée,* published by Arnauld and Lancelot in 1660, is extremely helpful. This work is tightly related to the *Logique* published by Port-Royal at about the same time (1662), related to the extent that Arnauld and Nicole transcribed several pages of the *Grammaire* in the *Logique*'s section on verbs (II, 2). The two works also share the same view of mental operations and their relative importance, a view which has been helpful in understanding Pascal's views of the thought process and the communication of knowledge and which is crucial to their view of the role of language.

In the first part of this chapter, I discussed Pascal's conception of a special style for part of the *Pensées,* a style that would be direct and natural so that it could represent the thoughts behind it as accurately as possible. He associated thought at its purest level with the *jugement,* the direct combination of two ideas. It follows, then, that a style that would represent such a combination would consist of ideas in direct combination or opposition. The *Logique* makes it clear that this type of thought and this type of language are basically the same—"jugements sont des propositions qui sont composées de diverses parties: il faut commencer par l'explication de ces parties, qui sont principalement les Noms, les Pronoms, & les Verbes. Il est peu important d'examiner si c'est à la Grammaire ou à la Logique d'en traiter" (p. 103).

When the *Grammaire* takes up the subject of how words are put together, the discussion begins with the same mental operations discussed in the *Logique (concevoir, juger, raisonner, ordonner),* except that *ordonner* is not included. This latter operation deals with the organization of language, not with its use, and is the domain of rhetoric more than of grammar. For similar reasons, Pascal gave it almost no attention in *De l'Esprit géométrique,* and Arnauld and Nicole considered it the least important mental operation.

The *Grammaire* begins with a discussion of mental operations because, just as they were important in understanding Pascal's method, an understanding of them is essential to understand grammar and to interpret language: "la connaissance de ce qui se passe dans notre esprit est nécessaire pour comprendre les fondements de la Grammaire. . . . On ne peut bien comprendre les diverses sortes de significations qui sont enfermées dans les mots, qu'on n'ait bien compris auparavant ce qui se passe dans nos pensées" (pp. 22, 23). We must understand the human thought process so we can adapt language to it, since language is to be a direct representation of thought: "une des plus grandes preuves de la raison, c'est l'usage que nous en faisons pour signifier nos pensées" (p. 22).

Like the *Logique,* the *Grammaire* identifies judgment as the most important mental operation. *Raisonnement* is merely a combination of *jugements,* and conceptions (intellectual and material) are rarely an important aspect of language except when combined in a *jugement:*

> Raisonner, est se servir de deux jugements pour en faire un troisième. . . .
>
> La troisième opération de l'esprit [raisonnement] n'est qu'une extension de la seconde [jugement]; et ainsi il suffira, pour notre sujet, de considérer les deux premières, ou ce qui est enfermé de la première dans la seconde; car les hommes ne parlent guère pour exprimer simplement ce qu'ils conçoivent, mais c'est presque toujours pour exprimer les jugements qu'ils font des choses qu'ils conçoivent. (p. 23)

Conceptions constitute the "objet de notre pensées," terms of a *jugement* (proposition) which are joined by the operation of the judgment. The essential operation, however, is the linking of these two terms: "la liaison apartient à la seconde [mental operation, i.e., judgment], qu'on peut dire être proprement l'action de notre esprit, et la manière dont nous pensons" (p. 24).

According to this view of thought and language, words ("signes pour marquer tout ce qui se passe dans leur [de l'homme] esprit"; p. 24) can be divided into two types: those signifying the objects of our thought, our conceptions (nouns, articles, pronouns, adjectives, prepositions and adverbs) and those signifying the manner (verbs, conjunctions and interjections). And, since the manner of our thought, what we think about objects, is more important than the objects, these latter parts of speech, and especially verbs and conjunctions, are the most important. Moreover, these words and their functions are natural, "tous tirés, par une suite nécessaire, de la manière naturelle en laquelle nous exprimons nos pensées" (p. 24).

We notice in these quotations from the *Grammaire* not only a view of the human thought process that is similar to Pascal's, but a similar concern with natural, direct expression of thought. In both works, thought and language constitute "un des plus grands avantages de l'homme au-dessus de tous les autres animaux"; similarly, Pascal cannot "concevoir de l'homme sans pensée. Ce serait une pierre ou une brute" (143/111). The best language is that which is "conforme à l'expression naturelle de nos pensées" (p. 106), and that in which words exist precisely to signify thoughts. In addition, it is the disposition of words and thoughts (see 575/696), the "manière de nos pensées," that is most important; once we have agreed on the meanings of words (conception, definitions) and resisted the temptation to let the words that express them distort our understanding of them, the most important thing is to combine them properly into judgments, or principles.

The *Grammaire,* like Pascal and the *Logique,* insists also on the difference between thought and language. According to Arnauld and Lancelot, people often tend to follow "plus le sens de leurs pensées, que les mots dont ils se servent pour les exprimer" (pp. 106–107). This precedence of thoughts over words is the origin of figures of speech, and it is the danger of confusing thought and language that makes Pascal insist so much on careful use of language to reflect thought accurately. He was aware of the differences between deep and surface structure; his interest in capturing the former helps explain his frequent use of simple syntax (noun-*être*-noun, for example). Furthermore, many of the occasional ambiguities in the *Pensées* result from the fact that the words do reflect the deep structure of his thought rather than the surface structure of syntax. (See the discussion of 225/192 in the next chapter, and chapter 12.)

The most important similarities, however, are not between Pascal's ideas about language and the ideas of the *Grammaire*, but between his ideas about language and the use he makes of it. Does the style of all or part of the *Pensées* correspond to his view of language, which is itself based on his view of thought? If it does, then this correspondence would be a primary reason for admiring the style of the *Pensées* and considering Pascal one of the founders of French prose. Furthermore, the admiration would be one to which even the saintly Pascal, portrayed by his sister and others with hagiographic tendencies, would not object. The admiration would be based not on an artificial conception of beauty of style, but on the expression of worthy thoughts and thought processes.

To study the correspondence of a style in the *Pensées* to Pascal's view of language and thought, we must isolate grammatical and syntactical features that would reflect such a view and then search for them in the *Pensées*. We would expect to find them more frequently in fragments that deal with the presentation of human nature and religion to the unbelieving reader, rather than in those that furnish proofs and historical evidence (miracles, prophecies, history of the Jews, etc.) to the reader already willing to listen to *raisonnements*. From what we can ascertain from Pascal's preliminary plan for a projected apology, fragments of the former type would suggest judgments for a reader to make on his or her own, while those of the second type would try to demonstrate in a more traditionally logical way why Christianity, which has been shown to correspond to human needs, is also justified by human and divine authority.[9]

The most obvious of these stylistic features is an emphasis

---

[9]We would also expect to find fragments of this first type occurring more frequently in the *Pensées* than in other works by Pascal (except perhaps in the first five *Provinciales*), as well as in works by other authors. Comparisons are extremely difficult to make; because of the fragmentary form of the *Pensées*, it is almost impossible to compare short fragments to much longer texts. Such comparisons are beyond the scope of the present analysis, which is concerned with different styles in the *Pensées* themselves.

on simple, direct connection of subject and predicate which would correspond to simple *jugements*. The example given by both the *Logique* and the *Grammaire* is "ayant conçu ce que c'est que la *terre*, et ce que c'est que *rondeur*, j'affirme de la *terre*, qu'elle est *ronde*" (*Grammaire*, p. 23; see *Logique*, p. 37). Two ideas are combined through the use of the verb *être*, the most fundamental and really the only necessary verb. Verbs should serve only to "marquer la liaison que nous faisons dans notre esprit des deux termes d'une proposition," but only *être* has remained "dans cette simplicité." Other verbs have had some other meaning added to their expression of affirmation (joining propositions), such as the idea of being alive which is added to the affirmative capacity of the verb "vit" in the expression "Pierre vit" (*Grammaire*, p. 67). Thus, an unusual number of occurrences of *être* is a first important stylistic feature to search for in the *Pensées*.

The other main type of word that signifies the way we think rather than the object of our thought is the conjunction (*Grammaire*, pp. 102–103). In a style designed to convey thoughts directly and to allow a reader to come to his or her own conclusions, a second stylistic feature to search for would be a fairly low number of conjunctions, especially of subordinating conjunctions that imply the author's opinion, such as *puisque* and *de sorte que*. *Et* is the weakest conjunction and, along with simple conjunctions such as *mais*, *ou*, and *ni*, should occur relatively more frequently than subordinating conjunctions. Conjunctions that imply consequence, such as *donc*, should be fairly rare, though they imply a logical conclusion rather than a personal, subjective one, and are thus not necessarily incompatible with a style that reflects thought as directly as possible.

A third feature is the repetition of certain words, especially nouns. In 452/515, Pascal objects to the automatic proscription of repeating a word, an objection related to his preference for a digressive method to include many ideas related to a final point, even though the result may seem disorderly (329/298, 457/532). If one proposition (in its barest form, two nouns linked by *être*) suggests another, the second proposition may contain at least one of the nouns of the preceding proposition. Rather than have a main clause followed by a string of subordinate clauses—as in the classical periodic style (see Houston, pp. 33–50), that is, one idea followed by a string of explanations and opinions—we would expect several independent clauses in a row, with few strong (subordinating) conjunctions between them. Repetition of this nature would help clarify a sentence or paragraph that contains few links between clauses, by creating points of reference and by making the all-important *rapports* evident at a glance. A paragraph could thus contain considerable digression, have only a few links between clauses to explain the relationships, and still be comprehensible. That is, the paragraph would still be comprehensible to any reader who noticed each *jugement* and the fact that the *jugements* were related, and who worked out the nature of the relationships for himself or herself.

The following chapters will discuss these three stylistic features: (1) frequency of occurrence of *être;* (2) frequency of occurrence of repetition, especially of nouns; (3) frequency of occurrence of conjunctions and other connectives, with particular attention to any large difference between the frequency of occurrence of subordinating conjunctions and that of *et* and other simple conjunctions. After giving examples of these features in various combinations, it will be necessary to see where they occur most frequently in the *Pensées* and to draw conclusions from the analysis of the features and of their distribution.[10]

[10]See the appendix for more information about the computer programs I have used to count these features; see also the bibliography for works on style by Antoine, Auerbach, Charles, Croll, Demorest, Dumonceaux, Hentsch, Houston, Lanham, Le Guern, Lubbock, Maggioni, Magnard, Mercanton, Mesnard, and Topliss.

9

Style in the *Pensées*—*Etre* and Repetition

The main goal of this and the following chapter is to point out and to analyze fragments of the *Pensées* that contain an extremely high or low frequency of occurrence of certain stylistic features. These stylistic features have been chosen in light of Pascal's methods (as described in the preceding section). At this stage of discussion, finding and describing important examples of Pascal's styles is more important than explaining why and how often he uses a particular style; the latter will be the subject of the last two chapters.

The length of a fragment is an essential factor in the analysis. Different stylistic features occur with different frequencies in longer or shorter fragments, and we must be aware of the differences in order to make meaningful comparisons between the styles of two or more fragments. I have thus determined relative frequencies of occurrence of these stylistic features, taking fragment length into account; my method is described in the appendix on computer methodology. I will concentrate on fragments with a length near the median of fifty words. While the average length is 105 words, fewer than 25 percent are longer than this average length, and only 10 percent are longer than two hundred words. I will not neglect longer fragments, nor extremely short ones altogether, but it is more meaningful to consider fragments that are of typical length.

The most striking examples in the *Pensées* of Pascal's use of *être* as the primary verb for linking subject and predicate (conceptions) to form a clause (judgment) are found in relatively short fragments where *être* is the only or the dominant verb. Fragment 529/641, for example, consists of two similar independent clauses with *est:*[1]

[1]Sellier, in modernizing the punctuation, divides the fragment into two sentences.

529/641 Notre nature est dans le mouvement, le repos entier est la mort.

There are no connectives, and the interpretation of these two simple, equation-like clauses depends on the juxtaposition of the two subjects and predicates. "Mouvement" is followed immediately by its opposite, "repos," and the reader notices a chiasmatic ABBA structure developing in which the second A could be the opposite of the first, just as the second B was the opposite of the first B. "La mort" is not the exact opposite of "notre nature," but a reader who is aware of the relationships among the parts of the sentence can recognize easily that nature is alive, even though "notre nature" refers to characteristics of humanity rather than to life itself, as either "*la* nature" or "*notre* vie" would. The impersonal statement "le repos entier est la mort" thus fits in with "notre nature" since both are somewhat abstract, but the presence of *notre* reminds the reader that it is his or her own death which is in question, not just the concept.

The simple construction of this fragment can thus carry the meaning of a much more complex sentence, such as "Il est naturel que nous cherchions le mouvement, parce que nous mourrons si nous restons en repos, le repos entier étant la même chose que la mort." Rather than spell out the various conclusions and explanations, Pascal has presented the essential information in a way which makes the conclusions and explanations clear to the reader who reflects for a moment on the relationship among the elements of the sentence.[2] In this way the reader glimpses the complexity of the relationship between humanity and nature as well as of those between movement and rest, and life and death.

Fragment 31/412 makes a similar use of *être* to express a paradoxical situation, leaving the reader to work out the exact reasons for the paradox:

31/412 Les hommes sont si nécessairement fous que ce serait être fou par un autre tour de folie de n'être pas fou.[3]

---

[2]I certainly do not agree with Henri Lefebvre's statement that "l'abus de l'auxiliaire 'être' correspond chez Pascal à la formulation sans réplique des banalités éternelles" (*Pascal*, Paris: Nagel, 1949, 1954, II, 239). Lefebvre cites 486/586 as an example, and he does not seem to limit himself to the use of *être* as an auxiliary verb in compound tenses.

[3]Sellier inexplicably omits "être fou par."

That is,

parce que (homme = fou)
(homme = fou) = (homme ≠ fou)

The fragment consists of little except forms of *être* and *fou;* the reader is thereby forced to reflect upon what it is to be crazy, and thus what it is to be human, in order to make some sense out of what seems completely illogical at first reading. If two seemingly opposite judgments can be equated though *être,* the simplest and most straightforward of all verbs, we must reevaluate our definitions of the terms involved, our ideas.

Pascal often uses one clause joined only with *être* to be the subject of another *être* clause, such as in 518/625, or in a more complex way, in 50/16:

518/625 Que la présomption soit jointe à la misère, c'est une extrême injustice.

50/16 Qu'une chose aussi visible qu'est la vanité du monde soit si peu connue, que ce soit une chose étrange et surprenante de dire que c'est une sottise de chercher les grandeurs, cela est admirable.

In such cases *être* sometimes serves as an auxiliary verb, part of the passive or the *passé composé,* but the result is much the same—a noun (*présomption, vanité*) is joined to a qualifier and this combination is joined to another qualifier through *être.*[4] In neither case is there an explanation of why *c'* and *cela,* which sum up the opening judgments in each fragment, are so unjust or so ironically admirable. There are no subordinating conjunctions or strong connectives, so each reader must consider definitions of the words involved and establish relationships among them. As in the case of 529/641 and 31/412 discussed earlier, the establishment of these relationships is made easier by parallel constructions.

In 50/16, for example, there are two long noun clauses that

---

[4]This use of *être* as an auxiliary to link a noun to a qualifier is especially characteristic of 430/849: "La charité n'est pas un précepte figuratif. Dire que Jésus-Christ qui est venu ôter les figures pour mettre la charité ne soit venu que mettre la figure de la clarté pour ôter la réalité qui était auparavant, cela est horrible."

begin with *que,* and the *que . . . soit* construction of the first half appears immediately in the second, with only *ce* in between. A chiasmatic construction is clearly involved (visible vanity : little known :: strange : foolish search for greatness), and the obvious similarity between *peu connue* and *étrange et surprenante* makes the reader aware of the somewhat less obvious connections between [*être*] *visible que* and *dire que* in the middle of each noun clause, and between *vanité du monde* and *sottise de chercher les grandeurs.* Furthermore, when we follow the parallels to the extreme, we find Pascal has established a connection between *monde* and *chercher les grandeurs* (he thus characterizes worldly people) as well as between *vanité* and *sottise:*

Il	est admirable
que	voir que monde
est	vain
soit	peu connu.

Il	est admirable
que	dire que chercher grandeurs
est	sottise
soit	étrange et surprenante.

Obviously, many fragments with a high concentration of *être* involve definitions or, at least, as in 31/412, they force the reader to pay careful attention to the meaning of the words involved. The implications of this insistence on the meanings of certain words can be presented, as in 529/641 and 50/16, through parallel (including chiasmatic), equation-like structures, but also through logical developments, such as in 91–92/58 and 135/103, both of which deal with justice and tyranny. (Fragment 530/645, which also deals with justice, has the highest concentration of *être* in the *Pensées,* but several of the occurrences take the form of auxiliary verbs, functioning in association with transitive verbs rather than independently.)

These fragments that contain logical developments are necessarily longer than the fragments discussed up until now; the latter usually have few strong connectives and a high frequency of occurrences of *être*. Generally, the shorter fragments have the highest concentrations of *être*; the longer fragments that do contain numerous occurrences of *être* are usually characterized by a high frequency of occurrence of subordinating conjunctions as well. In fact, of all twenty-seven of the fragments that have a significantly high frequency of occurrence of *être* and that also are longer than one hundred words, only 500/602 and 290/259 have a lower than average frequency of occurrence of subordinating conjunctions or of conjunctions in general.[5]

Both sections of 91–92/58 begin with a definition ("La tyrannie consiste au désir de domination . . ."; "La tyrannie est de vouloir avoir . . ."); both discuss different types of tyranny and point out statements that are false and tyrannical. Once the definition of tyranny has been established as something "hors de son ordre," it is easy for Pascal to show when two parts of a discourse, or of a syllogism, do not coincide ("Ainsi ces discours sont faux"). For example, "je suis beau, donc on doit me craindre" represents faulty reasoning, since beauty and fear are not in the same "ordre." Most of the connectives in the fragment come in these syllogisms, not in the establishment of the definitions; it is when Pascal feels the need to explain the implications of his definitions that we find longer fragments of this type and more connectives.

In 135/103, justice is not as easily distinguishable from injustice (and especially not from force) as tyranny was from justified desires in 91/58. Although there are several sentences in 135/103 that use *être* just as do the shorter fragments discussed above ("La justice sans la force est impuissante, la force sans la justice est tyrannique," for example), there are also more logical connectives such as "il est juste que," "il est nécessaire que," "parce que," "donc," "pour cela faire que," "aussi," and "ainsi." The fragment can be seen as a long series of judgments leading,

---

[5]For a definition of "significantly high frequency of occurrence," see the appendix. It is especially important to take into account the length of a fragment when analyzing the repeated words.

Fragment 500/602 has only a slightly significant frequency of occurrence of *être*, and the presence of numerous relative and substantive clauses makes it quite different from fragments which consist of simple combinations of ideas.

not to a real, logical solution, but to the best way out of a problem; such a long series requires at least some connectives to guide the reader along.[6]

It is possible that many of these fragments with a high frequency of occurrence of *être* and without strong connectives would have been revised to include stronger verbs as well as stronger connectives. I will return to this question in more detail in chapter 11, but it is useful at this point to consider a fragment such as 626/756 which, though fairly long (seventy-one words), seems to be notes Pascal intended to fill out later. Such fragments often consist of a series of sentences with *être* as the predominant verb and with few logical connectives or explanations.

626/756 Pensée.

> Toute la dignité de l'homme est en la pensée, mais qu'est-ce que cette pensée? qu'elle est sotte?[7]
>
> La pensée est donc une chose admirable et incomparable par sa nature. Il fallait qu'elle eût d'étranges défauts pour être méprisable, mais elle en a de tels que rien n'est plus ridicule. Qu'elle est grande par sa nature, qu'elle est basse par ses défauts.

The first paragraph (after the one-word title) is an addition; it is perhaps intended as a brief, temporary explanation of the next sentence which begins the second paragraph. The "donc" of this sentence is the only conjunction in the fragment which is what I will call a "ductive" conjunction, that is, it leads to a conclusion. "Donc" is out of place near the beginning of an argument—the admirable, incomparable nature of thought cannot be stated so strongly without some justification. There is certainly not enough justification to support the sentence which follows, but it does state Pascal's position and pose questions that could be answered in justification of this position. The question mark after "qu'elle est sotte" suggests that the foolishness of thought is something to be established also, not just an exclamation expressing a point that a reader would be ready to accept. Similarly, the punctuation

---

[6]The presence of *jugements* and of logical connectives in the same fragment produces a problematic discontinuity which will be explored in chapters 11 and 12.

[7]I follow the text of the manuscript here, not that of Sellier's edition which gives an exclamation mark instead of a question mark.

of the last sentence (we might expect exclamation marks) suggests something to be shown through examples, not something already established.

Except for the last sentence, there is little of that parallel structure we found in the fragments discussed earlier, little that could guide a reader toward establishing relationships and drawing conclusions. Assumptions are made without examples to back them up, questions are unanswered, and in general the fragment depends on others with the same theme (143/111, 231/200, 513/620, and 628/759, for example). This may be the way Pascal intended it, or this fragment may be a sketch for or a rejected version of another; it will be easier to decide after further discussion of Pascal's style.

Many fragments of the *Pensées* which contain a high frequency of occurrence of repeated words also appear to be notes for more developed fragments. For example, 381/349 and 315/283, which have the third and eighth highest relative number of repeated words, respectively, are little more than lists. Fragment 381/349 is a list of examples of "figures" which have a double nature, that is, a literal and figurative interpretation: "Figures particulières. Double loi, doubles Tables de la Loi, double temple, double captivité." Fragment 315/283 is little more than an indication that Pascal was considering the cyclical interpretation of history described in St. Augustine's *De Genesi contra Manicheaos,* (I, 23; see the note in the Sellier edition) as he put together the dossier "Perpétuité": "Les six âges, les six pères des six âges, les six merveilles à l'entrée des six âges, les six orients à l'entrée des six âges." The extremely high percentage of repeated words in these fragments cannot, however, be explained solely by their note-like nature. The concentration and elimination of all but the most necessary words calls attention to the fact that Pascal was thinking about several related aspects of one idea; if we are taking notes about a number of points to be made in an argument, each point is more likely to be different from the preceding one than so close that it can be expressed with almost the same words.

Pascal's tendency to consider related aspects of an idea is also evident in fragments that are somewhat more than brief notes but still extremely concentrated, such as 420/831, which has the seventh highest number of repeated words for its length of any fragment in the *Pensées:*

420/381 Le second miracle peut supposer le premier, le premier ne peut supposer le second.

The first clause generates the second through a reversal of subject and predicate, and a negation of the verb; no new material is introduced, and there are no connectives. Such a fragment provides an excellent example of Pascal's thought process at work—one thought occurs, and consideration of it leads to a recombination of its elements and thus to a new thought.[8] In neither clause is an explanation given, either because Pascal did not need to remind himself or because he felt the reader could figure it out. The conclusion to be drawn—again, it is not given directly—is of methodological importance to any consideration of miracles, and concerns the dangers of making an assumption (first miracle can *supposer* the second) based on a similar one (second miracle can *supposer* the first) without a careful examination of what happens to the relationship (verb) between subject and object when their positions are reversed.[9] More generally, when we combine ideas to form judgments, we should consider all possible combinations. This essential aspect of Pascal's method is a form of the "renversement du pour au contre" on which he insists in the dossier "Raison des effets," and is expressed admirably by the structure of the fragment.[10]

In an even more direct way, 77/43 shows Pascal's thought process functioning by negating the verb:

77/43 Peu de chose nous console parce que peu de chose nous afflige.

In this case, however, the second statement is an explanation of

---

[8]This process is certainly not unique to Pascal, but it is rare to find a writer whose published works reflect the original thought process so closely; Montaigne's self-revealing essays are a notable exception.

[9]Fragment 454/527 is a discussion of this type of faulty reasoning. I have discussed it in detail in "Editing and Interpreting Fragmentary Texts: A Justification of Pascal's Text in MSL 527–Br 40," *TEXT* (New York: AMS Press, 1985), 197–208.

[10]Fragment 439/860, which has the eleventh highest relative number of repeated words in the *Pensées,* operates in a similar way, presenting an alternative second clause through the conjunction *ou* rather than through negation of the verb.

the first; *parce que* links the statement and explanation, perhaps because the two clauses are so similar that a reader would not understand the two statements in direct juxtaposition with no linking words. When subject and predicate are reversed, as in 420/831, a reader is led to expect a different result, but if nothing is changed except the verb, it is hard to know if the two clauses are meant to express a similar or different meaning.

Rather than recombine elements of a sentence, many fragments use repeated words to go on to a second, related sentence, such as in 645/784:

645/784 Les mots diversement rangés font un divers sens. Et les sens diversement rangés font différents effets.

The direct object of the first sentence becomes the subject of the second sentence, which has a new object; the resulting structure is ABBC (*mots-sens-sens-effets*) rather than the ABBA structure of 420/831. This latter fragment is a perfect example of the content of 645/784, since it creates a different meaning by rearranging the same words. Here it is rather a matter of fitting a word into two places in the same structure (with the minor difference of "divers'" and "différents"), which necessitates a new object, and thus "un divers sens." We cannot, of course, make just any rearrangement of words and still have meaning, since we must consider the rules of syntax. We have more liberty in rearranging a series of meanings (arguments) in almost any order, since the rules for the ordering of points to be made in a discourse are less rigid than those of syntax, especially if we are using a method that depends more on juxtaposition than on formal chains of arguments.[11]

The five fragments just discussed (381/349, 420/831, 439/860, 77/43, and 645/784) are chosen from the fifteen fragments with the highest relative number of repeated words of all the fragments in the *Pensées.* The remaining fragments discussed in this chapter are among the most typical and the most interesting of the other one hundred fragments with a significantly high number.

---

[11]See the discussion in the next chapter of fragment 575/696, which is an amplification of 645/784.

Pascal often uses repetition to mention several (preferably all) possibilities before going on to a related sentence or clause:

24/405 Je blâme également et ceux qui prennent parti de louer l'homme et ceux qui le prennent de le blâmer et ceux qui le prennent de se divertir et je ne puis approuver que ceux qui cherchent en gémissant.

The repetitions here are concentrated by the use of the same verb (*blâmer*) in the independent and dependent clauses of the first part of the sentence, and by the similarity (in sound and meaning) of *approuver* in the last independent clause to *louer* in the first dependent clause, as well as to *blâmer* through opposition. Furthermore, the repetition of the phrase "ceux qui le prennent" links "se divertir" to "louer" and "blâmer," both of which are already linked by their antithetical relationship and identical direct objects (*homme*).

As a result of all this repetition—repeated words are only the surface indication of various types of repetition—the reader has the impression that all the possibilities have been exhausted.[12] A dialectical progression has led to the idea of diversion (neither praise nor blame, but a third possibility which negates both of the first two). This would normally be the final step, but the "Je blâme également" which began the sentence has made it clear that none of these three possibilities is satisfactory. The one that is acceptable ("chercher en gémissant") is presented as tightly related to what has come before (through the similarities of "approuver" and "ceux qui" to the rest of the sentence), and as the opposite of the third possibility (itself an alternative to or a synthesis of the first two). These tight, semantic and syntactic relations make it a very convincing fragment, one that reflects both Pascal's beliefs and his thought processes very well as it leads the reader to accept them. No reasons are given for why any of these possibilities should be blamed or praised, or for why "chercher en gémissant" is the only alternative to "se divertir." The fragment is more persuasive than logically airtight; to "convaincre des athées endurcis" (690/449) who insist on perfect

[12]For an example of a fragment with a large number of repeated words but without much structural repetition, see 240/208, discussed in the next chapter.

logic, Pascal would have to use an even tighter structure or convince the nonbelieving reader to accept a less geometric method. The same question thus arises as with the note-like fragments—is this how Pascal would have left them? And if he did leave this fragment as it is in the manuscript, was he relying more on rhetoric than on logic? Again, these questions cannot be answered without a discussion of other aspects of Pascal's style in the *Pensées.*

Fragments that contain a high percentage of repeated words often contain a high frequency of occurrence of *être* as well, such as 135/103 discussed above. Many of these fragments involve definitions and contain clauses which begin in a similar way but end differently:

90/57 Il n'est pas bon d'être trop libre.
Il n'est pas bon d'avoir toutes les nécessités.[13]

The identical beginnings of the two sentences force the reader to consider the relationship between "être trop libre" and "avoir toutes les nécessités," and to ask why neither is good—again, Pascal offers no explanations. Once we have decided what being too free means, we realize that it is quite similar to having all the necessities, and thus that being somewhat in want is not necessarily bad. By expressing a similar idea with different words, but at the same time introducing both statements with the same words, Pascal forces the reader to search for an explanation that is not explicitly stated. Then, perhaps, he could relate the idea of needs to the ideas of tyranny and justice that make up much of this dossier ("Misère").

Fragment 680/424 presents a more complex definition process:

680/424 C'est le coeur qui sent Dieu et non la raison. Voilà ce que c'est que la foi. Dieu sensible au coeur, non à la raison.[14]

There are no phrases or structures repeated, but several nouns,

---

[13]Fragment 90/57 has the fifth highest relative number of repeated words of all fragments containing more than one occurrence of *être;* fragment 18/399 has the highest. Fragment 135/103 has the highest *percentage* of repeated words of all fragments.

[14]I follow the punctuation of Lafuma and of the manuscript.

verbs, articles, and prepositions are. The first sentence describes one aspect of the heart, but the second and third sentences define faith. There is no preparation for the change of subject between the first and second sentences, which would explain why Pascal added a third sentence to explain the "ce" of the second and to restate the first. In this restatement, the grammatical subject has changed from the heart to God (if we consider the last sentence as an ellipsis for "Dieu [est] sensible . . ."), God being the true subject of faith, whereas the heart is only an instrument, an operation (see chapter 3). This is an excellent example of how Pascal's thought often moves ahead of the syntax that expresses it, requiring him to repeat several words in order to make all the relationships clear.

Fragment 680/424 is, in the Sellier classification, only part of a long fragment that is made up of fragments 418–426 in the Lafuma classification and that contains the famous wager. The shorter texts (Lafuma 419–426) were written in the margins beside Lafuma 418, and each contains at least an average percentage of repeated words; in addition, they develop related themes in a fascinating example of the way Pascal made associations.[15] There are remarkable stylistic similarities among some of them as well, and these similarities suggest that the associations could be syntactic as well as thematic. My comments on these fragments are partially the result of one of the side benefits of a statistical analysis of literary texts. My lists of fragments with a high relative frequency of occurrence of repeated words included several neighboring fragments in the Lafuma classification; this proximity led me to look at these fragments more closely, and then to turn to Brunet's analysis. It is certainly possible to come to the same results without statistical analysis, but my lists made it much easier to find these interesting examples of stylistic and thematic similarities.

Lafuma 421 and 425 use similar structures ("nulle religion";

---

[15]There are even more repeated words in this fragment if we include the variants. For details on the composition of Sellier 680, see Georges Brunet, *Le Pari de Pascal* (Paris: Desclée de Brouwer, 1956). Brunet also includes a brief discussion (pp. 116–18) of related fragments that were written on the same sheet of paper as Sellier 680 but were later inserted into other dossiers.

"la seule science") to begin fragments that discuss the paradoxical nature of the perpetuity of Christianity. Lafuma 426 uses a similar structure ("Il n'y a que la religion chrétienne") to begin a discussion of an equally paradoxical and related subject, itself related to the main argument of the wager. Lafuma 425 is especially interesting because a variant shows that Pascal was consciously creating the parallel structure. He began the second half of the fragment (after "nature des hommes") with the direct "a toujours," but changed it to "est la seule qui ait toujours," obviously under the influence of the "la seule science qui est" which begins the fragment. This structure not only adds to the number of repeated words, but also to the occurrences of *être*, making the fragment more like an equation between two seemingly different situations. It is also an equation without any arguments leading up to it, containing modifiers of each half of the equation ("seule . . . qui est") but no connectives except the *et* in the first dependent clause.

Groups of similarly constructed fragments which also show thematic similarities (such as Lafuma 425–426) are found fairly often in the *Pensées*, and not always in the same dossier nor on the same sheet. Fragments 146/114 and 225/192 both contain repeated structures dealing with our simultaneous awareness of our misery on the one hand, and of our grandeur (146/114) or of God (225/192) on the other. The second sentence of 146/114 contains two notably parallel parts, differing only in the substitution of "grand" for "misérable" and "connaître qu'on est" (emphasizing the more conscious, rational process) for "se connaître" in the second half: "C'est donc être misérable que de ~~être~~ [se] connaître misérable; mais c'est être grand que de connaître qu'on est misérable." The hesitation between "être misérable" and "se connaître misérable" seems due to a desire to make the sentences as parallel as possible and is probably responsible for the omission of *se*. Similarly, the first two sentences of 225/192 are the same except for the reversal of *Dieu* and *misère*, which results in different objects of *fait*.

These similarities are particularly necessary in 225/192, since the possessive *sa* in the first sentence and the pronoun *celle* in the second are ambiguous without them. Pascal's tendency to use parallel syntax to express similar thoughts seems to make him less conscious of such smaller, grammatical details, as if the deep structure of his language is more important than the surface structure. This tendency is hardly surprising from a writer who held that "l'éloquence est une peinture de la pensée," and who criticized artificial (i.e., surface) symmetry (481/578, 466/559). It is the nature of fragments that contain similar structures—often joined though the simplest of all verbs with very few connectives—to express related thoughts. One thought (judgment), and often one component (conception) of a thought, suggests another, and fragments such as those discussed in this chapter are an extremely direct way to put them on paper. This directness is due especially to the lack of connectives in the sentences preceding the concluding sentence of each fragment. The first sentence of 146/114 and the first two of 225/192 contain no examples, no explanations, and no transitions, but rely on repetition and parallel for their clarity and force. As in 24/405, we could question the assumptions behind these preliminary sentences, and thus the conclusions that follow, but the very structure of the fragment seems so "right" that we would not necessarily object, especially if other fragments on the same general subject have reinforced these assumptions. This direct juxtaposition of thoughts is one of Pascal's favorite methods, "la digression sur chaque point" (329/298) until the point is sufficiently reinforced to allow a strong, authoritative presentation such as that in 225/192—now the author needs to add nothing except the bare facts.[16]

Such parallel constructions are less prevalent when Pascal takes the time to state carefully the reasons behind a somewhat paradoxical statement such as "c'est être grand que de connaître qu'on est misérable," as he does in 155/122. This fragment discusses various opinions about mankind's greatness and misery and is considerably longer than 146/114 and 225/192 (164 words

[16]That Pascal did not include every step of a carefully logical process does not mean he was using faulty logic; nor was he trying to cover up logical weaknesses with a style—"rhetoric" in the pejorative sense of the term—that leads the reader to neglect arguments that could weaken his case. Pascal may have been taking notes for himself, or trying to make the reader do much of the thinking, but it is doubtful that he was trying to be dishonest.

compared to 42), but arrives at exactly the same conclusion: "Il [l'homme] est donc misérable puisqu'il l'est, mais il est bien grand puisqu'il le connaît."[17] Pascal uses the same words as in 146/114, though he is able to replace "l'homme" with "il" and "être misérable" with "le." Still, there are interesting differences. Whereas in 146/114 Pascal made a special effort to change "être misérable" to "(se) connaître misérable" (for the sake of parallel construction), in 155/122 he uses "puisqu'il l'est" at the end of the first clause of the last sentence and "puisqu'il le connaît" at the end of the second. Furthermore, the noun clauses beginning with "que de" are replaced with subordinate clauses beginning with "puisque." The sentence is thus briefer because pronouns have replaced nouns and *être* has replaced *se connaître,* but it is a less direct combination of ideas because of the subordinate clauses. The noun clauses of 146/114 are direct representations of a judgment and can serve as the subject of another judgment without any connectives, whereas the subordinate clauses of 155/122 represent a *raisonnement* based on the preceding discussion.

The final sentence of 155/122 is, like that of 146/114, high in occurrences of *être* and of repeated words, but different in that it contains more conjunctions (4) as well (544/662 is another such fragment). This important difference is even more pronounced in the preceding sentences—those of 155/122 contain numerous logical conjunctions, as well as expressions such as *conclure* and *au contraire;* those of 146/114 and 225/192 contain none. Fragment 155/122 is an example of a fragment that could reinforce another fragment such as 146/114, that is, back up its preliminary statements.[18] Fragment 155/122, on the one hand, has a fairly high relative number of repeated words, even excluding the extremely high number found in the last two sentences, because it digresses around a point. On the other hand, it has a high concentration of *être* only in the last two sentences, and it has a large relative

[17]I follow the punctuation of Lafuma and of the manuscript.

[18]In the nine fragments discussed above that contain a high relative number of repeated words, there is only one example of what I call ductive conjunctions (i.e., those leading to a conclusion): "parce que" in 77/43. Jean Mesnard's article "Pourquoi les *Pensées* de Pascal se présentent-elles sous forme de fragments?" contains an excellent discussion of fragments which are developments of shorter "noyaux."

number of subordinating conjunctions and of other connectives throughout. Fragment 146/114 has an unusually high relative density of repeated words throughout, which reflects the density of its form and content—related thoughts (judgments) presented to the reader with few explanatory connectives.

In the next chapter I will return to the question of subordination and the types of fragments in which it is found. First, however, it is important to look at fragments even longer than 155/122, itself three times longer than the median fragment length of fifty. We find that longer fragments that are unusually high in repeated words compared to others of similar length are usually less direct than shorter ones with a similar relative frequency of repeated words, that they contain numerous connectives, and that the repetition is less a structural device than the necessary result of a lengthy discussion—usually in a highly periodic style—of a subject. I will discuss these longer fragments in the following chapter, which deals with conjunctions, even though some of the fragments have a high relative frequency of repeated words.

In 480/577, however, repetition does play an important structural role in the development of the argument. Of all fragments longer than 155/122, only 229/198 and 290/259 have a higher relative number of repeated words, and they are considerably shorter (211 and 213 words, respectively, compared to 308). Like 146/114, 225/192, and 155/122, and like many longer fragments, 480/577 is an example of how Pascal argues a point—in this case the "règle des partis"—which he has already thought about carefully. His argumentation is a somewhat different type here, however. On the one hand, unlike the three fragments just discussed, 480/577 does not end in a sentence relatively high in *être* and repeated words. In addition, the connectives are stronger and spread throughout the fragment, rather than concentrated in the last sentence. Even a simple conjunction such as *mais*, absent from 146/114 and 225/192, occurs in 480/577 three times more often than in the average fragment.

On the other hand, this is a fragment dealing with the probable, and the logical connectives are accordingly weak—"il n'est pas certain que," for example—and are applied to statements such as "nous voyions demain," statements whose truth cannot and does not have to be proved formally. Pascal proceeds from one such statement, or an example, to another related (often opposite) one, so that the reader will get the point that we need not deny the existence of religion just because it is uncertain. Pascal never says this explicitly, however, nor does he offer a definitive, formal proof. He finishes the second paragraph and the first part of the fragment, by mentioning two other cases in which we accept something that is uncertain: "Or quand on travaille pour demain et pour l'incertain, on agit avec raison."[19] He makes his point through examples and comparisons, and each part of the argument needs to be expressed in such a way that its relationship to other parts is immediately clear. Such an argument obviously requires repetition of some words, and the use of *certain, incertain,* and *certainement* in conjunction with each statement and example is largely responsible for the high relative percentage of repeated words. (The number would be even higher if *incertain* and *certainement* were counted as forms of *certain.*)

The second part of the fragment (paragraphs 3, 4, and 5) explains the reasoning that led to the implicit conclusion of the first part and shows how the "règle des partis" reveals the causes behind the effects. This reasoning is a matter of determining whether or not to base our actions on the possibility of an event's taking place, and that determination depends on the probability of the event as well as on what we stand to gain by assuming it will or will not take place. In the case of 480/577, the chances of tomorrow's arriving or of a successful completion of a sea voyage are great, and we certainly have a lot to gain by assuming that our lives will go on; we should thus assume that tomorrow will arrive, and we should act (make plans) accordingly. Pascal then adds that we can make similar assumptions about the existence of religion—the possibility of its existence is no more doubtful than that of the arrival of tomorrow.

This type of reasoning, based on something that is so likely

---

[19]One should use Sellier's text to see the correct paragraph divisions, which are indicated by "traits de plume." These divisions are ignored by many editors.

it might as well be certain, is also known as illative reasoning. The best known discussion of it is in Cardinal Newman's *Essay for a Grammar of Assent,* and uses the great fire of London as an example. The occurrence of such an event is unlikely, but after we have heard several independent accounts of it, the accumulation of individual bits of evidence reaches the point where we believe the event has occurred and we act accordingly. (In the case above, the arrival of tomorrow has happened so often that we might as well assume it will happen again, though there is no certainty that it will.) Filleau de la Chaise uses the example of the fire in his *Discours sur les* Pensées *de M. Pascal où l'on essaye de faire voir quel était son dessein,* and says that "ce serait être fou d'en douter, et de ne pas exposer sa vie là-dessus pour peu qu'il y eût à gagner" (*Pensées,* ed. Tourneur-Anzieu, II, 269).

In such cases, the amount of gain is of little importance, since the chances of winning are so great. The opposite case is described in its most extended and best known development in 680/418 (the "pari"). This case depends on the hypothesis that the chance of a large, and especially infinite, gain can make up for a small chance of winning. For example, one chance in ten of winning one hundred dollars is preferable to nine chances in ten of winning ten dollars, since 1 × 100 (first example) is 100, while 9 × 10 (second example) is only 90. We thus act "avec raison" when we hope for, count on, something that is not certain; in 480/577, we count on the safe completion of a journey, the appearance of tomorrow, or—by comparison only—the existence of religion.[20]

It is quite possible that Pascal would not have included an explanation of his reasoning in any kind of published version of this fragment. More importantly, this second part of the fragment—which forms such an obvious extension of both the content and the syntax of the second paragraph that many editors have ignored Pascal's line separating the two—shows that Pascal was acutely aware of methodological questions as he wrote. Fur-

[20]See 5/386, 186/153, 187/154, 190/158, 191/159, 324/293, and 358/326 for other examples of this aspect of Pascal's theories on probability. I am indebted to the late Professor D. J. Walker for this explanation of the *pari.*

thermore, Pascal continues to repeat many words and phrases. Even in this explanatory section, he does not use formal demonstration but continues to juxtapose related statements and examples. We should not be surprised when we consider Pascal's approach to probability. He looked at each possible case that could result from a given situation and, even when he had reduced the complexity of the various possibilities to a general rule, based his explanations on comparisons, on an enumeration of the possibilities, so that any reader could follow them. Rather than reduce results to formulas, as in the analytic geometry of Descartes, he preferred a visually comprehensible presentation—such as his famous triangle, or the diagrams, with lines of various colors that were his solutions in projective geometry.[21] In a very similar way, an argument based on clear and related statements and examples, often using *être* as the main verb and using some of the same words, is much easier for the average reader to follow than is a formal demonstration.

It is possible, however, to carry the process of stating and comparing related examples to a point where it does become hard to follow. An obvious case is the elliptical mention of an example to be found in another text, such as "Saint Augustin a vu qu'on travaille pour l'incertain: sur mer, en bataille, etc.," immediately following the hypothesis ("on doit travailler pour l'incertain, par la règle des partis") that opens the second part of 480/577. A reader could, *à la rigueur,* understand that the "incertain sur mer" refers to the uncertainty of a safe completion of a voyage at sea and that the "en bataille" refers to the uncertainty of living through a battle, but what are we to do with the "etc."? We could ignore it, or supply our own examples—after all, Pascal often leads the reader to form his or her own conclusions—but in any case it subtracts from the simplicity and directness of the argument.

The problem is compounded with the reference to Montaigne. The example of the "esprit boiteux" and of his opinion that "la coutume peut tout" are perhaps familiar to many readers, but they have nothing to do with "travailler pour l'incertain." Rather, they are examples of an effect which is reached without knowl-

[21]On Pascal's work in projective geometry, see chapter 6, note 4.

edge of its true cause, just as Saint Augustine understood that we must act without complete certainty of success and without understanding exactly why. (An additional complication presents itself here—if Saint Augustine could not understand, how can an average reader? Pascal's pride seems to be showing, since he has gone further than his master.) The initial subject of the fragment and of the paragraph has thus been abandoned for a discussion of cause and effect, and of the relative merits of those who see causes and effects compared to those who see only effects.

Again, the question of what Pascal would have done with such a text if he had prepared it for publication is of little importance here. Reading it with the paragraph divisions found in the manuscript, a reader feels a need to reconstruct the text, just as an editor feels the need to add footnotes to explain the references to Augustine and Montaigne. By reducing his text below a certain level of simplicity and directness, Pascal forces his readers to work out certain aspects of it for themselves (What is the "incertain sur mer"? What is the relation of Montaigne's comment on the "esprit boiteux" to uncertainty?) It is not that the text becomes less clear, but that Pascal is supplying even fewer explanations than in the first part of the fragment. By the end of the fragment he has reduced his explanation to almost mathematical terms: "ils sont à l'égard de ceux . . . comme ceux . . . à l'égard de ceux . . . ." Obviously, there will be many repeated words.

10

Style in the *Pensées*—Conjunctions

In the preceding chapter, I pointed out two stylistic tendencies in the *Pensées,* tendencies which correspond to the two styles I described at the end of chapter 8 and which reflect two different methods. One tendency, especially suitable to the expression of mental operations without drawing conclusions from them, is characterized by simple, direct expression of thought, by frequent use of *être* and of repeated words, and by infrequent use of conjunctions, especially strong, logical ones; fairly short fragments with a high concentration of *être,* such as 50/16, are the best examples. The other tendency, more suitable to the presentation of historical evidence and proofs, is characterized by less direct expression of thought, by logically developed arguments. Some fragments with this tendency, such as 91/58 and 158/103, have a high relative frequency of occurrence of *être* but also contain numerous logical connectives such as "il est nécessaire que," "parce que" and "donc."

I pointed out examples of these same two tendencies in fragments with numerous repeated words. Fragments 645/784 and 680/424 are good examples of the simple, direct tendency, and 155/122 contains a large number of repeated words as well as some logical connectives that characterize the other tendency. Fragment 480/577 is an example of a fragment with a somewhat different use of repetition and with numerous logical, but weak, connectives.

We find examples of these same two tendencies when looking at Pascal's use of conjunctions in the *Pensées* and at how they reflect his methods. It is important to consider fragments that contain both a high and low relative number of connectives, since it is fragments with a low relative number of conjunctions that we would expect to characterize the simple, direct method and style, whereas those with a high relative number would be indicative of other methods Pascal uses. In addition, there are several different types of conjunctions, from the fairly neutral *et* to the subordinating conjunctions that imply why the reader should agree or what he or she should conclude from what has come before (*puisque* or *par conséquent*, for example; I call these "ductive" conjunctions, since they lead to a conclusion). In this chapter, I will thus look first at fragments that contain few conjunctions and then at those that contain high relative numbers of the various types of conjunctions.

Most fragments of the *Pensées* that contain few conjunctions also contain high relative numbers of *être* or repeated words, and typical examples have already been presented in the preceding chapter. For example, 529/641 (discussed at the beginning at chapter 9) contains two independent clauses with no conjunctions to join them, though we might expect a conjunction such as *tandis que* to emphasize the opposition between movement and repose. The main reason for the absence of conjunctions, however, is the lack of a conclusion drawn from the two *jugements*, the lack of the third term of the syllogism—if we avoid movement, then we go against our nature, and the result is death. It is not a difficult conclusion to draw, and the reader who has noticed the relationship among the four nouns does not need Pascal to spell it out step by step (one possible way to spell it out is given in chapter 9).

This fragment, along with 90/57, 31/412, and 518/625, is typical of shorter fragments with a high concentration of *être*—nouns linked by *être* into clauses that do not have strong connectives to indicate their relationships. The relationships are made clear by parallel structures, often involving numerous repeated words, and explanations are rarely given. The result is fragments consisting of several clauses or sentences with no conjunctions.

There are fragments without *être* which function in a similar way but rely more on repeated words to hold clauses together without conjunctions. Fragment 225/192 (discussed toward the end of chapter 9), like 529/641, could be written in much longer fashion, making all the connections obvious: "Quand on connaît Dieu et en même temps on ne connaît pas sa propre misère, le résultat est l'orgueil, parce que . . . ." The briefer, stronger version has the force of a maxim, seems "right," while my hypothetical, longer version makes the reader more aware that there are debatable assumptions and points being made (it is possible to know God; mankind is miserable; pride is the necessary result of knowing God without great humility; pride is bad). If an author does not explain an assumption or a conclusion, we tend to assume that an explanation is not necessary, especially if we agree with Pascal, and Arnauld and Nicole, that conclusions, *raisonnements*, are easy to draw once we have the proper principles to base them on.

I do not mean to imply that Pascal is cheating, that he is creating an *imposture* by turning moral philosophy and religion into deceptive rhetoric.[1] In the first place, we cannot make such accusations against an incomplete, unpublished work; in the second, there is no evidence that Pascal doubted his readers' abilities to draw proper conclusions. Rather, I see his goal as convincing the reader of the soundness of his—Pascal's—own observations and assumptions, so that he would not need a formal, periodic style such as that of my hypothetical longer version. He did not find excessive explanations, and the accompanying conjunctions, persuasive: "On se persuade mieux pour l'ordinaire par les raisons qu'on a soi-même trouvées que par celles qui sont venues dans l'esprit des autres" (617/737). Conjunctions are a sure sign that ideas have already been formed in someone else's mind; otherwise, how would we know which conjunction to use?

Pascal does use a conjunction to conclude 225/192, perhaps because he has introduced a new "term," Jesus Christ, without any transition between the second and third sentences. He does not state the problem (something else is needed because neither pride, the result of sentence 1, nor desperation, the result of sentence 2, is acceptable), but he does explain how Christ can be seen as a solution. And he does it, of course, largely by repeating words from the first two sentences.

Fragment 645/784, discussed in chapter 9, is an example of repetition of an entire sentence except for a change in one of the

---

[1]Roger Duchêne, in *L'Imposture littéraire dans les* Provinciales *de Pascal,* makes such an accusation against Pascal's method in the *Provinciales,* accusing him of making the "provincial" reader feel capable of judging matters that should be left to professional theologians.

nouns and for a reversal of subject and object. The resulting structure is strong and convincing, and the extreme repetition calls such attention to itself that a reader automatically compares the two sentences, even though there is no stated connection. From this point of view, the "et" added between the two sentences is an innocent connector, and the fragment could stand without it. Why, then, is it there—a word that is supposed to indicate similarity—unless perhaps it is not so innocent after all? Does it suggest an exact chiasmatic reversal of the two nouns? If so, it is not innocent at all, since *mots* in the first sentence becomes *effets* in the last, for reasons discussed in the previous chapter. Or does it suggest simply something similar, a repetition of the idea of "diversement rangés" though not of what is rearranged? Could it, and should it not be, replaced by *mais,* to emphasize that something different happens when we rearrange meanings than when we rearrange words, despite the similarity of the process of rearrangement? Or does it only imply similarity between the two occurrences of the word *sens,* regardless of what happens to *sens* when it becomes the subject of a new sentence? Pascal gives an "answer" when he uses "aussi bien que" in a differently worded version of this fragment (575/696, discussed below as an example of "comparing" conjunctions). The main points here are: first, even the inclusion of a simple conjunction like *et* can change the meaning of a fragment, especially when Pascal often uses no conjunctions at all; and second, *et* can be quite difficult to interpret.

Before going on to a discussion of fragments where *et* and other conjunctions occur frequently, it is important to look at a fragment such as 767/943 in which there are no conjunctions but also few occurrences of *être* and of repeated words. Such fragments, unless extremely short, are rare, and they normally occur when Pascal is commenting, interpreting, rather than when he is making original observations (joining ideas with *être*):[2]

767/943 Il me semble que Jésus-Christ ne laissa toucher que ses plaies après sa résurrection.

---

[2]Croll finds the frequent use of *and* to be characteristic of the "stile coupé," because it has "no logical *plus* force whatever" (*Style, Rhetoric and Rhythm,* p. 215).

> *Noli mi tangere.*
> Il ne faut nous unir qu'à ses souffrances.
>
> Il s'est donné à communier comme mortel en la Cène, comme ressuscité aux disciples d'Emmaüs, comme monté au Ciel à toute l'Eglise.

The only form of *être* is an auxiliary, and the only repeated words are simple function-words: *il, que, à* and *comme.* The last sentence of the first paragraph is a conclusion based on the first sentence, but there are no conjunctions to make this clear. The second paragraph has a three-part structure but is so elliptical as to avoid any connectives except the prepositions *comme* and *à.* This structural repetition—even if there are not many individual words, and no nouns and adjectives, repeated—holds the sentence together; otherwise, something like "et à un autre niveau il s'est donné . . ." would be needed to join the second and third parts of the sentence to the first. The content and structure of the fragment, and especially the "Il me semble" at the beginning, suggest that these were notes for Pascal's own use; he knew which points he wanted to make, and how, and there was no need to explain it to himself.

When Pascal uses conjunctions in the *Pensées, et* is by far the most frequent.[3] The highest relative number of occurrences is found in short fragments like 258/226 and 296/265, in which Pascal, as he so often does, is discussing a subject that has two sides:[4]

258/226 Toute la foi consiste en Jésus-Christ et en Adam et toute la morale en la concupiscence et en la grâce.

296/265 Figure porte absence et présence, plaisir et déplaisir.

---

[3]Pascal uses *et* both to create extension (581/703, for example) and to combine elements (144/112, for example). He also uses it often in fragments that are based on Biblical passages; see 718/483, 720/485, and 735/489, for example.

[4]It is difficult to make meaningful comments on fragments shorter than twenty-one words (the average length for fragments with one conjunction). Of fragments with more than twenty-one words and no conjunctions, thirteen (10 percent) have a relative frequency of *être* and repeated words that is not significant.

> Chiffre à double sens. Un clair et où il est dit que le sens est caché.

The second fragment is especially remarkable since its subject is this same two-sidedness illustrated by the high concentration of *et:* both *figure* and *chiffre* have two sides (*absence-caché* and *présence-clair*). The second paragraph serves as an elaboration of the first, though there are no connectives to indicate a relationship between them, nor to give any idea of what kind of a relationship there could be. The thrust of the fragment is the existence of the double nature of *figures*—not an explanation of it—and the structure of the fragment reflects this thrust.

The binary nature of the fragment, and the lack of explanatory words, makes the second part of the first sentence difficult to interpret. First of all, does *plaisir* correspond to *absence,* following the order of the first clause, or to *présence,* following that of the last sentence? We might assume that *plaisir* and *présence* go together, but in exactly what way? It is as if there is a "worldly" connection, based on the pleasure we take in being with someone or in having something. This hardly seems appropriate in the context of Old Testament law and prophecy, however, and a more likely connection would be based on the pleasure present in understanding something. In that case, though, would there be more pleasure in understanding the clear (present) or the hidden (absent)? We thus return to the first question, to what do *plaisir* and *déplaisir* correspond? However we decide to interpret the fragment, it is clear that we must pay careful attention to the structure of the fragment, since there are no connecting, explanatory words except *et,* a word that—as I pointed out in discussing 645/784—is not always an innocent indication of similarity. Indeed, where is the similarity between *absence* and *présence,* between *clair* and *caché*? *Et* indicates duality here, but not necessarily similarity.

Fragment 258/226 contains a similar use of *et,* except that there is no difficulty in working out the relationships here; Christ is clearly associated with grace for any reader even slightly familiar with western civilization. Faith and morality are both double, made up of two conflicting extremes, and Pascal expresses them in a chiasmatic order,

Christ : Adam :: concupiscence : grace,

as if to suggest that Christ is the beginning and the end.[5]

In somewhat longer fragments, *et* is used to link several dependent clauses to a main clause, as well as to link elements in a single clause, and also to extend sentences—and ideas—by adding additional independent clauses. Fragment 24/405, discussed in the preceding chapter, is a good example. The first three occurrences of *et* introduce three possibilities: three dependent clauses serving as objects of *blâmer;* the fourth occurrence introduces a new orientation, a new independent clause with *approuver* instead of *blâmer.* The somewhat ambiguous character of *et* is again apparent, as the first three occurrences link three different types of people to a common fate; the fourth occurrence introduces a related idea, expressed in a similar way, but it uses a verb that has the opposite meaning of *blâmer* and governs a type of person completely different from the first three. *Et* thus links related elements of the fragment, but they are related only because they are opposite. Pascal's thought process is such that, in considering both sides of a question, he often links opposites with a conjunction of similarity; the presence of a relationship is clearly more important than its nature.

Pascal also uses *et* to extend a sentence by adding an idea that goes one step beyond the idea expressed in the preceding clause. He does this in 152/120 and then uses *et* again to introduce a second sentence that is similar to the first but that also contains elements opposed to it.

152/120 Nous sommes si présomptueux que nous voudrions être connus de toute la terre, et même des gens qui viendront quand nous ne serons plus. Et nous sommes si vains que l'estime de 5 ou 6 personnes qui nous environnent nous amuse et nous contente.

The first *et* extends "toute la terre" to include posterity, that is,

[5]Pascal uses both ABBA and ABAB constructions and, when there are no connectives to indicate which one is appropriate, we must rely on previous knowledge, on accepted principles such as those discussed in chapter 2. This reliance on accepted principles is one way in which he is able to make direct presentations of his thoughts. See also the discussion in chapter 11 of what de Man calls "chiasmatic reversal."

those who are not even on earth now. The second *et* seems to introduce a similar idea, since it starts with the same "Nous sommes si . . . que" structure and since *vain* is close to *présomptueux* in meaning, but it then opposes five or six acquaintances to all humanity present and future. There is no conclusion stated after these two similar but opposite sentences, and there are no connectives other than *et* to indicate how they fit together. (In contrast, see 225/192, where a similar presentation of humanity as characterized by *orgueil* and *désespoir* is followed by a statement that Christ can offer something in between.)

In fragments such as 102/68, Pascal uses *et* to double elements of a clause or phrase in order to increase the intensity, the emotional impact. He is speaking, as in the famous fragment on the "disproportion de l'homme," of extremes in size and duration:

102/68 Quand je considère la petite durée de ma vie absorbée dans l'éternité précédente et suivante . . . le petit espace que je remplis et même que je vois, abîmé dans l'infinie immensité des espaces que j'ignore et qui m'ignorent, je m'effraie et m'étonne de me voir ici plutôt que là, car il n'y a point de raison pourquoi ici plutôt que là, pourquoi à présent plutôt que lors. . . .

Each occurrence of *et,* as well as the three of *plutôt que,* make eternity, or space, or our time on earth, seem doubly large, or doubly arbitrary. If "que j'ignore" and "je m'effraie" are not enough to frighten the reader, "qui m'ignorent" and "m'étonne" should greatly increase the impact. Furthermore, a point is made more emphatic by the mention of the future (as in 152/120) and the past.

Et is often strengthened by the addition of another word, often another conjunction. *Même* is used in this way in 102/68, to increase the emotional impact, whereas *ainsi* is often used to increase the logical force. Fragment 207/176 is a good example:

207/176 Ceux qui n'aiment pas la vérité prennent le prétexte de la contestation et de la multitude de ceux qui la nient, et ainsi leur erreur ne vient que de ce qu'ils n'aiment pas la vérité ou la charité. Et ainsi ils ne s'en sont pas excusés.

The first occurrence of *et* serves to double the "prétexte" of the first clause, as in the fragments discussed above, but the addition of *ainsi* to the other occurrences adds an element that is missing from these other fragments, an explanation of the parts of the fragment containing *et*. The main point of this fragment seems to be that the people described in the first sentence cannot be excused, rather than that such people exist, and the fragment thus builds through two logical connections to its conclusion. In a fragment such as 152/120, on the other hand, the emphasis seems to be on pointing out the presumptuousness and vanity of some people (in case the reader had never noticed) rather than on the obvious conclusion that this is not intelligent behavior. There is an important difference between people who are presumptuous and vain—all of us ("nous sommes . . .") have a natural tendency to be like that—and people who oppose truth (207/176), since the latter make a conscious and rationalized effort. In the case of the latter, Pascal formulates an argument against them; in the former, it is enough to call our attention to our conduct.

Other simple, linking conjunctions (*ou, ni, tantôt*) are used in much the same way as *et*—though their meaning is more precise—leaving little doubt about whether the connection is between similar or different elements. Such conjunctions are sometimes used to extend a sentence, such as in 389/357:

389/357 Nul n'est heureux comme un vrai chrétien, ni raisonnable, ni vertueux, ni aimable.

This is a concise way of expressing four simple statements in which *être* joins a person and a descriptive adjective, and *ni* thus serves less to oppose two or more elements of a phrase or clause than to suggest variations on the original clause.

It is much more common for these linking conjunctions to oppose two or more elements of a sentence, usually within a clause or phrase. Fragment 624/754, which, along with 389/357, has the highest concentration of these linking conjunctions, is a good example:

624/754 Premier Degré: être blâmé en faisant mal ou loué en faisant bien.

Deuxième Degré: n'être ni loué, ni blâmé.

The first sentence presents what could be considered a normal state of affairs, associating blame with bad and praise with good through the participial construction and suggesting a relationship of cause and effect between actions and the reactions to them. We might assume that this is as far as we need to go, since this is the way things should be and the way they usually are. When Pascal goes on to a second level, however, we expect—knowing Pascal—a reversal of the first sentence, a statement of the unjust condition in which one is praised for bad deeds and vice versa. Instead, he negates both parts of the first sentence, replacing *ou* with *ni.* He also leaves out the two explanatory participial clauses, so that we do not know under what circumstances such a negation could take place or where the reversal of the first *degré* would fit in; the result is a fairly cryptic fragment. We can of course suggest interpretations—a state of grace, perhaps before the Fall, where earthly actions are of little importance; or, as Havet quite plausibly suggests, a connection with fragment 97/63, which deals with school children who receive praise.[6] It is more difficult to interpret than most of the fragments discussed above where explanations were left out, but not as difficult as it would be without the parallel construction and repetition.

Although these linking conjunctions most often join elements of a phrase or clause, they sometimes join clauses, such as in 105/71. (I quote this fragment after Tourneur and the manuscript; the text differs slightly from that of the Lafuma edition, and the punctuation from that of both Lafuma and Sellier.)

105/71 Contradiction

Orgueil, contrepesant toutes les misères. Ou il cache ses misères, ou, s'il les découvre, il se glorifie de les connaître.

After the participial clause which opens the main part of the fragment (quite unusual for Pascal), *ou* introduces the two means of counterbalancing one's misery, means that could also be said

[6]The first degree would be children who are admired for good actions, the second degree those who do not receive the "aiguillon" of admiration. Havet's interpretation would explain the lack of a reversal in the first sentence.

to counterbalance each other since they are opposites ("découvre" here has the meaning of "uncover," or "reveal"). The second means is expressed in a more complex way. Pascal did not oppose "cache ses misères" and "se glorifie de les connaître" directly, since there is a more direct relation, or opposition, between "cache" and "découvre," and since he needed to emphasize the paradoxical idea of taking pride in something we normally hide. The expression "se glorifie" obviously goes best with "orgueil" and reminds the reader that we would be just as prideful in claiming not to have any *misèresm* when in fact they were only hidden—as in revealing them. Nevertheless, the main opposition, which gives structure to the fragment and brings out the paradox, is between hiding and showing.

The conjunctions which I have placed in the "comparing" category are more precise than simpler conjunctions like *et, ou,* and *ni,* but they have similar functions, extending a clause or sentence or, somewhat less frequently, opposing related elements of a sentence. The end of 575/696 is a good example, as Pascal refers back to the same idea expressed in 645/784 ("Les mots diversement rangés . . .") to show that "la disposition des matières est nouvelle," even if he is using old material:

575/696 Et comme si les mêmes pensées ne formaient pas un autre corps de discours par une disposition différente, aussi bien que les mêmes mots forment d'autres pensées par leur différente disposition.

It takes twenty-seven words (not counting "Et comme si . . . ne . . . pas," which link the sentence to the rest of the fragment) to state what was stated in sixteen words in 645/784—"corps de discours" replaces the somewhat vague "effets," phrases beginning with *par* replace the briefer participial expressions ("diversement rangés"), and "aussi bien que" replaces "et." This additional length results from Pascal's efforts to make a more careful defense of his originality, which in turn requires that the relationships among all the parts of the fragment be explicit. This care with relationships explains the explicit connectives such as "Et comme si" (as well as the earlier "J'aimerais autant") and the "aussi bien que" which replaces the ambiguous *et* (see the discussion of 645/784 toward the beginning of this chapter); this care also explains the phrases beginning with *par*, so that the "disposition" of the first sentence can be repeated.

Fragment 575/696 has only slightly more than the average relative number of repeated words, while 645/784 has the fifteenth highest relative frequency of occurrence. This frequency reflects the extended, amplified form of the former fragment, its careful choice of words to make relationships clear, as opposed to the tendency in 645/784 to repeat words as well as structures in a brief statement of two related phenomena. It also reflects, of course, Pascal's method in 575/696 which could be called proof by comparison. First, there is the comparison to the *jeu de paume*, then, in a new paragraph, the comparison, or reduction, of *matières* to *mots*. This step allows him—*if* we accept the comparison—to defend himself by showing that he is doing nothing unusual, since every speaker of a language uses the same words. Once this is accepted, he states with great care the already implied comparison:

pensées : mots :: corps de discours : pensées (matières).

This comparison states nothing that the careful reader has not already noticed after the first sentence of this paragraph, but it serves as a sort of concluding Q.E.D. How different from the forceful concision of 645/784!

The comparing conjunctions ("Et comme si," "aussi bien que") in 575/696 serve less to extend the fragment by introducing new material—after all, the subject was the *arrangement* of material—than to conclude it. Extension is more typical, as in 4/385:

4/385 Mais ce n'était pas assez que les prophéties fussent, il fallait qu'elles fussent distribuées par tous les lieux et conservées dans tous les temps.

Et afin qu'on ne prenne point tout cela pour un effet du hasard, il fallait que cela fût prédit.

Il est bien plus glorieux au Messie qu'ils soient les spectateurs et même les instruments de sa gloire, outre que Dieu les ait réservés.[7]

[7]Much of this fragment is extremely difficult to decipher. Sellier reads the second

The "ce n'était pas assez" makes it clear from the beginning that there is more to come, that argument will follow argument. There are two groups introduced by "il fallait," the second doubled through the use of *et;* then the "bien plus glorieux" indicates that there is even more to come. It is at this point that the comparing conjunctions themselves appear, as *et* is reinforced by *même;* just when we think the series is over, "outre que" introduces one more element. This last clause is a marginal addition, introducing a new syntactic structure which does not flow very well from the "Il est . . . que" with which the sentence begins; this break in the rhythm of the sentence makes the extension seem even greater.

The existence of prophecies has thus been extended to include their distribution in all places and all times (first sentence) and their prediction (second sentence). The whole extended idea of prophecy is then extended to include a discussion of the Jewish people ("ils" in the third sentence) who are not only spectators of the accomplishment of the prophecies but are even participants in it. This extension is achieved through various means—simple conjunctions like *et,* and more specific ones like *aussi bien que;* expressions like *pas assez* and *bien plus;* and double, parallel structures. Finally, another comparing conjunction introduces one more extension; even though it is hard to tell what Pascal wrote after "outre que," the conjunction and the way the last words are crammed into the corner make it obvious that it was an idea that came to him after the sentence had been more or less completed. It seems clear that this fragment is less a written version of a development that Pascal had worked out than a development that was taking place as he wrote it.

The "Mais" with which 4/385 begins suggests that this fragment was itself the extension of something else,[8] probably a dis-

sentence as "Et afin qu'on ne prît point l'avènement . . . ," and the first copyist read the end of the fragment as "outre que Dieu en tire son mystère." These last words, after "outre que," are especially difficult to make out.

[8]There are numerous examples in the *Pensées* of fragments that seem to be extensions or developments of others. See the discussion of 155/122 and 146/114 in the preceding chapter, and Mesnard's article about "noyaux" ("Pourquoi les

cussion of the existence of prophecies. *Mais* and other conjunctions of opposition function in much the same way as do *et* and other linking, comparing conjunctions, opposing related elements of a sentence or extending a clause or sentence. They are used to indicate a fairly strong opposition, since Pascal often uses *et* where one would expect *mais,* to emphasize the similarity even among opposites (see the discussion of 645/784, 296/265, and 24/405 above). Fragment 224/191 has the highest relative number of occurrences of *mais:*[9]

224/191 Il est non seulement impossible mais inutile de connaître Dieu sans Jésus-Christ. Ils [those who search for God through Christ] ne s'en sont pas éloignés mais approchés. Ils ne se sont pas abaissés mais *quo quisque optimus eo pessimus si hoc ipsum quod sit optimus ascribat sibi.*

Like 4/385 discussed above, this fragment seems to be an extension of another fragment, perhaps 221/189. The strongly negative first sentence supposes a previous discussion of how to know God, and the "Ils" that begins the second sentence has no antecedent in what has come before. The first *mais,* along with the *sans,* thus extends the original idea, opposing but relating what follows to what has preceded; the other two *mais* link adjectives that are opposite in meaning and create the paradox of knowing something (God, in this case) better indirectly than directly. (The quotation from St. Bernard, about becoming worse as one becomes better, adds to the paradoxicality of the fragment.) There are no explanations of exactly why this indirect knowledge is better, but the strong, concise, parallel form—this fragment contains an extremely high relative frequency of both *être* and repeated words—is quite convincing, although we would need the discussion of which this fragment is an extension to be completely convinced. Here, Pascal did not even seem to feel the need

---

Pensées de Pascal se présentent-elles sous forme de fragment?"). Fragments such as 4/385 differ from those that depend on commonly received principles (such as 258/226 discussed above) or on previously furnished information (as in 224/191), since there is a *grammatical* suggestion that something is missing.

[9]Fragment 680/418 (the *pari*), in which Pascal counters the arguments of his imaginary interlocutor, has a similarly high relative frequency of occurrence of *mais.*

to finish the fragment—after "éloignés mais approchés," what could follow "abaissés mais" but *élevés,* or some word with the same meaning?

Mais is often used in conjunction with *et,* to introduce a negative side before or after a positive statement. In 754/925, for example, we find the same type of paradoxical statement with *mais* as in 224/191, but followed by a positive final sentence with *être* as the main verb and extended by the addition of a phrase beginning with *et:*

754/925 La loi n'a pas détruit la nature, mais elle l'a instruite. La grâce n'a pas détruit la loi, mais elle la fait exercer.

La foi reçue au baptême est la source de toute la vie du chrétien, et des convertis.

Following Church tradition, Pascal progresses from nature to law to grace, using *mais* to show that, paradoxically, that which surpasses nature does not void it, nor is it voided by the grace that in turn surpasses it; *mais* joins the two parts of the sentence rather than separating them.[10]

The last sentence introduces several new elements, but we can interpret it successfully by following what was most likely Pascal's thought process—faith combines law and grace and is thus a logical subject to follow the first two sentences. Furthermore, although all Christians have the same faith, a recent convert might know the law but not yet have received grace (Richelet defines *convertir* as "mettre sur la voie du salut"). This is not the place for a discussion of extremely fine points of theology, but rather for looking at how Pascal's thought process goes from paradox to resolution and includes a separate category ("convertis") as an afterthought.

A close look at the manuscript makes this process clearer. The first clause with *mais* is an addition, but the second is not; the idea to add this first clause probably occurred to Pascal after he had started the second sentence and planned to include "mais elle la fait exercer"—he seems to have decided that the addition

[10]See the quotations in the Tourneur-Anzieu edition of the *Pensées,* II, 48, n. 4. Additions and changes to the manuscript are also indicated in this edition.

of a similar clause would strengthen the idea of paradox and the structure in the first paragraph. He next wrote "La gloi," probably the beginning of "La gloire," but he replaced it with a new sentence that followed logically from the first two. Finally, he added "et des convertis," probably because he saw he could make his closing statement stronger by making it more inclusive.

Fragment 583/705, with an extremely high concentration of *et* and *mais,* is an example of a series of positive statements joined by *et,* followed by a clause introduced by *mais:*

583/705 Les grands et les petits ont mêmes accidents, et mêmes fâcheries, et mêmes passions. Mais l'un est au haut de la roue, et l'autre près du centre, et ainsi moins agité par les mêmes mouvements.

Everything is double in the first half of the fragment, including the triple series *accidents–fâcherie–passion,* but *mais* introduces a difference, itself double so as to include both *grands* and *petits.* The final *et,* though strengthened by the addition of *ainsi,* makes the conclusion drawn from the comparison to the wheel seem simple and a natural continuation. The three *et* at the beginning extend the fragment to give us the impression that everything is the same; but this impression is quickly broken by *mais,* as Pascal, through a "renversement du pour au contre," reveals a "pensée de derrière" which shows the true nature of things. All of this is done with remarkable concision and becomes especially clear if we compare this fragment to the passage in Montaigne (II, 12) from which it obviously derives, except that Pascal takes it a step further.[11]

The fragments discussed above have all contained sentences in which most of the conjunctions indicate the presence of a connection—similarity or difference—without saying much more about the nature of the connection or about the author's opinions. Coordinating conjunctions such as *et, mais, ou,* and *ni* do just what their name implies, and from this perspective Pascal's use

[11]Pascal takes this process of concision even further in 395/363, where, rather than repeat the first half of the fragment with the addition of comparing and opposing conjunctions, he sums it up with "au contraire": "Ils laissent agir la concupiscence et retiennent le scrupule, au lieu qu'il faudrait faire au contraire."

of them is not unusual. What is unusual is that he uses them when we would expect a stronger conjunction to indicate the exact nature of the connection. I mentioned above how Pascal used *et* where we might expect *mais* in 24/405. But there are also cases in which we would expect a conjunction that indicates the exact relationship (or at least what the author thinks the relationship should be) among the key words in the fragment, such as in 645/784. These stronger, ductive conjunctions are certainly not absent in Pascal, but they are rather rare in the shorter fragments; indeed, in fragments shorter than the median length of fifty words, only five (one percent) have a relative number of occurrences of subordinating conjunctions greater than the average relative number of occurrences for all conjunctions in fragments of that length; only twelve have more than one subordinating conjunction, and none has more than two. The rest of this chapter, devoted to Pascal's use of subordinating conjunctions, will thus deal mainly with fairly long fragments and, for the sake of simplicity and brevity, mostly with extracts from these fragments.

Si is by far the most common subordinating conjunction in the *Pensées*. Pascal uses it as a sort of double-edged shortcut to a point: if the reader accepts the condition in the "if" part of the sentence, he or she must accept the result in the other part; or, conversely, if the reader accepts the result and the "if" part does not agree with it, then there is something wrong with the "if" part. These conclusions are obvious and need not be stated; from this point of view, *si* is similar to the coordinating conjunctions, since it does not always lead to a stated conclusion, but it still leads quite directly to an implied one.

Fragment 18/399 is an excellent example of this "shortcut" type of reasoning (there are no question marks in the manuscript):

18/399 Si l'homme n'est fait pour Dieu pourquoi n'est-il heureux qu'en Dieu.

Si l'homme est fait pour Dieu pourquoi est-il si contraire à Dieu.

Intermediate steps of the reasoning process are omitted but a complete *raisonnement* would be something like (1) are we made for God? (2) not made for God has no need of God, and conversely, made for God has need of God; (3) we have need of God (to be happy); (4) therefore we are made for God. Pascal treats step (4) as accepted and begins the next sentence with it, but step (2) is missing. For such an abbreviated reasoning process to be convincing, the reader would have to accept the implications of the missing step, and we can probably assume safely that Pascal would have relied on fragments that treat human nature and human needs (see 40/6, for example) to prepare the reader for the argument presented here in 18/399. Such a use of several fragments to complete an argument is an excellent example of the "digression sur chaque point qui a rapport à la fin" method (329/298).

Fragment 18/399 is typical of fragments in which *si* is used in conjunction with a high relative frequency of occurrence of *être* and of repeated words, where they help connect four fairly different *jugements*. Each sentence combines two *jugements* in a seemingly objective manner and poses questions, but the *si . . . pourquoi* structure makes it clear that Pascal believed the second *jugement* in each sentence (following *pourquoi*) to be true. In this fragment, the *pourquoi* in the second part of the first sentence presents what follows as a fact and, at the same time, presents the first part of the sentence as false, since it (the first part) does not explain the second part. Pascal can thus begin the second sentence with the opposite of the first part of the first sentence, join it to another fact introduced by *pourquoi,* and lead the reader to accept a paradoxical conclusion (we are made for God and are also contrary to Him), since both parts of the sentence are true even though they seem contradictory.

Pascal presents his thoughts directly here, with no verbs except *être,* and does not really state his beliefs, but the structure of the fragment, and especially the conjunctions, lead a reader to accept them. In most of the fragments discussed in the previous chapter, Pascal simply presented, with no or few connectives, ideas about the human condition and relied on human reason to lead the reader to the same conclusion he himself had drawn. In this fragment, however, the conclusions are a bit more complex—

from negative to positive to paradox—and the use of *si* offers the reader some guidance.

Still, Pascal does not go on to discuss the paradoxical conclusion, and in this way 18/399 resembles other brief fragments with high concentrations of *être* and of repeated words—it presents ideas, or opinions, without elaborating on them. When Pascal does elaborate, he usually uses stronger subordinating conjunctions, as in 514/621:

514/621 Guerre intestine de l'homme entre la raison et les passions.

S'il n'avait que la raison sans passions.

S'il n'avait que les passions sans raison.

Mais ayant l'un et l'autre il ne peut être sans guerre, ne pouvant avoir paix avec l'un qu'ayant guerre avec l'autre.

Aussi il est toujours divisé et contraire à lui-même.

The two sentences beginning with *si* have conclusions so obvious that Pascal did not even feel the need to complete them, especially since he was not using a conclusion from the first sentence to begin the second, as in 18/399, but simply reversing the two nouns and stating two contradictory possibilities. Since neither of the unstated conclusions is acceptable, the two conditions (introduced by *si*) must be false ("Mais . . .") and Pascal goes on to explain this and its implications. *Si* is replaced by connectives—present participles in particular—which imply both that the condition ("ayant l'un et l'autre") is true and that the conclusion which follows ("il ne peut être sans guerre") is logically inevitable; there is nothing conditional now, only the logical.

Nevertheless, this conclusion derives from conditional statements, which Pascal now restates in a much more positive way: "ne pouvant avoir paix avec l'un qu'ayant guerre avec l'autre." It becomes clear that the missing conclusion of the second and third sentences, for example, must be "il pourrait avoir paix avec elle [la raison]" or "il pourrait avoir paix avec elles [les passions]." These two in turn could lead to two more conditions, "s'il avait guerre avec les passions" and "s'il avait guerre avec la raison," followed by results of each condition. Pascal has skipped these intermediate steps, however, and the conditional has given way to more ductive statements, "ayant l'un et l'autre . . ." and "ne pouvant avoir. . . ." He can then make the final statement with certainty, and without the war-peace metaphor: "Aussi il est toujours divisé et contraire à lui-même." The connectives tell the story—*si* is rejected by *mais*, the participial expressions explain why, and *aussi* presents the inevitable conclusion.[12]

The last two sentences of 514/621, with their high concentration of ductive connectives, serve as an explanation and elaboration of the first part of the fragment, itself made up of two highly similar sentences (not counting the first sentence, which is a sort of title). This concentration of ductive connectives in explanations is common in the *Pensées*, and the rare short fragments that contain subordinating conjunctions are usually explanations or elaborations as well, but of something expressed much more concisely (and not always in the same fragment). In 372/340—which, along with 530/645 (discussed below) has the highest relative number of subordinating conjunctions of the fragments with fewer than fifty words—is an elaboration of a brief Latin quotation:

372/340 *Non habemus regem nisi Caesarem.* Donc Jésus-Christ était le Messie, puisqu'ils n'avaient plus de roi qu'un étranger et qu'ils n'en voulaient point d'autre.

The two clauses beginning with *puisque* explain the conclusion introduced by *donc* and make the fragment seem conclusive. However, the fragment remains difficult to understand unless we are familiar with the scriptural tradition that interprets the Jews' unwillingness to accept a king—other than the foreign one they already have—as an indication that an eternal king was at hand (Genesis 49: 8–10). Twenty–five words is hardly enough to describe and compare the Old Testament prophecy and the conditions during the reign of Caesar.

Fragment 530/645 is another short fragment that contains an explanation of a brief statement. It is quite unusual because it has the fourth highest relative number of occurrences of *être* in

[12]Fragment 511/618 is another, and more complex, example of *si* giving way to stronger and stronger connectives.

the *Pensées,* and twice the average number of repeated words for fragments of similar length, but it also has a high concentration of ductive conjunctions. This can be explained by the subject of the fragment, justice, which in the *Pensées* always involves a paradoxical relationship with force and custom:

530/645 La justice est ce qui est établi. Et ainsi toutes nos lois établies seront nécessairement tenues pour justes sans être examinées, puisqu'elles sont établies.

A statement, or definition, is made at the beginning, using *être,* and then conclusions are drawn. The fragment can thus be seen as an elaboration of the simple idea that could be expressed "La justice est ce qui est établi et ce qui est établi est tenu pour juste," for example; it can also be seen as a considerably more concise statement than 135/103, which deals with the same subject but in a step-by-step way that avoids the need for quite so many connectives (considering the length of the fragment, 160 words as opposed to 25).

It is more typical for fragments with a high concentration of ductive conjunctions to be longer than 372/340 and 530/645 (25 words). Ductive conjunctions are found frequently in the dossier "Raison des effets" and in other fragments where, as in fragments dealing with justice, Pascal uses the "pensée de derrière" to go from one level of understanding to higher ones. Fragment 126/92 is an excellent example, though one could also look at 100/66, 115/80, 119/85, 127/93, and several others; 126/92 is also another example of a fragment which is clearly an extension or elaboration of another fragment:

126/92 Il est donc vrai de dire que tout le monde est dans l'illusion, car encore que les opinions du peuple soient saines, elles ne le sont pas dans sa tête. Car il pense que la vérité est où elle n'est pas. La vérité est bien dans leurs opinions, mais non pas au point où ils se figurent. Il est vrai qu'il faut honorer les gentilshommes, mais non pas parce que la naissance est un avantage effectif, etc.

Every clause is introduced by some sort of connective which indicates what the reader should think of what is to come (I am interpreting the first "car" as introducing the clause "elles ne le sont pas . . ."). These connectives are all fairly strong, indicating opposition, cause and effect, or concession—even the "bien" in the second sentence has the same concessive function as the "Il est vrai" in the third; indeed, the weaker conjunctions such as *et, ou,* and *ni* do not appear at all.[13]

It is unusual to find fragments such as these, with a high relative number of occurrences of *être* and of repeated words and with this many strong connectives.[14] Normally, when Pascal makes simple statements with *être* and repeats the same structure—the beginnings of sentences one and three, for example, or the last parts of sentences two and three—he does not add explanations, since his main purpose is to present ideas, opinions, observations, and so on, and to show the reader the *way* to a conclusion, not the conclusion itself. Here, however, the main point of the fragment is the reasons behind the paradoxical statements ("Il est vrai, . . . mais," for example), not the statements themselves, which serve as examples.

I suggested at the end of chapter 8 that fragments that deal with reasons and explanations, that try to demonstrate in a more traditionally logical way why Christianity is justified by human and divine authority, are likely to be more common in the dossiers that come after the "Transition de la connaissance de l'homme à Dieu"; these dossiers deal more with explaining the truth of Christianity and the falseness of other religions, whereas the earlier ones deal more with making convincing observations about human nature. Explaining prophecy, for example, can be quite complicated, since we have to discuss the prophecy, its fulfillment, and the connection between them, as in 4/385 (discussed above as an example of comparing conjunctions). It becomes even more complicated, however, when we have to deal with false and true prophecies at the same time, as in 416/968:

416/968 Si la fable d'Esdras est croyable, donc il faut croire que l'Ecriture est Ecriture sainte, car cette fable n'est fondée

[13]There are only three other fragments in the *Pensées* that are longer than 126/92 and that do not contain *et, ou,* or *ni*—124/90, 195/163, and 794/957.

[14]Of the thirty fragments with a significant relative number of occurrences of *être* and of repeated words, 17 percent have a significant relative number of occurrences of subordinating conjunctions.

> que sur l'autorité de ceux qui disent celle des Septante, qui montre que l'Ecriture est sainte.
>
> Donc, si ce conte est vrai, nous avons notre compte par là. Sinon nous l'avons d'ailleurs. Et ainsi ceux qui voudraient ruiner la vérité de notre religion, fondée sur Moïse, l'établissent par la même autorité par où ils l'attaquent. Ainsi par cette providence elle subsiste toujours.

This is not an easy fragment to understand, even with all the connectives to point the way. First of all, we must know the story in the apocryphal books of Esdras about the Scripture's being destroyed and reconstituted by Esdras, and know that it undermines the authority of the five books of Moses ("notre religion, fondée par Moïse"). We must also know about the Septuagint, the Greek translation of the Old Testament books made by the "Septante," without which the New Testament loses much of its authority. We must also know that both these authorities (Moses and the "Septante") were of great importance to Pascal. Even so, the "par là" and "d'ailleurs" at the beginning of the second paragraph are not immediately clear, and we must follow the connectives carefully.

The first sentence is paradoxical—if a fable, which Pascal would prefer not to believe, is true, then we must believe that Scripture is holy! An explanation is needed quickly, and the "car" introduces it—since the only authority behind this fable is the same authority that establishes the authenticity of the Septuagint, anyone discrediting the books of Moses because of Esdras simultaneously gives credit to the Septuagint. The importance of this is not clear until, in the second paragraph, we realize that the main concern is the truth of Christianity, which can be established by going back either to Moses or to the Septuagint; thus, believing Esdras and denying Moses gives credence to the Septuagint and can serve the same purpose for Pascal that the books of Moses served. It is really only when we understand this, in the next to last sentence, that the first sentence of the second paragraph becomes clear—"par là" is through the Septuagint (the last mentioned authority) and "d'ailleurs" is through Moses, whose authority is challenged only by the account of Esdras (at least that is all Pascal mentions here).

The connectives play an important role, introducing each part of the argument so the reader knows how they all fit together. There is also a good bit of repetition of words and structures, as one would expect in a text dealing with two authorities that establish the same truth. (The fragment has a higher than average, but not significantly higher, relative frequency of occurrence of repeated words.) The essential phrase "fondée sur" is repeated, as are certain key words such as "sainte" and "Ecriture," but more important are the parallel structures, such as "qui disent/ qui montre," "si/sinon," "ceux qui voudraient ruiner l'établissent/l'attaquent." These repetitions are not enough to hold the fragment together, however, nor are simpler conjunctions such as those found in 18/399; the strong connectives such as "donc," "car," and "ainsi" are necessary as well.

We also find this high concentration of strong connectives and of repetition in fragments that deal with methodology, since there are fine points which must be explained. Indeed, if they did not require explanation, Pascal probably would not mention them; after all, he does not seem to have had a treatise on methodology in mind as he wrote the *Pensées.* Fragment 454/527 (referred to in the discussion of the type of reasoning in fragment 420/831 in chapter 9, note 9) is an excellent example, especially since, like 804/972, it is difficult enough to understand that many editors have changed Pascal's text. I have discussed these changes in considerable detail in an article devoted to this fragment,[15] but it is important to look briefly at it here. The fragment is an important example of how Pascal presents something that is less than obvious, but it is also important because of what it says about repeated, and especially about reversed, structures:

454/527 Les exemples qu'on prend pour prouver d'autres choses, si on voulait prouver les exemples on prendrait les autres choses pour en être les exemples.

Car, comme on croit toujours que la difficulté est à ce qu'on veut prouver on trouve les exemples plus clairs et aidant à le montrer.

---

[15]"Editing and Interpreting Fragmentary Texts: A Justification of Pascal's Text in MSL 527- Br 40." I follow the text of the manuscript.

> Ainsi, quand on veut montrer une chose générale, il faut en donner la règle particulière d'un cas, mais si on veut montrer un cas particulier il faudra commencer par la règle particulière. . . .

The first sentence, with only "si" (weakened by the conditional tense) as a connective, is tautological and can be summarized as follows, with A standing for "exemples" and B for "autres choses": we take A to prove B; if we want to prove A, we take B. Pascal does not point it out, but it is clear that B depends on A and thus cannot be used to prove it. The next sentence, introduced by "car," explains why we could make this error—people tend to assume that anything not being proved does not need to be proved—and is followed by what seems to be a restatement of the first sentence, with "règle particulière" replacing "exemples," and "chose générale" replacing "autres choses." The "ainsi" indicates, however, that what follows is a logical conclusion, not a restatement; an error has been pointed out, and now it is necessary to show the solution that imposes itself—if we want to use A to prove B, then to prove B, we must use something else, in this case the "règle particulière" of a case that was itself a "règle particulière" of the "chose générale." We must take the process (general to particular) one step further, rather than reverse a process that is working perfectly.

Pascal is writing about the dangers of interchanging elements of a thought process; the fragment that expresses these dangers needs logical links to show that some things have changed, in spite of the repeated words and structures, and that sentence 3 is not a restatement of sentence 1. Such a fragment needs "car" to set off the explanation and especially "ainsi" to prepare the conclusion, that is, the new version of the beginning. The rest of the fragment gives a more detailed explanation of why we tend to make an error of this type, and it too contains numerous strong connectives. This is not the type of fragment in which Pascal can simply state his opinion without the conjunctions that help justify it.

Many of the fragments with a high concentration of ductive conjunctions are developments of shorter fragments on the same subject. Some of these brief, point of departure fragments contain a fairly high concentration of simple conjunctions, such as *et* and *ni,* but no stronger conjunctions; it is as if the elements of the sentence are joined loosely, simply, to be joined more tightly later as the fragment is developed. Fragment 249/216, for example, could be the point of departure for 237/205. Pascal's first version is "La vraie religion enseigne nos devoirs, nos impuissances et les remèdes." He then added "orgueil et concupiscence" as examples of "impuissances," and "humilité" and "mortification" as examples of "remèdes." The two occurrences of *et* are not absolutely necessary, especially the second, which Pascal omitted in a similar place between *humilité and mortification.* The "divines connaissances" could be those expressed by the "sagesse de Dieu" in the prosopopoeia in 182/149, where the incomprehensibility of the misery and grandeur of the human condition is explained directly, and where "preuves convaincantes des marques divines en moi" are also offered.

More frequently, however, these shorter, point of departure fragments are high in occurrences of *être* and of repeated words, but low in conjunctions, whereas the longer versions have the opposite characteristics. For example, 240/208 develops the idea, expressed briefly in 225/192, that Christianity can offer a middle ground between the two extremes of *orgueil* and *désespoir/paresse,* of *grandeur* and *bassesse.* It is obviously intended to follow a discussion of Christianity's "divines connaissances," which could be contrasted to the *orgueil* and *désespoir* that result from imperfect human knowledge.[16] A long paragraph elaborates and explains what was presented so succinctly in 225/192, using a style that differs from any of those in the fragments discussed above.

240/208 Sans ces divines connaissances qu'ont pu faire les hommes sinon ou s'élever dans le sentiment intérieur qui leur reste de leur grandeur passée, ou s'abattre dans la vue de leur

[16]See Mesnard, "Pourquoi les *Pensées* de Pascal se présentent-elles sous forme de fragments?" The theme of the two extremes of the human condition is a frequent one in the *Pensées,* and there are several fragments that can best be understood when read together; see, for example, 249/216, 17/398, 683/430, 683/431, and 690/449. Tourneur thinks 240/208 is a variant of 164/131, but it makes more sense to read it as a development than as a variant.

> faiblesse présente? Car ne voyant pas la vérité entière ils n'ont pu arriver à une parfaite vertu, les uns considérant la nature comme incorrompue, les autres comme irréparable, ils n'ont pu fuir ou l'orgueil ou la paresse, qui sont les deux sources de tous les vices, puisqu'ils ne peuvent sinon ou s'y abandonner par lâcheté, ou en sortir par l'orgueil. Car s'ils connaissaient l'excellence de l'homme, ils en ignorent la corruption, de sorte qu'ils évitaient bien la paresse, mais ils se perdaient dans la superbe, et s'ils reconnaissent l'infirmité de la nature ils en ignorent la dignité, de sorte qu'ils pouvaient bien éviter la vanité, mais c'était en se précipitant dans le désespoir. . . .

There are of course parallel structures, as Pascal balances the two extremes, but the vocabulary shifts each time—*orgueil* is associated with *nature . . . incorrompue, excellence, superbe, dignité,* and *vanité,* whereas *paresse* is associated with *nature . . . irréparable, lâcheté, corruption, infirmité,* and *désespoir.* The only key word that is repeated is "ignorent," and most of the repetition is in the seven occurrences of *ils.* It seems clear that he is making a consistent effort to use a different word each time the ideas of *orgueil* and *désespoir* are to be expressed, in order to impress on the reader the varied dangers associated with human knowledge when divine knowledge is missing.[17] The fragment reads like a list of sins and only concludes when it arrives at the noun which was one of the basic pair in the first two sentences of 225/192, *désespoir.* This sentence thus comes to a strong conclusion and leads to a second paragraph which, though not developed here, would discuss the various sects that correspond to the various combinations of pride and laziness.

Now that divine and human knowledge have been discussed at length, the even longer third paragraph elaborates on how Christianity can provide a solution, not by replacing one extreme with the other but by getting rid of both and replacing them with "la simplicité de l'Evangile." So much has been said about the two extremes by now that they seem inevitable, and such a solution thus seems almost miraculous. As in the first paragraph,

---

[17]This is a good example of the lack of a general rule about repeating words; see 452/515.

a fairly simple idea is elaborated with a constantly changing vocabulary, so that the reader receives the same information in different ways.

This fragment as a whole is a good example of Pascal's use of conjunctions without a high concentration of repeated words or of *être.* This does not mean that there are not parallel structures, but that the two parts of the parallel do not often use the same words. The shifts in vocabulary permit more elaboration, more diversity, more stylistic effects (sounds, rhythms, etc.), but they take away the comprehension-at-a-glance that is so characteristic of fragments discussed in the previous chapter, as well as of many of those in this chapter, in which a high concentration of connectives is accompanied by numerous repeated words.[18] The style in the paragraph quoted above is effective and beautiful, and it uses well-balanced cadences to express the evils associated with imperfect human knowledge, but Pascal does not write so well when he develops a formal argument.

In 615/734, Pascal is concerned with making his argument seem as rigorous as possible. This argument resembles those of his work in geometry, in which he establishes a point in one case and then applies the conclusion to other cases.[19] Pascal could have expressed the main idea of the fragment in a brief, paradoxical fragment such as "On sait qu'il y a de vrais miracles parce qu'il y en a tant de faux," much as he did in 544/661, or even more cryptically as in 421/832, "Il y a de faux et de vrais." Here, however, he chose to use complex syntax (the fragment, along with the extremely similar 616/735, contains ten of the fifty-five occurrences in the *Pensées* of the imperfect subjunctive forms *eût, eussent* and *fussent*). The fragment provides numerous examples and considers several possible explanations and potential objec-

---

[18]There are also a few fairly short fragments, like those discussed in the previous chapter, that have a high concentration of repeated words and structures but also of conjunctions; 544/662 is a good example. See also 126/92 (discussed above) and 476/573.

[19]See chapter 5 on Pascal's methods in science. The axioms (principles) are not defined, but this is because, as with such concepts as time, he is dealing with common experience ("comme il y [a] eu quantité de remèdes qui se sont trouvés véritables"). See *De l'Esprit géométrique, O.C.*, p. 350.

tions, thus adding considerably to the length of the fragment as well as to its complexity.

This fragment was dictated by Pascal to his sister Gilberte. The style shows that he was dealing with a subject to which he had devoted considerable thought, and that he was more interested in explaining it to others than in writing it down for himself. In the main body of the fragment (after the title)—which in the manuscript is one long paragraph—each sentence begins with some sort of strong connective ("de même," "il faut raisonner de la sorte," etc.), so that the reader is led from one point to the next. The only exception is the last sentence, in which Pascal suggests some possible objections without stating them completely; this sentence would obviously have to be developed and reworked to explain each objection and the "etc." if it were to be used with the rest of the fragment.

This main body of the fragment is a rigorous formal argument. Pascal states the problem ("ayant considéré . . .") and his hypothesis ("il m'a paru . . .") in the first sentence. He next examines both possibilities (remedies exist or do not exist) and the conclusions that follow. He then discusses similar circumstances before arriving at the subject of miracles (expressed in the title but not in the first sentence) and finally of religion. This type of argument explains the presence of the numerous connectives, both of explanation and of comparison. The following extract is a good example of this type of argument and of the style that expresses it:

615/734 . . . Il en est de même des prophéties, des miracles, des divinations par les songes, des sortilèges, etc. Car si de tout cela il n'y avait jamais rien eu de véritable on n'en aurait jamais rien cru: et ainsi au lieu de conclure qu'il n'y a point de vrais miracles parce qu'il y en a tant de faux, il faut dire au contraire qu'il y a certainement de vrais miracles puisqu'il y en a tant de faux, et qu'il n'y en a de faux que par cette raison qu'il y en a de vrais. . . .

The unusually high frequency of repeated words in this sentence—the entire fragment has about an average frequency—comes not only from the opposition of similar ideas, but from repeating the same structural words in various arguments. The repeated words are not only the key nouns and adjectives such as *miracle, vrai* and *faux,* but all sorts of introductory phrases (*il faut, si . . .*) and connectives (*de même, parce que, car, comme*).

The title of the fragment (the first sentence, which Pascal had Gilberte add at some point after he had begun dictating) shows a similar use of repetition but also an important difference. It is longer than 407 fragments of the *Pensées,* and it resembles the heading of a chapter of one of Arnauld's treatises more than it does a Pascalian fragment.[20] It states the main idea of the fragment fairly directly, but the second "on ne croit" could be omitted, as could the "ou pour rajeunir":

615/734 Titre.

> D'où vient qu'on croit tant de menteurs qui disent qu'ils ont vu des miracles et qu'on ne croit aucun de ceux qui disent qu'ils ont des secrets pour rendre l'homme immortel ou pour rajeunir.[21]

The sentence is remarkably parallel and formal in construction, since the "D'où vient" at the beginning allows each clause to begin in exactly the same way. This form reflects less Pascal's tendency to think in associated pairs than his desire to express the association in a way that makes it obvious to the reader at first glance; he is associating formal syntactic structures more than he is associating ideas. Thus, though some parts of the fragment have as high a relative number of occurrences of repeated words as some of the fragments discussed in the previous chapter, it is hardly the same type of repetition. This latter type of fragment offers information, ideas, and solutions which the reader can combine, whereas the title of 615/734 poses a question and does not even mention the key words *vrai* and *faux* around which Pascal's argument revolves, nor does it use *être* to combine ideas. What distinguishes this title sentence from the rest of the frag-

---

[20]See Sainte-Beuve's comments on Arnauld's method and style, in the *Fréquente communion,* with its propositions followed by refutations like a "démonstration de géométrie" (*Port-Royal,* Paris: Gallimard, 1953, Book II, ch. 12, I, 636–37). As Sainte-Beuve, and also Roger Duchêne (*L'Imposture littéraire dans les* Provinciales *de Pascal,* ch. 1), point out, Arnauld's style is far less heavy than that of most of his contemporaries, but it is still characterized by rigor and by point-by-point demonstrations.

[21]The word "Titre" is found in the manuscript and in Lafuma but not in Sellier.

ment is the absence of any conjunction stronger than *et* to join the two clauses. Pascal is simply posing the question and stating two related observations; he is not yet ready to suggest any other relationship between them than the one present in the negation of the second *croit*. The strong connectives will come as he develops his argument.

This fragment hardly shows Pascal at his stylistic best. The title sentence would be more at home in a theological treatise and, in the extract discussed above, the three pairs of opposing clauses after "au lieu de conclure" make the sentence cumbersome and difficult to comprehend, in spite of the logic and balanced construction. This is the way Pascal argues with a nonbeliever or with a recent convert; it is not the way he presents human nature to the average reader. Similarly, it is the way Louis de Montalte counters the arguments of Annat and the other Jesuits; it is not the way he talks to his provincial friend.

11

Stylistic Multiplicity and Fragmentary Form

In the preceding two chapters, I discussed two stylistic tendencies in the *Pensées* which reflect Pascal's thought processes and are characterized by the relative frequency of occurrence of *être*, repeated words, and connectives. These tendencies correspond to Pascal's *esprit de finesse* and *esprit de géométrie*, and I will call them the "subtle" and the "geometric" styles.[1] Together with the figurative style, which I discuss in this chapter, they make up the three main styles Pascal used to communicate his ideas. The subtle tendency is most obvious in the *Pensées* where, Pascal was convinced, such topics as human nature and needs were not suited to formal demonstration. It permits a direct presentation of his thought and thought processes without necessarily stating a conclusion, and it uses *être* to connect nouns (ideas) directly; there are few connectives between clauses (members) of the sentence (period). This tendency is found to a lesser extent in

[1]Jean-Jacques Demorest, in *Pascal écrivain* (Paris: Minuit, 1953), was perhaps the first to distinguish carefully between something like these two styles. He sees a "style ferme et analytique," related to the *esprit de géométrie*, as typical of the *Provinciales*, and a "style clair, dense et synthétique," related to the *esprit de finesse*, as typical of the *Pensées* (pp. 132–33).

Mesnard, in "Pourquoi les *Pensées* de Pascal se présentent-elles sous forme de fragments?," also identifies two similar styles, which he calls "coupé" and "périodique." His views are especially pertinent to my discussion here, since he arrives at this stylistic distinction from an analysis of Pascal's methods. This article appeared about the same time I arrived at similar conclusions in a similar way and is a welcome confirmation.

Davidson (*Blaise Pascal*, pp. 102–107) does not distinguish among styles, but he mentions two rhetorics, two methods, and four modes of discourse in the *Pensées*. His geometric and dialectical modes of discourse, like his geometric and theologically dialectical rhetorics and his mathematical and dialectical methods, correspond roughly to my geometric and subtle styles, though I am wary of calling anything in Pascal strictly dialectical unless we insist strongly on the process rather than the result. For example, Davidson says "in Pascal's dialectic one does not reach a truly clear intuition of the principle until the end" (p. 103); it is often hard to see where this end would be. It is in combining his dialectical mode with that of "spontaneous self-expression" (p. 106) that we come closer to what I call the subtle style.

the first ten *Provinciales,* and to an even lesser extent in the last eight, which are addressed directly to the Jesuits.

In their most basic form, fragments typical of this subtle style consist of what Pascal and Port-Royal called *jugements,* two nouns linked by *être* in something resembling a mathematical equation (noun^1 = or $\neq$ noun^2). These fragments may consist of only one *jugement,* in which case they are somewhat like maxims, or *sententiae,* often suggesting a definition or a redefinition of a well-known word; more commonly they are somewhat longer, presenting several *jugements* or extending the definition or other opening statement. The first, or combining, type juxtaposes *jugements* and is often dual or antithetical. The reader is led to examine two sides of a question, the relationship between which is often underscored by the presence of some of the same words in the statement of each side. This repetition suggests comparison and contrast, and often a recombination of thc words to make a more accurate statement.[2]

The second, or extending, type of fragment often begins with a fairly complete statement of the main point of the fragment, frequently a definition. To this opening statement Pascal adds examples, explanations (both possible and definite), various counterstatements, and often increased intensity. Many possibilities, many points of view, are presented in what he calls the "digression sur chaque point qui a rapport à la fin" (329/298). There are more connectives than in the combining type, but they indicate linking (*et, ni*), comparing (*comme*), or contrast (*mais*), and they relate members of the period without implying cause and effect. We often find two of Pascal's favorite procedures, the "pensée de derrière" and the "renversement du pour au contre" (see chapters 7 and 12) in such fragments.

It is rare to find a definite conclusion in either of these types of direct presentation of thoughts. This is not to say, however, that there is no way for the reader to arrive at a conclusion, that there is no certainty; juxtaposition, comparison, inference (illation),

---

[2]The possibilities of recombination inherent in the subtle style, as well as problems with its use (especially in conjunction with other styles), will be discussed from a more theoretical point of view in the next chapter.

analogy, and probability can all be used in such fragments to suggest a conclusion. In many cases, juxtaposition of ideas, a sort of informal definition, is enough—there is no reason for Pascal to explain the relationship between the ideas, and fragments of this type usually do not contain any connectives stronger than *et*. Comparison establishes a somewhat more explicit type of juxtaposition and can be negative or positive, depending on the type of connective used (*mais* or *comme*, for example). The manner of expressing the comparison suggests to the reader what kind of relationship Pascal saw between the two (or more) elements being compared. Further, it suggests that the reader consider that relationship as a key to arriving at a conclusion.

Pascal is able to suggest a conclusion inferentially by presenting enough individual observations, enough separate reasons, so that the reader finally reaches a point at which he or she accepts the more general point being made. (This type of reasoning, also called illative, was discussed in more detail in chapter 9, along with the concept of the *règle des partis*, part of Pascal's work on probability.) This method is well-suited to the more extended fragments in which the numerous points of view, the numerous digressions around one point, cause the reader to lean more and more toward Pascal's view of the point in question.

Inference is a type of probability, and though Pascal could say in the fifth *Provinciale*, "Je ne me contente pas du probable, je cherche le sûr" (p. 389B), the "sure" is much more difficult to attain once we leave the order of divine authority and revelation. Pascal does not use rigorous mathematical probability in this direct expression type of fragment (as he does in 680/418, the *pari*, for example), but he does present possible explanations for such conditions as human misery and grandeur. These explanations fit the human condition so well that we are tempted to accept them as true even though they are only probable, that is, analogies instead of undebatable explanations.[3] He presents these explanations both in fragments that consist only of simple jux-

[3]This is not at all the same as the "opinions probables" of the Jesuits that Pascal criticizes in the *Provinciales*. The acceptability, or probability, of an explanation depends not on one person's having held it, but on its conforming to the facts.
For a good example of analogy, see 480/577.

taposition and in others that present several examples or explanations or a combination of both; if the process is one of building up numerous examples, however, it is more properly called inferential, or illative.

The combining and extending types of the subtle style are very close to what Morris Croll calls the curt and loose periods that characterize the Senecan or baroque style.[4] His criteria for the curt period are (1) main members without syntactic links; (2) short members; (3) first member as a statement of the period as a whole; (4) asymmetrical members. The first two are definitely present in what I have called the combining type, and the third is often present; symmetrical members are quite possible, however, especially when they are made up of two similar *jugements* which Pascal expresses with repetition of some of the words. Croll's loose periods are characterized by coordinating conjunctions, absolute participial constructions, and parenthetical statements. Coordinating conjunctions are one of the main features that distinguish what I call the extended type from the combining, and parenthetical statements are very much a part of Pascal's digressions. Absolute participial constructions are rather rare, however, especially when one compares Pascal to other seventeenth-century writers. In short, this subtle style does have much in common with the way Croll sees styles of other writers of the period, but it also has some distinctive features.

We see the distinctiveness of Pascal's style even better when we look at the geometric stylistic tendency. If Pascal were typical of the seventeenth century as Croll and others describe it, the opposite tendency of his simple, direct (Senecan) presentations would be a Ciceronian style, emphasizing formal beauty rather than expressiveness (Croll, p. 207) and characterized by carefully constructed complex periods in which form and balance are more important than the direct expression of the thoughts behind

---

[4]"The Baroque Style in Prose," *Studies in English Philology*, ed. Malone, et al. (Minneapolis: University of Minnesota Press, 1919), 427–56. I cite the article from Croll's *Style, Rhetoric and Rhythm*, ed. J. Max Patrick, et al. (Princeton: Princeton University Press, 1966), 207–33; it is also found in Chatman and Levin, eds., *Essays on the Language of Literature* (Boston: Houghton Mifflin, 1967), 341–61.

them; in short, it would be the "fausses fenêtres pour la symétrie" that Pascal criticizes in 466/559. This is hardly the case—Pascal's geometric style is not like the curt or loose style, but it is certainly not Ciceronian; it is as concerned with the careful expression of thought as is the subtle style. The point is that, as in the two *esprits,* there are different principles involved and different "sortes de raisonnements" (670/512; the quotations in the following paragraph are all from this fragment).

In the *esprit de finesse* and the corresponding style, there is the question of presenting ("faire sentir," in the intellectual sense of *sentir* as described in chapter 1) principles which are "choses tellement délicates, et si nombreuses . . . sans pouvoir le plus souvent le démontrer par ordre comme en géométrie." "Il faut tout d'un coup voir la chose," and Pascal's subtle style permits this by presenting ideas and *jugements,* juxtaposed so that they may be grasped together, or by digressing and expanding the original statement so that more of the numerous points can be presented. In the geometric style, on the other hand, the principles are more "nets et grossiers," and we can proceed "par progrès de raisonnement." First, though, we must establish definitions and principles that can be "si stériles, qu'ils [les fins] n'ont point accoutumé de voir ainsi en détail, qu'ils s'en rebutent et s'en dégoûtent." This process is precisely what Pascal wanted to avoid in much of the *Pensées,* both because his subject was not suited to such a linear order (457/532) and because working with such principles would alienate ("dégoûter") his readers.

This geometric style does have longer and more complex periods than the subtle, and more strong connectives (what I have called ductive conjunctions), but these reflect the complexity of the subject matter rather than a desire for formal beauty. Fragments in which this style is found elaborate a previous statement, but rather than presenting more points of view, as in the extended type of the subtle style, they concentrate on the reasons behind the previous statement. They contain rigorous arguments, leading—via connectives—from principles to conclusions, and often show an awareness of methodology. There are often parallel structures (more often for clarity than for aesthetics) but rarely the repeated words that make it so easy to establish the relations between the parallel elements. It is two arguments, rather than two ideas, that are being compared, and this is not the sort of judgment that can be made "d'une seule vue." The process is much more linear, "par progrès de raisonnement," and each subsequent step is prepared by the preceding one rather than simply being juxtaposed to it—thus the necessity for strong, ductive connectives, for fewer repeated words, and for a variety of verbs, all stronger than *être;* there is a movement toward a stated, prepared conclusion rather than a dependence on juxtaposition, comparison, or probability.

The subtle and geometric styles are certainly not the only styles in the *Pensées.* For example, we could certainly make a case for the existence of a "biblical" style, especially in the translations from the Bible and in such works as the "Mystère de Jésus" and the "Mémorial." However, such texts remain peripheral to the fragments that interest us here, since they (those texts) are not intended mainly to express the truths that Pascal had found. Of greater interest are some of the best known, best loved fragments, and if I have not quoted these fragments often, it is because they are better known, because their stylistic features have been more extensively discussed. I have concentrated on Pascal's efforts to create a style that corresponds as directly as possible to his thought processes, from simple juxtaposition to complex logical sequences. There are, however, numerous fragments in which his imagery and other rhetorical figures suggest a much greater concern with influencing, persuading, the reader. I call the style of these fragments figurative; it could also be called rhetorical, in the traditional, often pejorative sense of the word.

There is little need here for extensive analysis of these oft discussed fragments; a quick look at 230/199 ("Disproportion de l'homme") will furnish numerous examples. There are rhetorical questions ("Qu'est-ce que l'homme dans l'infini"); there are many types of repetition: anaphora ("Que l'homme" at the beginning of several sentences) and epanaphora[5] ("trop de bruit . . .

---

[5]Several members of a sentence start with the same word. The distinction between anaphora and epanaphora is a useful one, though not all works on rhetorical figures make it. For example, see Bernard Dupriez, *Gradus: Les procédés littéraires* (Paris: 10/18, 1984).

trop de lumière . . . trop de distance et trop de proximité . . . trop de longueur et trop de brièveté de discours . . . trop de vérité"); and there are as well the famous graduated enumerations of the infinitely large and small. The sonorous effects are remarkable: onomatopoeia (*craque, glisse*); alliteration ("Qui se con*s*idérera de la *s*orte *s*'effraiera de *s*oi-même"); paronomasia (the repeated /e/, /nu/, /i/ of "et nous quitte, et si nous le suivons il échappe à nos prises, nous glisse et fuit d'une fuite éternelle"). This last quotation is also an example of a highly rhythmic final clausula. And of course, there is the peroration at the end: "Enfin pour consommer . . . ," even if Pascal did not finish it.

There are numerous examples of other figures in the *Pensées*, especially in the longer, more developed fragments. There is the famous prosopopoeia in 182/149, and the antiphrasis ("Plaisante justice qu'une rivière borne") and the par'upanoian (unexpected cause and effect: "Pourquoi me tuez-vous . . . ? Et quoi, ne demeurez-vous pas de l'autre côté de l'eau") of 94/60 and 84/51. Pascal enters into dialogue with the reader with apostrophe ("Connaissez, donc, superbe, quel paradoxe vous êtes à vous-même" in 164/131, itself dealing with the figure of paradox) and with apodioxis (indignant rejection of an absurd argument: "Qui souhaiterait d'avoir pour un ami un homme qui discourt de cette manière?") after putting words in the mouth of the unbeliever in 681/427.

If all of the examples above are from what I call Pascal's figurative style, this does not mean that there are not figures in his subtle and geometric styles, but that they are more frequent in the figurative style and are of a different nature. A consideration of a list of figures (such as those in Dupriez, in Fontanier's *Les Figures du discours*, or in the glossary of Alvin Eustis's *Anthology of Seventeenth-Century French Literature*), reveals many which are as common in these former two styles as they are in the figurative style, though they are usually found in more compact form and without the more traditional, "flowery" figures I have just mentioned (peroration, apostrophe, alliteration, for example).[6] Such figures are more like what the Port-Royal *Gram-*

[6]Pierre Fontanier, *Les Figures du discours*, ed. Gérard Genette (1830; Paris: Flam-

maire (part II, chapter 24) and Fontanier (part III) call "figures de style" than they are true tropes or "figures de construction."

Figures such as antithesis, paradox, and chiasmus are found in both the subtle and geometric styles, depending on whether we are juxtaposing and comparing ideas and simple *jugements* or relating more complex arguments with strong connectives. (For examples, see the fragments discussed in the preceding two chapters, especially 626/756, 31/412, and 50/16 for the subtle style and 530/645, 514/621, and 454/527 for the geometric.) In the subtle style, these figures of opposition are often reduced to the form of a *sententia* or maxim (77/43), and the lack of conjunctions can produce asyndeton as well as ellipsis and anacoluthon. For an example of asyndeton, see 529/641, where *repos* is juxtaposed to its opposite *mouvement* with no conjunctions and no preparation for the change from positive to negative. Fragment 514/621 is a good example of ellipsis, and Croll gives an excellent example of anacoluthon: "Le plus grand philosophe du monde . . . son imagination prévaudra" (78/44; Croll, p. 229). We also find oxymoron in the subtle style, as in 117/83.

The presence of repeated words is found in the subtle, geometric, and figurative styles, most especially in the subtle (see chapter 9 for examples of repetition in the subtle style; see the discussions of 240/208 and 615/734 in chapter 10 for examples in the geometric). A figure that involves a specific type of repetition, such as anadiplosis (repetition of last word of a clause at the beginning of the next) is more common in the subtle style (420/831, 31/412), while a freer type of repetition such as epanorthosis (repetition with slight changes) is found in both subtle and geometric (77/43, 615/734). More extended fragments in the subtle style create conglobation (piling up of examples and proofs), as in 135/103.

Some figures involving repeated words are used in the subtle and geometric styles in a quite logical way, whereas they are used

marion, 1977). Alvin Eustis, *Seventeenth Century French Literature . . . A Critical Anthology* (New York: McGraw-Hill, 1969). See also Du Marsais, *Des Tropes* (Paris: Brocas, 1730), and Bernard Lamy, *La Rhétorique ou l'art de parler,* 4th ed. (1699; Brighton: Sussex Reprints, 1969); the first edition is from 1665. Figures are especially rare in longer fragments in geometric style.

more to *agréer* and for their rhythmic effects in the figurative style (see the examples from 230/199, above). In the geometric style, epanaphora is used to introduce reasons (the two clauses beginning with *puisque* in 372/340), and in the extended subtle style to list examples ("devoir. . devoir. ." in 91/58). Anaphora is used in the brief, combining subtle style to create in each sentence the symmetrical patterns that allow the reader to grasp the fragment at a glance.

Imagery is less evenly distributed among these three styles than are stylistic figures. It is of course quite prevalent in the figurative style, and has been studied extensively by Michel Le Guern and others.[7] It is much less common in the geometric style (Le Guern points out that Pascal rarely uses imagery in his scientific writings except when there is no available non-figurative word; p. 205). In the passages discussed as examples of the geometric style in the preceding chapter, only 514/621 contains what could be called a real image, that of the "guerre intestine" between reason and passion.

Imagery is more common in the subtle style, but certainly not as common as in the figurative. The examples discussed in chapters 9 and 10 contain words used in the figurative sense such as *coeur* (680/424), *cercle* and *lumière* (155/122), *boiteux* (480/577), *abaissés* (224/191), and *espace, durée, infini* (102/68); the use is similar to that in 230/199. The majority of the fragments in this stylistic category do not contain imagery, however, but either abstract nouns—representing the ideas involved—or concrete nouns—in the examples. This is what we would expect in a style that aims at presenting thought as directly as possible; when there is a word which corresponds directly to a thought, there is no need for figurative language, which Pascal (and his colleagues such as Arnauld and Nicole) definitely mistrusted.[8]

---

[7]Michel Le Guern, *L'Image dans l'oeuvre de Pascal* (Paris: Armand Colin, 1969). Gérald Antoine, "Le Langage de Pascal," *La Table Ronde* 171 (1962): 56–71. Dom Michel Jungo, *Le Vocabulaire de Pascal* (Paris: Editions d'Autrey, 1950).

[8]The *Logique* refers to the reader's need for ornaments as a weakness (p. 22), and the *Grammaire* praises the French language for being natural and clear, able to attain beauty without excessive figures. Davidson, in *Audience, Words and Art*, p. 113, points out that Pascal was much more interested in instruction than in moving and pleasing, that he had no interest in ornaments.

Le Guern's division of Pascal's use of imagery into three categories—example, comparison, and metaphor—corresponds exactly to the distribution of imagery among Pascal's styles that I have just described. Metaphor is found most frequently in the figurative style and is the least logical of the three (p. 208). Still, in harmony with Pascal's distrust of form for the sake of form (466/559, 609/728), metaphor has a "valeur affective" or a "valeur explicative" even if there is also a "valeur esthétique" (pp. 206–207). Metaphor is meant to be persuasive ("l'art d'agréer") even if it is not strictly logical and rational ("l'art de convaincre"). The subtle style is characterized precisely by example and comparison, especially in longer, extended fragments. According to Le Guern, Pascal uses comparison to establish values rather than to explain, and he does this by juxtaposing ideas and *jugements,* often omitting the comparing words, that is, connectives (pp. 197, 202). Examples permit proof by analogy, which is very much like the inferential, illative method described at the beginning of this chapter; see also the end of chapter 9. Pascal does not lead the reader step by step to a conclusion but presents him or her with more and more evidence. Imagery is not necessary to this process, to this method (which works quite well with direct, literal language), but it is by no means incompatible with it; it is sometimes even necessary in this fallen world where everyone does not follow reason.

It is not surprising that none of Le Guern's three divisions corresponds well to the geometric style. In its purest form, this strictly logical style, and the method behind it, needs only to define its terms and establish its principles, and the conclusions follow easily. One word corresponds to one idea—see Pascal's discussions of definitions in *De l'Esprit géométrique,* and chapter 5 above—the principles (axioms) are clear and accepted by all, everyone reasons to the same conclusion, and there is no need for anything but the careful processing of literal language. Figures and images are rare in this style, especially in fragments longer than the median (50 words).

The categories of Croll and Le Guern are very helpful in understanding Pascal's styles, especially in the *Pensées,* but both neglect the geometric style.[9] It is not a very interesting style from

---

[9]Le Guern does not really neglect it; he is aware of how Pascal writes in his

a traditional point of view, probably because of its origins in the realm of science. We can hardly neglect it, however, since it is precisely his scientific background that makes Pascal such an unusual figure in the history of literature. The world of science was definitely where Pascal was "coming from" as he entered the polemical fray of the *Provinciales*; it was certainly not only his worldly experience that made his associates at Port-Royal think of him as a possible author of a polemical work but also his reputation as a geometrician, as someone who was a master of the scientific method of argument.[10]

Keeping the importance of Pascal's scientific background in mind, we can turn to the categories of Richard Lanham for another way of looking at Pascal's styles, even though Lanham's is once again a two-sided view which leaves out one (the subtle) of the three styles I am concerned with here. Still, the two extremes provided by Lanham's categories form an excellent framework for understanding Pascal's most distinctive style. Lanham has suggested that Western literature be seen as "the symbiotic relationship of the two theories of knowledge, theories of style, ways to construct reality."[11] In a similar way, Pascal's *Pensées* can be seen from the point of view of the styles I have described, and from that of the theories of knowledge that lie behind these styles. Furthermore, there are opposing world views in the *Pensées* reflected in these styles and theories of knowledge.

In Lanham's convincing presentation of two styles of life, the serious, central, essential self (something like the soul) is opposed to the rhetorical, social self. The serious style of life posits the existence of a divinely certified reality, of true referentiality of language, of one value structure; it is sublimely religious and tragic. The rhetorical style of life, on the other hand, sees no reality beyond language and recognizes several different value

---

scientific works, and this style with its paucity of images has little connection with the subject of his book on imagery. Demorest's "style ferme et analytique" corresponds to the geometrical style, but he does not give any examples of it from the *Pensées*.

[10]For more details, see my "Chez les Jésuites et chez les honnêtes gens: Methods and Styles in the *Provinciales*," in *Biblio 17* 21 (1984): 57.

[11]*Motives of Eloquence* (New Haven: Yale University Press, 1976), 34. The two styles he refers to are the serious and the rhetorical.

structures; it is worldly and sentimental. The serious style of life favors transparent style, clarity of idea, and sincerity of feeling, whereas the rhetorical favors excessive style, imitation, and representation. The conflict between these two styles of life and the literatures associated with them is an essential part of the Western tradition.

It is not difficult to see how these categories can be applied to Pascal and his time: the serious is Jansenist and *dévot,* the rhetorical is Jesuit and *honnête.*[12] In the more specific realm of the *Pensées,* the serious is associated with the grandeur of mankind in the pre-Fall state, with the true and unique self and its divine spark, and with clear, demonstrable—no interference from the "puissances trompeuses"—concepts; the rhetorical is associated with the misery of mankind after the Fall, with the constantly changing, *haïssable* social self, and with the gap between "les choses . . . simples en elles-mêmes" and ourselves "composés de deux natures opposées" (230/199). As forms of expression, the serious is the *art de convaincre,* a classical and transparent style; the rhetorical is the *art d'agréer,* a baroque and excessive style; in the terms I have established to describe Pascal's styles, the serious is the geometric and the rhetorical is the figurative.

From the actual state of the manuscript of the *Pensées,* we can surmise that, in developing a possible apologetic strategy, Pascal would have wanted to establish the superiority of the serious style of life over the rhetorical, and the superiority of the religious style with its one way over the worldly style with its diverse, diversionary *divertissements.* It would follow that he would use a serious method and style, argumentative and periodic, but this is clearly not the case in many of the fragments. Does he then go to the opposite extreme and adopt the method and style most familiar to a worldly, non-believing audience in the 1650s—obviously and traditionally rhetorical, full of figures?—hardly, in spite of the presence of this style in many frag-

[12]Racine derides the overly serious style of the Jansenists who criticized him for his association with the theater in his "Lettre à l'auteur des 'Hérésies imaginaires' ": "Retranchez-vous donc sur le sérieux, remplissez vos lettres de longues et doctes périodes, citez les Pères . . . : vous êtes appelé à ce style" *(Oeuvres complètes,* ed. Pierre Clarac, Paris: Seuil, 1962, 311B).

ments. There is definitely a third style in the *Pensées*—the subtle—which falls precisely in between the serious (geometric) and the rhetorical (figurative) styles, between the way he learned to write as a scientist and a more traditional, worldly style. Intended as a direct expression of thought (ideas combined into *jugements*) without chains of *raisonnements,* the subtle style is both serious and rhetorical—serious in that it is simple and clear, but rhetorical in that it is hardly free from figures.

More importantly, the style of life that corresponds to the subtle style falls in between those of Lanham's serious and rhetorical styles since it posits the existence of a divinely certified reality but recognizes that language is not truly referential. Longing for pre-lapsarian clarity in a fallen world, it believes in the existence of ultimate truth and in the possibility of true referentiality, but it recognizes the need to express this truth with a language in which referentiality is not only arbitrary (as in scientific discourse) but also confused and corrupt (as in everyday discourse). This is why Pascal's subtle style calls attention to itself, often by its very simplicity, its bareness, in the same way that the underdressed woman with no makeup calls as much attention to herself as does the overdressed woman who represents rhetoric or, more specifically for Pascal, excessively ornate poetry (486/586; Lanham, p. 30).

Paul de Man noticed this paradoxical nature of Pascal's styles in the *Pensées,* and for de Man the resulting "disjunction" between sign and referent, word and thing, not only calls attention to itself but threatens to undermine any hope of complete understanding.[13] Such a threat cannot be dismissed lightly, especially

[13]On de Man's concept of disjunction, see "The Rhetoric of Temporality," which first appeared in 1969 and is reprinted in *Blindness and Insight,* 2nd ed. (Minneapolis: University of Minnesota Press, 1983), 187–228. His application of this concept to Pascal is in "Pascal's Allegory of Persuasion," in *Allegory and Representation: Selected Papers from the English Institute, 1979–80,* ed. Stephen J. Greenblatt (Baltimore: Johns Hopkins University Press, 1981), 1–25. Page references below will be to this article unless otherwise specified.

I have some general reservations about de Man's interpretation of Pascal, and it is important to state them at the beginning. A false opposition between the "Art de persuader" and epistemology in the *Esprit géométrique*—Pascal refers to both of them as "preuves méthodiques parfaites—causes de Man to neglect the intellectual side of performative statements, that is, of what I call

since de Man's "preliminary hints" go straight to the heart of Pascal's stylistic multiplicity. It is important to examine these hints closely before going on to look at how and where Pascal uses his various styles. Only then can we decide if de Man is right or if there is a way of understanding Pascal so that his text remains convincing and persuasive rather than seductive, intelligible in spite of its stylistic and methodological complexity.

De Man describes an ironic awareness in Pascal that allows us to go beyond our inauthentic "empirical self"—a self oblivious to the complexities of existence and knowledge—to create a "self that exists only in the form of a language that asserts the knowledge of this inauthenticity" ("The Rhetoric of Temporality," p. 214). This awareness stems from oppositions between real and nominal definitions in *De l'Esprit géométrique,* and, in the *Pensées,* between what he calls cognitive, propositional statements and modal, performative statements; the former set out propositions that can be judged true or false, whereas the latter "perform what they enunciate regardless of consideration of truth and falsehood" (p. 21). The cognitive statements, with their highly logical, linear content, are expressed mainly in what I call the geometric style; the performative statements are expressed mainly in the subtle. De Man discusses 158–159/125–126, 164/131, and 155/122 in terms of chiasmatic reversals of binary oppositions, revealing the existence of multiple possibilities, combinations, and *jugements*—if the reader is willing to investigate all the possibilities. In 158–159/125–126, for example, Pascal first sets up the following schema, in which the elements in each line are paired with each other:

nature	first	constant
custom	second	erasable

the subtle style. Performative (modal) statements in these fragments are based on the very intellectual processes of *sentiment* as much as they are on pleasure and seduction (p. 23). This misunderstanding also seems to be the cause of de Man's accusing Pascal of "bad faith" in not being able to explain the "art d'agréer" (p. 5). He seems to think Pascal is using the "rhetoric of seduction" in these performative statements, whereas it is much more a case of using *sentiment* and the subtle style. Furthermore, Pascal is talking about being able to *explain* the "art d'agréer" and give rules for it, not about being able to *use* it.

He then proceeds, however, to reverse the pairings, so that we end up with a different schema:

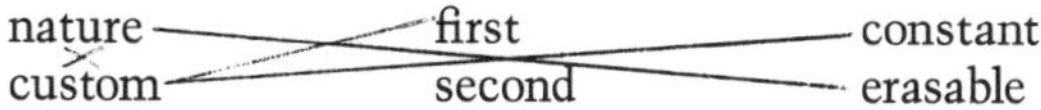

For de Man, contradictions exist in these fragments, but there is a chance for totalization, for making them intelligible through a dialectical movement, which, though infinitely postponed, remains possible.[14]

This chiasmatic reversal works best in fragments written in the subtle style, a style that can be associated with performative statements because it states a case directly and with few logical connectives, whether the case should be (is true enough to be) so stated or not.[15] Such statements can express what *is logically* if they contain a valid *jugement,* or what *is practically* if they are basically a description. In addition, they can suggest new statements of what is or should be by allowing for recombinations of the words, such as in the chiasmatic reversals described by de Man.

The main problem, or disjunction, that de Man discusses comes when performative statements, in the subtle style, are confronted with cognitive statements in the geometric, especially in 135/103 but already in 164/131 and 155/122. Fragment 164/131

---

[14]De Man sees any instance of such a postponement or disjunction as ironic, but this infinite postponement of the very possibility that can provide hope for arriving at true understanding is also ironic, in the more traditional sense of the word, as well as paradoxical.

See also Davidson, *Blaise Pascal,* p. 87. Davidson is more positive than de Man, since he sees an end to the dialectical process (pp. 93, 103). I am not sure we can ever reach this end in such a fragmentary, incomplete text, but Davidson is correct to point out that Pascal does at least provide immediate satisfaction to the reader by means of his digressive method (p. 93).

[15]Fragments 158–159/125–126, for example, contain no subordinating conjunctions in 148 words—(the strongest logical word, *donc,* occurs only in an ironic question: "Quelle est donc cette nature sujette à être effacée?"). Both have numerous repeated words, and 159/126 has a very high frequency of occurrence of *être.*

Fragment 158/125 has only one occurrence of *être,* but it nonetheless uses few strong verbs. Rather, there is a sentence with no main verb at all, two occurrences of "il y en a" with a meaning similar to that of *être,* and reflexive or intransitive verbs such as "se voit" and "dépend" which present explanations in a performative way, with no explanations.

is so long and complex that de Man cannot identify chiasmatic reversals here by juxtaposing neighboring words but has to combine words from different parts of the fragment—we are a long way from typical fragments in the subtle style where similar statements are juxtaposed and often share key words.[16] In 155/122, Pascal states the chiasmus himself—('Il est donc misérable, puisqu'il l'est. Mais il est bien grand, puisqu'il le connaît"), but here he uses the geometric style, including what de Man calls "apparently deductive propositions" characterized by *donc* and *puisque* (p. 18).

In fragments such as these, and especially in 135/103, de Man sees the dialectical process as disrupted—the performative statements, which, like *jugements,* ideally should stand by themselves, prove to be inadequate and need to be backed up by propositional statements (*raisonnements*) which furnish some sort of proof. The poles of what is and what should bc become reversed: logical, propositional statements, rather than describing what is in a world where everything is as it should be, posit what should be—but isn't—in a fallen world ("Il est juste que ce qui est juste soit suivi"); performative statements, rather than describing an arbitrary vision of what one person would like to have happen, describe things as they are in this fallen world ("La justice sans la force est impuissante").[17] Thus the "ainsi" of the last sentence of this fragment ("Et ainsi ne pouvant faire que ce qui est juste fût fort, on a fait que ce qui est fort fût juste") is that of a despot and not that of Descartes (p. 23), an ironic indicator that the existing state of affairs—that which is strong is considered just—is the result of a corrupted logic in a fallen world rather than of a carefully reasoned decision. For de Man the geometric style, like

---

[16]In 158–159/125–126, the words that de Man juxtaposes (*nature/coutume; première/seconde; ineffaçable/sujette à être effacée*) are found in close proximity in the text; in 164/131, *pyrrhonien, dogmatique, vérité,* and *nature* do not occur in the same paragraph except in variants.

I will return to these last three fragments in chapter 12; they are well chosen examples, and by using similar examples the similarities and differences between my approach and his will be clearer.

[17]Pascal speaks of justice in a way that describes perfectly a performative statement: "La justice est une qualité spirituelle dont on dispose comme on veut" (119/85). Force, on the other hand, is a "qualité palpable" and should not be subject to performative statements.

cognitive logic, has failed, and rather than supporting performative statements and the subtle style, it calls attention to their mutual weaknesses and to their ultimate incompatibility (disjunction).

Before discussing the success or failure of a style and before deciding how radical is the heterogeneity of styles in the *Pensées*, I would like to look more closely at where and how these different styles are used. It is of course hypothetical to ask which style(s) Pascal would have used in a non-existent, or at least incomplete, apology, but we can look at the content of the various sections of the manuscript of the *Pensées* and then draw our conclusions based on what we know of his methods, of his views on thought and language, and of his intentions.[18] Is there evidence of a tendency for one style to predominate? Do certain styles characterize certain sections of the *Pensées* or the discussions of certain subjects? Are there shifts in style to suggest a progression from a worldly, rhetorical style of life to a serious one as a similar progression takes place in Pascal's style of writing?

If Pascal were to be perfectly true to the stylistic implications of his methods (which I have described in chapters 7 and 8), he would employ the subtle style quite consistently, at least when dealing with ideas (conceptions) and principles, with the human condition and needs. It is hard to imagine that he would have used the geometric style, since he found it adaptable neither to the complexities of his subject nor to the tastes of his readers; and we doubt that he would use an overly figurative style, given his avowed dislike of eloquence which is anything but "une peinture de la pensée" (481/578). We could then expect to find the subtle style—with its characteristics of high relative frequency of occurrence of *être* and repeated words, and low relative frequency of occurrence of ductive conjunctions—in dossiers (*liasses*) dealing with these subjects. This would include particularly dossiers 2–16 of the Sellier classification, through "Transition" (the first fifteen dossiers of the Lafuma classification);

[18]I describe these sections of the *Pensées* below; see the beginning of chapter 7 for a description of the *Pensées* as Pascal left them.

dossiers 17–28 contain more proofs, and we would expect to find in them more examples of the geometric style. We would expect to find the subtle style in the "liasse-table" of the Sellier classification—if this is indeed a "table des matières plus étoffée" (p. 31)—but less in the "développements de 1659–1662," which are longer, more polished, and more tightly reasoned, and thus more likely to contain the geometric and figurative styles. It would be hard to know what style(s) to expect in the dossiers from the "phase préparatoire" (1656–1658), since it is probable that they predate the classification of fragments into dossiers.

We do indeed find the subtle style in the places we would expect but no more frequently than we find other styles; we also find each style quite frequently in places where we would not expect to find much evidence of it.[19] In fact, when we compare the different sections of the *Pensées,* we find very few differences that could not be attributed to the random distribution of stylistic features; the main exception is found in the distribution of ductive conjunctions among the first twenty-eight dossiers of the Sellier classification.

The six main sections as described by Sellier in his edition of the *Pensées* are:

1. Dossier 1, the "liasse-table."
2. Dossiers 2–16, through the dossier "Transition," dealing with the human condition, reason, and needs.
3. Dossiers 17–28, dealing with figures, proofs, prophecies, and so on.
4. Dossiers 29–35, the "phase préparatoire" (1656–58), dealing mostly with Esdras and miracles.
5. Dossiers 36–44, 1659–62, dealing with geometry, authority, and miscellaneous subjects.
6. Dossiers 45–61, 1659–62, developments of earlier fragments.

There are no significant differences in the occurrence of *être,*

[19]See the appendix for information on the computer programs I used to identify these styles and to determine their relative frequency of occurrence in the various sections of the *Pensées.*

repeated words, conjunctions, or ductive conjunctions—either individually or in combination—between the classified dossiers of the 1658 project (2–28) and the earlier or later ones, except for the "liasse-table," nor between dossiers written in 1656–58 and those written between 1659–62. Nor are there any when comparing the classified dossiers to sections 4, 5, and 6 individually, with the slight exception of section 6, the developments. Differences among these last three sections are not statistically significant, but they are more significant than differences between the classified dossiers and sections 4 and 5, except in the case of ductive conjunctions. In particular, the developments contain fewer repeated words than any other section.

The only comparison which reveals significant differences in the occurrence of *être* is that between sections 2 and 3. Section 2 (dossiers 2–16) contains considerably more occurrences of *être* and fewer fragments with an unusually low relative frequency of occurrence. It does not contain any more occurrences of *être* than do the developments, however.

Differences among the first twenty-eight dossiers taken individually are more significant than those between these dossiers as a group and the rest of the *Pensées*, but they are still not statistically significant, except in the case of ductive conjunctions. In particular, the fragments in the "liasse-table" have a considerably lower relative frequency of occurrence of ductive conjunctions than those in any other section. As a whole, section 2 (dossiers 2–16) contains more ductive conjunctions than section 3 (17–28),[20] but fewer than the other sections (4–8). Among dossiers 2–28, the distribution of ductive conjunctions varies much more widely than that of other stylistic characteristics. Dossiers with a high relative frequency of occurrence include (in descending order) "A.P.R.," "Le Souverain bien," "Preuves de Moïse," "Figures particulières," "Divertissement," "Commencement," and "Raison des effets"; those with a low relative frequency of occurrence include (in ascending order), "Rabbinage," "Conclu-

[20]This is the most surprising exception to the expectations I suggested at the end of chapter 8 and in the discussion of fragment 416/968 in chapter 10.

sion," "Rendre la religion aimable," "Philosophes," "Ennui," and the "liasse-table."

We can draw some conclusions from these findings that match the expectations I have established. The style of the developments (the dossiers in section 6) is more geometric than subtle, except that there is a high relative frequency of occurrence of *être*. The lower relative frequencies of occurrence of repeated words and the higher of ductive conjunctions (though not as low and high as one might expect) is typical of the periodic, geometric style, as Pascal explains more carefully what he has earlier stated more directly. The unexpected presence of *être* is probably due to Pascal's general preference for this verb, a preference which would explain the lack of significant differences in his use of it throughout the *Pensées*.[21]

The "liasse-table" stands out as having extremely high concentrations of repeated words and low concentrations of *être* and of ductive conjunctions. The first and third characteristics are to be expected, but the second is not. The second is mostly attributable to fragments such as 16/397, 17/398, 25/406, and 36/417 in which phrases without *être* are repeated; these fragments have a strong comparative, antithetical character. In general, the dossier is characterized by condensed expressions of related points to be made, of items that could be compared and developed. In short, it is exactly what we would expect in a "table des matières plus étoffée."

Though the concentration of stylistic features, and of ductive conjunctions in particular, is not what we would expect in each of the two main sections of dossiers 2–28, the distribution of these conjunctions among the individual dossiers is less unexpected. The unexpectedly high relative frequency of occurrence of ductive conjunctions in the dossiers in section 2 comes from five dossiers: three of these ("A.P.R.," "Le Souverain bien," "Commencement") come from the end of the section, after Pascal begins to discuss the "seconde partie" (181/148), in which he offers explanations for human misery and explains how faith in

[21]Details on the use of *être* in the *Provinciales* are given later in this chapter; it is used there 24 percent less frequently than in the *Pensées*.

God can lead to a solution. Seen in this way, opposing dossiers 2–10 to 11–28 makes more sense than comparing 2–16 to 17–28. The two dossiers between 1 and 11 that have a high relative frequency of occurrence of ductive conjunctions, "Divertissement" and "Raison des effets," are more anomalous. In the case of "Raison des effets," it is obvious that the subject lends itself to the use of numerous logical conjunctions to introduce the reason behind the effect at each level. The high concentration of conjunctions in "Divertissement" is mostly due to 168/136, itself a development of fragments such as 165–166/132–134, similar to those in section 6. This dossier also contains a fragment (137/135) which seems to have very little to do with *divertissement,* and which is very high in ductive conjunctions.

Looking at dossiers which have a lower concentration of ductive conjunctions than we would expect from their place in section 3, we find that "Rabbinage" and "Rendre la religion aimable" are more like the "liasse-table," because they contain mostly lists of ideas and facts to be developed. They contain only two fragments each and are not typical of the section. The other dossier in this section with fewer occurrences of these conjunctions than we would expect is "Conclusion," in which we would expect to find a restatement of ideas and opinions rather than the new developments or explanations we find in fragments such as 413/381 and 414/382.

Although we can offer explanations (such as the ones above) for the characteristics of individual dossiers in sections 2 and 3, the fact remains that there is little stylistic unity within these sections, less than one would expect in a well-worked out plan. More importantly, given Pascal's tendency to adapt his style to his subject matter and to his readers, there is less stylistic *difference* than we would expect when we compare these sections as wholes to other sections, but there is just enough to suggest that we are not amiss in looking for it.

When we look at a more completed work such as the *Provinciales,* we find that a stylistic comparison of the various sections reveals precisely the differences we would expect. For example, in chapter 6 I pointed out methodological differences among three groups of letters: in letters 1–4, Pascal concentrates on definitions; in 5–10 on principles; and he resorts to *raisonnements* in letters 11–15. Excluding the quotations, which make up a larger and larger proportion of the letters, we find that the first ten letters contain 14 percent fewer conjunctions than the last eight, and 18 percent fewer logical conjunctions. The first letter has the highest frequency of occurrence of *être,* and the first five letters have 7 percent more occurrences of *être* than do the last eight; the first ten and the last eight, however, have the same percentage. Being 42 percent longer than the first ten letters, the last eight have a slightly higher (7) percentage of repeated words, but 33 percent less when we compensate for length.[22]

There is, of course, not a perfectly consistent progression of all of these features. Letter 11, for example, has 30 percent more conjunctions than letter 10, as one would expect, but almost exactly the same percentage of occurrences of *être.* In most cases, the percentage of occurrence of *être* is not consistent and does not reveal much about the individual letters. *Etre* appears 24 percent less frequently than it does in the *Pensées,* probably because the *Provinciales* are dealing with a more formal subject and with a vocabulary that is to a large degree dictated by the circumstances, whereas in the *Pensées* Pascal is freer to combine his own observations about the human condition ("l'homme est . . ." or ". . . est vrai," for example).

It is the use of conjunctions in the *Provinciales* that is the most interesting and the most revealing about the methods at work. *Et* makes up about 40 percent of the total conjunctions, and though its use does not diminish in the last eight letters, its frequency relative to other conjunctions does. The use of logical conjunctions increases drastically in some of the last eight letters, occurring twice as often in letters 13 and 17, as in letters 3 and 5, for example; there is a similar increase in the occurrence of other ductive conjunctions.

While the use of these ductive conjunctions increases, that

[22]In this case, I compensated for length by dividing by the average word count. This is a less than perfect method, but there are not enough data to calculate predicted values, as I did for the *Pensées.*

of comparing conjunctions decreases in the last eight letters. This decrease is most noticeable between letters 10 and 11, in which it drops 80 percent, although the overall use of conjunctions increases by 30 percent. These usages confirm the expectations generated by a study of Pascal's methods in the various letters—there is more comparison in the first ten letters and less argumentation. Pascal does not need to connect many of his statements with logical conjunctions, because the comparisons are clear—the doctrines of the Jesuits are not the same as those of the Church, and the conclusion is equally clear: the Jesuits are wrong. It does not take complicated syntax to express such comparisons and conclusions, but it does take somewhat more complex language to convince the holders and inventors of those doctrines that they are wrong. There is less comparison and more demonstration in the last eight letters, less statement of right and wrong and more explanation of why a particular opinion is wrong.

If the *Provinciales,* then, show definite stylistic differences that reflect the methodological differences, does the relative absence of such stylistic differentiation among the sections of the *Pensées* mean simply that Pascal did not have time to complete his planning, his writing, and rewriting?[23] To suggest an answer to this question, we must go beyond statistical generalizations and look at some fragments that would be likely to play key roles in any plan suggested by his preliminary classification of his *Pensées.*

The *Provinciales* offer a perfect example of the adaptation of method and style to content and reader, and much of their continuing success is due to Pascal's having been able to avoid the overly formal, periodic, geometric style, especially in the first ten letters. He could count on the Jesuits, and on Annat in particular, to read his more argumentative—full of *raisonnements*—letters, since they had a vested interest, a need to respond. He could not count on this interest from the typical reader of an apology who

[23]We can never be sure about how much time Pascal had, or how much healthy time, but he did work on the *Pensées* for six years, and he found time during the last two to work on the three *Discours sur la condition des grands* and on the *carosses à cinq sous.*

must be told why he or she should be interested in religion and must be shown that Christianity is "aimable" (dossier 18); nor could he have counted on such an interest from the "ami provincial" in the first few *Provinciales.* The strategy of "Nous étions bien abusés" (letter 1) is much like that of convincing the reader of an apology that he or she has been wrong in being indifferent to eternal life and to religion—the author must catch and hold the reader's interest.

Pascal's discussion of *divertissement,* for example, is clearly intended for just such a purpose, that is, to show the reader that there are more important things to be interested in. Such a discussion would thus come fairly early in an apologetic plan, as it does in the classification of the dossiers in the *Pensées.* But would it come in the form of a formal argument, full of ductive conjunctions, as in 168/136: "Quand je me suis mis quelquefois à considérer. . ."?[24] Similarly, how effective would the long, skillfully argued 164/131, about the relative merits of skeptical and dogmatic philosophies, be to an indifferent reader, or at least to one who preferred a lighter style such as that of the *Provinciales*? Other long fragments in the first ten dossiers (78/44, 94/60, for example) are more readable, more typical of the subtle style than of the geometric.

I have used these two fragments (164/131 and 168/136) as examples of texts that do not seem to fit in their places in Pascal's preliminary classification, because they are clearly texts on which he spent considerable time but which are, from the point

---

[24]See Pascal's justification of his style in the *Provinciales,* as reported by Marguerite Périer: "si j'avais écrit d'un style dogmatique, il n'y aurait eu que les savants qui l'auraient lu" (Lafuma 1002). See also Racine's sarcastic criticism of the overly serious style of the theologians at Port-Royal, quoted earlier in this chapter, n. 12.

Jean Mesnard, in "Pourquoi les *Pensées* de Pascal se présentent-elles sous forme de fragments?," is very aware of the need to hold the reader's interest ("Une déduction abstraite et contraignante risque de le rebuter"; p. 645); he also uses 168/136 as an example. He sees it as an incomplete (compared to 230/199, for example) development of shorter fragments, the major piece of a "noyau" on the theme of *divertissement.* He cites these fragments as an example of how Pascal gives the geometric method more "souplesse et vie," as an "analyse d'une situation commune contre laquelle il convient de réagir" (p. 645). I see 168/136 in particular as lacking in *souplesse,* as leading readers to a conclusion rather than allowing them to react at their own pace.

of view of the methods and styles I have described, quite different from others that surround them. I doubt they would hold a typical reader's attention any more than would the multi-leveled complexity of much of "Raison des effets" (126/92 and 127/93, for example); such complexity is almost impossible to express in anything except the geometric style.[25] Even if these two fragments did hold a reader's attention, the great difference in methods and styles would be disconcerting and not what we would expect to find.

These examples (126/92, 127/93, 164/131, and 168/136) are only a few specific and well-known illustrations of the frequent presence of the geometric style in the early dossiers, of an absence of stylistic consistency and differentiation to be found throughout the *Pensées.* If Pascal was going to develop these fragments into anything like a traditional apology, with carefully worked out and ordered arguments written in a consistent style, he had a long way to go. Even if this lack of progress was due only to a lack of time, it suggests that what we have in the *Pensées* is further from being a completed apology than many people think. The classification into dossiers suggests a possible arrangement based on content, but this is only a first step.[26] Pascal seems far from having worked out the application of the original and successful method and "subtle" style he developed in the *Provinciales,* to a subject matter more complex than that of texts and debates and to principles like those of the *esprit de géométrie:* "les principes sont palpables mais éloignés de l'usage commun de sorte qu'on a peine à tourner la tête de ce côté-là, manque d'habitude: mais pour peu qu'on l'y tourne, on voit les principes à plein" (670/512). Pascal's success in the *Provinciales* comes from his ability to put these geometric, manageable ("palpables") principles in front of his readers' eyes without resorting to the geometric style.

[25]These fragments might interest a "libertin érudit," however, especially the idea of intellectual superiority over the *peuple* and the *demi-habiles.* It is certainly possible that this was the type of reader Pascal had in mind, a type of reader who would be more interested in the discussions of pagan philosophies and the *deux infinis* than a less erudite reader.

[26]The presence of what Mesnard calls "noyaux," and the development of briefer fragments into longer, more structured ones, may constitute a second step, but it is far from a definitive one.

His problem in the *Pensées* was of a different nature—to include all the principles, "si déliés et en si grand nombre," *and* be sure that the mind of his reader was *juste* enough not to "raisonner faussement sur des principes connus." Even if he could have controlled the extremely complex "digression sur chaque point qui a rapport à la fin," could he have presented everything in a style that would both be appropriate to the subject? Could he consistently catch and hold a reader's interest, even when presenting complex, paradoxical subjects such as *divertissement* or the "raison des effets," which require that the reader be lead through a series of *raisonnements*?

This lack of stylistic consistency and differentiation between the subtle and geometric styles is very much like what de Man calls a heterogeneity between two types of language: performative—"the language of pleasure (*volupté*) and of persuasion by usurpation or seduction"; and cognitive—"the language of truth and of persuasion by proof" (p. 20). He sees this heterogeneity as an ironic indication that there is little hope of complete understanding, of proceeding dialectically toward a state "in which oppositions are, if not reconciled, at least pursued toward a totalization that may be infinitely postponed, but that remains operative as the sole principle of intelligibility" (p. 20). We are faced with what he calls "the destruction of all sequence," or allegory (p. 23).

It is true that in the *Pensées* as we have them, regardless of the reasons for their incomplete state, there is a disconcerting mixture of styles, and we may wonder whether Pascal had any desire or intention of making his text less disconcerting. After all, one of his main goals—and perhaps the only one he ultimately felt capable of accomplishing—was to make the reader aware of the inadequacies of human understanding. Still, I do not think we have to be as negative as de Man is about the effects of this heterogeneity, or disjunction. The two styles (languages) both function well in many fragments,[27] and the "discomfort" that de

[27]De Man says not all fragments reveal the disruption of the dialectical process toward totalization (p. 20), but his concluding pages read as if he were generalizing for all fragments.

Man describes as a result of reading the final sentence of 135/103—where "ainsi" becomes despotic as a result of this disjunction—is clearly intended by Pascal; the "discomfort" can serve as an indication of the lack of logic and justice in a fallen world without denying all hope of understanding. Not all performative statements can be reduced to seduction, and it is precisely one of the major advantages of the subtle style that it can make statements that readers can accept or reject without the need for explanations in the form of cognitive statements in geometric style.

As I pointed out above in note 13, de Man neglects the intellectual side of *sentiment,* and its role in performative statements and in the subtle style. This style may coexist uncomfortably with the geometric in many places, but it is also a brilliant and unconventional tool that Pascal forged to express the complexities of the human condition. He did not complete a convincing apology, certainly not a traditional one, but he managed to suggest, through the interplay of loosely connected statements and fragments, the many points of view we must keep in mind. Rather than destroy all sequence, he pointed out the weaknesses of a sequential method and replaced it with "la digression sur chaque point qui a rapport à la fin" (329/298).

Is it not possible that Pascal was coming to believe that there was nothing wrong with this stylistic inconsistency, that the "véritable ordre qui marquera toujours mon objet par le désordre même" applies to style as well as to the arrangement of the fragments?[28] Wittgenstein describes a similar situation, in terms that suggest style as well as arrangement, in the Preface to the *Philosophical Investigations:*

> After several unsuccessful attempts to weld my results together into such a whole, I realized that I should never succeed. The best that I could write would never be more than philosophical

[28]Fragment 457/532. Mesnard ("Pourquoi les *Pensées* de Pascal se présentent-elles sous forme de fragments?," p. 638) thinks this fragment applies only to discussions of pyrrhonism; I think it can be applied more generally.

> remarks; my thoughts were soon crippled if I tried to force them on in any single direction against their natural inclination.[29]

Forcing thoughts against "their natural inclination" is a problem at the level of the clause and sentence as well as at the level of the arrangement of paragraphs and chapters, and Pascal's efforts toward natural expression, toward the portrait of thought, could have led him to accept the most appropriate means of expression, the most appropriate style, regardless of the style of surrounding passages. If a thought is expressed in the most natural way, why not leave it as it is rather than try to rewrite it to make it fit (try to make it different from the original, so that it becomes a *tableau* rather than a *portrait*). A digressive method and order can result in two neighboring passages having quite different subjects, and the subjects may require quite different styles if they are to be expressed naturally.

Whether or not Pascal was content with the stylistic diversity, or inconsistency, that characterizes the *Pensées,* such diversity in no way detracts from his great stylistic accomplishments in all the styles he uses. On the contrary, we are perhaps fortunate to have so many styles, to be able to enter into the workings of Pascal's mind in one fragment and then to fall under the spell of his rhetoric in the next. I would not go so far as Sartre to say that "La mort de Pascal sauva ses *Pensées* d'être composées en une forte et incolore apologie"—I am not sure that his death was the main cause of the incomplete state of the *Pensées,* nor that I would not like to see the completed work—but I am more than content with what we have.[30]

---

[29] 3rd ed. (New York: Macmillan, 1958), p. ixe.

[30] *Qu'est-ce que la littérature;* quoted in Ernst, *Approches pascaliennes,* p. 530.

Conclusion

12

The Fragmentation of Thought and Language in a Fallen World

In the preceding chapter, I discussed the presence of at least three styles in the *Pensées*—subtle, geometric, and figurative. The first two correspond closely to Pascal's two main thought processes, or methods: (1) the direct combination of words and ideas, with a relative absence of connectives, allowing for frequent digression and forcing the reader to reach his or her own conclusions, and (2) a carefully ordered, linear series of arguments. The first (subtle) involves the mental operations that Pascal and the Port-Royal *Logique* call *sentiment* and *jugement;* the second (geometric) involves what they call *raisonnement* and *ordre.*

We would expect Pascal to use one of these methods, and the corresponding style, consistently in sections of the *Pensées* dealing with the same subject or calling for a similar approach; furthermore, we would not expect him to use a seemingly inappropriate style, but my analysis of the styles of the fragments and dossiers (*liasses*) reveals numerous instances of this seeming inappropriateness and of stylistic inconsistency. The method, which worked so well in the *Provinciales,* of using the subtle style to catch his readers' attention and then using, in the last eight letters, the geometric style to argue specific points with the Jesuits, seems to have been harder to apply to the more complex subject matter of the *Pensées.* The classification of the *Pensées* into dossiers suggests that Pascal did consider a similar approach to them and a similar stylistic division—dossiers 2–16 would catch the reader's attention and show the inadequacies of our understanding; the remaining dossiers would present more specific proofs of the excellence of Christianity (prophecy, miracles, etc.). However, we find in almost all the dossiers the presence of multiple points of view, of digression to related subjects, and of appeals to the ability of the *sentiment* to make immediate judgments about how words and ideas are combined. These characteristics make it difficult to give an orderly presentation and to use the geometric style, yet much of the subject matter of these dossiers, such as the history of the Jews and the "raison des effets," demands—and receives—just such a presentation and such a style.

Pascal was thus faced with the need not only to develop a (subtle) style that was much more flexible than the traditional (geometric) style—a style that would disconcert many readers, including the editorial committee at Port-Royal—but also to combine it with the geometric and other styles, often within the same fragment. It is no wonder that he was not any further toward completing an apology, nor that there is much in the *Pensées* to suggest that he was considering using a fragmentary form and a diversity of styles. This fragmentation and diversity would occur not just on the larger scale of the organization of the text, but also on that of individual fragments. In short, although the *Pensées* are far from the completed "apology" that most editors and commentators have tried to reconstruct, they are equally far from being unsuccessful, stylistically or methodologically flawed, or non–convincing.

I reached the conclusions summarized above by analyzing methods and styles in Pascal's writings and by studying what he said about thought, method, and style. If we look at these same writings from a more philosophical-theoretical point of view, we can discern an attitude toward thought and language that is consistent with just the kind of fragmentary, seemingly disorganized text we have in the *Pensées.* The incomplete, fragmentary nature of the manuscript might result from Pascal's realization of the difficulty of accurate expression of thought as well as from his lack of time to complete and to organize a projected apology. It is not just that the means of expression available to a writer do not always match the complexity of thought—this has already been discussed in chapter 8—but that language and knowledge are flawed, fallen.[1] All three of the styles I described in the preceding

[1]For a more complete treatment of the importance of the concept of the Fall in the *Pensées,* see Sara Melzer, *Discourses of the Fall.*

chapter, both in themselves and in combination with each other, point to a highly problematic discontinuity between sign and referent, between word and thing.

The geometric style often reveals this discontinuity less, because it can rely on nominal definitions that make the relation between word and thing clear and unambiguous. Ultimately, however, the discontinuity becomes more critical than in the other two styles, because it is impossible to have perfect nominal definitions of every word. As a result, a discourse that has its reason for being in the absolute correspondence between sign and referent, in the possibility of defining all terms, is shown to be hopelessly flawed except when it is used with the arbitrary terms of mathematics.[2]

The other two styles, the figurative and the subtle, are equally prey to this discontinuity but are less seriously flawed by it, because they admit its existence and contain other means of representation than the direct one-to-one correspondence between word and thing. The figurative style depends on analogy, on figures such as metaphor and symbol, to suggest what words in their literal sense cannot. The subtle style, with its direct juxtaposition of words without explanatory connectives, allows for multiple relations between words and groups of words (ideas and *jugements*), for a plurality of levels. A word can suggest more than one thing or idea, be combined with other words in more than one way.

Of Pascal's two main thought processes, or methods, he considered the direct thought expressed by subtle style to be a more accurate representation of our fundamental mental processes than is the linear, discursive thought expressed by the geometric style (see chapters 7–8). The subtle style is more open to all possibilities, an essential capacity in a world where there is more than one way to look at things and where the best method for

---

[2]Davidson (*Blaise Pascal,* pp. 35–36) gives a good example of how Pascal attempts to overcome the discontinuity between words and things in his work on conic sections. Unfortunately, most of this work is lost, and we cannot know just how successful he was. Even here, as Davidson points out, the linear order of definitions, demonstrations, and conclusions must exist in parallel with "occasional corollaries or remarks added in parallel,"—and that order is hard to maintain.

communicating truth is "la digression sur chaque point qui a rapport à la fin" (329/298). Equally important, the subtle style forces the reader to recognize discontinuity, and the complexities and difficulties of attaining true knowledge. It creates an ironic perspective (see below, and chapter 11), that is, the ability to distance ourselves—through a Pascalian "pensée de derrière" and "renversement du pour au contre,"—from what we are saying, to be truly aware of the "raisons des effets" that allow us to go at least one step beyond standard behavior and attain a perspective from which to understand its deficiencies.[3] This continual shifting of perspective is essential to Pascal's thought. It is not enough to recognize the falsity of an opinion—"toutes ces opinions sont détruites" (127/93); we must realize that there is a point of view from which these same opinions are valid, and then that they are ultimately invalid because those who hold them do not hold them for the right reasons. How can we hope to reflect this complexity, this multiplicity, if we use a linear style that must state one opinion after the other? We can describe the situation using such a style, as Pascal does in 127/93, but it takes a much more subtle style to suggest some or all of the possibilities without going through the tedious process of identifying each level each time it is mentioned.[4]

The "renversement du pour au contre" and the "pensée de derrière" allow Pascal—and his readers—to go beyond mental complacency, beyond the habits of custom, to the highest level of understanding humans are capable of.[5] (There is also the "lumière supérieure" of the "chrétiens parfaits"; 124/90.) It is clear from many fragments, especially in the dossier "Ordre," that a major component of any apology he was considering writing would be to awaken readers from apathy about religion and the human con-

---

[3]See the dossier "Raisons des effets," especially 124/90 and 127/93; see also the end of chapter 7. There are several different levels of understanding, and we can only understand one level after attaining a higher one.

[4]Fragment 127/93 is interesting because it contains a high relative frequency of *être* and of repeated words but also a high relative frequency of conjunctions. Pascal makes simple statements (*jugements*) about similar situations, but he must add a considerable amount of explanation to make the relationships clear.

For examples of Pascal's use of the subtle style to express multiple possibilities, see chapter 9; see also the discussion of de Man in chapter 11.

[5]See chapter 2 on nature, custom, and the Fall.

dition: "Je ne puis approuver que ceux qui cherchent en gémissant" (24/405). Language plays an essential role in this process, since it is too easy to say things we are used to saying without thinking about them; Pascal was as aware of the dangers of a complacent, mindless use of language as he was of those of apathy.[6]

The subtle style thus served his needs well. In addition to representing the complexities of the human condition and the need to reconsider our opinions, it calls attention to the way language is being used and reveals the thought process behind it. The subtle style calls attention to itself most directly when, as in 127/93, it is confronted with the geometric style. Fragment 135/103 is a good example as are, to a lesser degree, 164/131 and 155/122. Fragment 164/131 contains a mixture of styles, though we might expect such a long, argumentative text to be dominated by the geometric style. There are in fact numerous occurrences of subordinating conjunctions, but also of *être,* as Pascal fills his text with numerous *jugements* without explanations—"Cette neutralité est l'essence de la cabale. Qui n'est pas contre eux est excellemment pour eux," for example. Still, the text is so long and complex that Pascal cannot hold it together simply by repeating words to relate one statement to another, and there are many ductive conjunctions and few repeated words. In 155/122, and especially in the last two sentences ("Il est donc misérable, puisqu'il l'est. Mais il est bien grand, puisqu'il le connaît."), there are numerous repeated words, and three of the last four verbs are *être;* but this concise, paradoxical conclusion cannot stand without the ductive conjunctions *donc* and *puisque* so characteristic of the geometric style. There is a definite *renversement du pour au contre,* carefully explained in the preceding sentences, but Pascal cannot seem to bring himself to say it "en un mot," that is, to write simply "Il est misérable et grand."

In fragments such as these and especially in 135/103, the *jugements,* which ideally should stand by themselves, need to be backed up by *raisonnements,* which furnish some sort of justifi-

---

[6]Many of the fragments in the dossier "Raisons des effets" deal with discerning the true reasons behind what is *said.* See, for example, 125/91 and 126/92.

cation. The subtle style, though it presents truth, is only describing things as they are in this less than perfect world ("La justice sans la force est impuissante"). The geometric style is not needed here to explain this very obvious truth but to point out the relative, corrupt character of this truth by stating what should be ("Il est juste que ce qui est juste soit suivi"). Ideally, the subtle style should suffice (for example, a sentence such as "Ce qui est juste est suivi."), and something is obviously wrong when simple statements (*jugements*) cannot be used to describe the way things should be. The "ainsi" of the last sentence of this fragment ("Et ainsi ne pouvant faire que ce qui est juste fût fort, on a fait que ce qui est fort fût juste") does not introduce a conclusion that is right or that we would want but only one that is expedient. Unfortunately, the conclusion is perfectly logical given the corrupted principles of the human condition. This kind of logic, this use of the geometric style, does not really support the subtle style; it only calls attention to it and to the discontinuity between them.

There are of course theological ramifications to this philosophical, linguistic view of the world, of the self and its search for knowledge. The problematic necessity of discursive language, of geometric style, reflects our fall from the direct knowledge that was possible in Eden, where *jugements* necessarily represented the true state of things: "En Dieu, la parole ne diffère pas de l'intention" (803/968). In the fallen world, *jugements* can be true or false, represent things as they are or as they should be; we often need discursive language, *raisonnements*, geometric style, to distinguish between the true and the false, the *is* and *should be*. But discursive language is also flawed, and the discontinuity between the two is, like the Fall, another rupture between words and things. There remains the possibility of revelation (the ultimate direct thought, subtle style), to make this distinction, to overcome the discontinuity, but this mysterious, unpredictable illumination is not something we can count on in our day-to-day affairs. There is little hope of making recognizable, sequential progress toward salvation, just as there is little hope that linear statements, expressed in geometric style, can lead toward true knowledge of the human condition, no matter how effectively they can lead toward mathematical certainty.

The awareness of the discontinuity between the subtle and the geometric styles, of the futility of sequential ordering, leads to that of the impossibility of reaching complete understanding through linear progression. We cannot develop an idea linearly (geometric style) without digressing to other ideas (subtle style); and when we try to use this subtle style to express thought directly, we cannot avoid insisting on the discontinuity between sign and referent as well as between the subtle and the geometric style. This awareness of discontinuity is ironic in the sense that it involves incongruity between the actual and the expected result—we would expect a rigorous, "scientific" style to lead infallibly toward indisputable truth. Furthermore, the failure of the geometric style leads us to turn to a style (subtle) and to mental processes (*sentiment, jugement*) that are themselves ironic, in the sense that they allow the use of words to express something other than their literal meaning and espcially that they allow statements (combinations of words) to suggest more than one conclusion. The geometric method, if it is successful at all, eventually comes to a dead end in the QED—there is nothing to do but to start another chain of reasoning, which usually involves choosing one of several possible directions and neglecting others. The ironic method of the *esprit de finesse,* however, omits the usual signs of certainty (connectives, careful linear progression, and clearly stated univocal conclusions) and thus allows for new and simultaneous perspectives and developments, both about the processes at work and about the words and ideas in question. This type of irony, like figurative language but without the need for figures, allows the presence of multiple, often conflicting ideas in one, allows more than one meaning to be generated by one statement. In this complex and fallen world, things can usually be seen from more than one point of view, and the best possibility of true understanding lies in this ironic reversal–substitution of signs, that is, in ironically multiple meanings.[7]

---

[7]I am indebted for some of this view of irony to the standard works by Booth and Muecke as well as two recent works: Jean Pol Madou, "Ironie socratique, ironie romanesque, ironie poétique," (*French Literature Series* 13 (1987): 62–73); and Gary Handwerk, *Irony and Ethics in Narrative* (New Haven: Yale University Press, 1985). See also Mesnard's chapter on irony in the *Pensées* in his *Les*

If ironic multiplicity is a primary structural principle of the *Pensées* and is the best way of understanding the human condition, what kind of text does it produce? What is the effect on readers? The subtle style is an improvement over the geometric for the subject matter of the *Pensées,* but can it really lead to a satisfactory understanding, can it really convince an unbeliever of the value of Christianity? By constantly calling attention to itself and to problems that it is perhaps incapable of overcoming, does it not go too far? Surely the typical reader would like to understand the text with as little effort as possible. In reading the *Pensées,* we find it necessary to perform the difficult task of viewing ourselves ironically from several points of view. The text and the self exist on multiple levels, and we must use the *pensée de derrière* to question every opinion. Furthermore, we must remain aware of the distinctions between Pascal's three orders (physical, intellectual, and divine; see 339/308), and of the definite gaps between each order. The self is discontinuous, and so is the text of the *Pensées.*

When we combine this discontinuity with the ironic subtle style which constantly calls attention to it, the traditional idea of a text comes apart—not just the idea of a traditional apologetic text which proceeds step by step toward a single goal, but also that of a traditional persuasive or convincing text. Still, there is no need to be negative about the ability of Pascal's text, discontinuous, incomplete and fragmentary as it is, to make its point. Even if we reject the argument based on religion—that all the text has to do is raise questions and prepare the reader to accept grace—the *Pensées* do not deconstruct themselves beyond repair. If a fragment like 135/103, with its paradox and mixture of styles, is not what we would expect in a traditional apologetic text, the explanation is not that Pascal did not know how to express himself. In addition to giving his opinions about force and justice, the fragment—through the discontinuity of its styles that call atten-

---

Pensées *de Pascal,* pp. 273–99. Mesnard insists on irony as a means of leading the reader, through the *esprit de finesse,* beyond his or her point of view to a more advanced, and often contrary, one: "l'ironie consiste à adopter le point de vue de l'interlocuteur pour amener celui-ci à le dépasser. . . . L'ironie est une forme de l'esprit de finesse" (p. 289).

tion to a corrupt human nature—makes the reader aware of the false basis through which force has become truth. The questioning of the possibility of complete human understanding is exactly what Pascal says he is trying to communicate: "Si l'homme s'étudiait il verrait combien il est incapable de passer outre. Comment se pourrait-il qu'une partie connût le tout?" (230/199). The human condition contains both *misère* and *grandeur* (155/122), and even if we are "incapables de savoir certainement," we are not condemned to "ignorer absolument" (230/199). Pascal can make his point, and his readers can understand it, even if the point is that we cannot understand everything.

The discontinuity between types of language in the *Pensées* is a discontinuity between two different languages of truth: truth through the method of geometry (expressed in the geometric style), and truth through the method of *finesse* (expressed in the subtle style). Statements using the subtle style can be based on the quite rigorous, intellectual power of the *sentiment* rather than on unfounded opinions. The language of the subtle style does not lead to geometric certainty, and when misused it can lead to unjustified or purposely falsified statements, but it can also lead the reader to a careful reconsideration of self and to a much better understanding of the human condition.

For the average reader, the only way to handle this discontinuity of the text and self is to remain suspended, to accept multiple points of view, styles, and methods, and to use the "renversement continuel du pour au contre" to go from one point of view to another. We must search for ways to reconcile the huge variety of often contradictory ideas, words, and things: "Pour entendre le sens d'un auteur il faut accorder tous les passages contraires" (289/257), whether the author is a human writer, nature, or God. From Pascal's perspective, remaining suspended means giving up hope of understanding everything, but not of attaining enough understanding to see the (fallen) world as it is, to learn to live in it, and to accept the hope of grace. Pascal, like his fragmentary text, has no patience for those who accept easy answers and refuse to search—any apology he might have written could not have helped those who have no interest in being helped, who refuse to accept discontinuity and suspension; the *Pensées* as we know them cannot reveal their true richness to those who are not willing to accept irony and fragmentation, in order to read in a new way.[8] This way of reading can lead to confusion and doubt, but it is also the best way Pascal gives us of comprehending a complex situation. Even without his faith in a divinely guaranteed understanding for those who truly search, even if the goal of complete understanding is infinitely postponed, we become a "habile" rather than a member of "le peuple" who, without the benefit of a "pensée de derrière," remains ignorant of why things are as they are.[9]

The fact that the *Pensées* can lead the reader to an essential awareness, to a valuable if incomplete knowledge, does not make them any less problematic as a text. They do not constitute a complete apology, or anything close to one. The way they are written suggests such an acute awareness of the problems of thought and language that we feel "an emotive reaction to the impossibility of knowing what it [language] might be up to"[10] as strongly as we do the anguish when confronted with the "deux infinis." The reader, much like the reader of a *nouveau roman*, needs not only to make his or her own sense of a disjointed text but also to follow this text toward a reconstruction of a lost, fallen state of direct communication and knowledge; the reader must then proceed to a recognition of the rupture between this fallen state and his or her current state, and ultimately to a decision about how best to overcome the rupture. And conversely, if such a decision is the ultimate goal of Pascal's text, in what better way could he write it than in a fragmentary, digressive form, in a form in which a linear, logical, geometric style is constantly contrasted

---

[8]See fragments such as 24/405, 39/5, and 195/163 for Pascal's insistence on the importance of searching. Ultimately, a finished apology would insist on more than searching and a new way of reading. As Davidson points out (*Blaise Pascal*, p. 90), Pascal would want to change not only the ideas of the reader but also his or her "moral posture," that is, to bring about a conversion.

[9]From this point of view, the question of whether or not the *Pensées* can convince an unbeliever of the value of Christianity becomes moot—either this was not Pascal's goal, or he was unable to achieve it. It makes much more sense to discuss these fragments in terms of what they can do in their incomplete state: clear up misunderstanding, present a way of looking at the world, and make Christianity seem worth looking into.

[10]Paul de Man, *Allegories of Reading* (New Haven: Yale University Press, 1979), 17.

to an open, subtle style that allows for multiple possibilities? In such a way, he keeps the reader aware of the ironic discontinuities between signs and referents, *is* and *should be,* human and divine.

As I was pondering the subject of this study years ago, Henri Peyre advised me against "reducing the tragic thinker to a man obsessed with language problems and desiccating him." My conclusion now is that it is only through a study of Pascal's language, and of the thought process behind it, that we realize exactly to what degree Pascal's thought is tragic without being despairing. Aware that the discontinuity of language is parallel to that of the human condition, he found a way to use language that would demonstrate its weaknesses while taking advantage of its strengths, to show that we need to be aware of our *misère* as we take advantage of our *grandeur.* His self is his thought, and his eloquence is truly a portrait of this thought-self (481/578, 167/135)—if his thought is tragic, then so is his language, and we cannot understand the one without the other.

Appendix: Computer Methodology

I. General

My study of Pascal's methods and styles suggested three principal stylistic features that would reflect (especially in the *Pensées*) his concern to express his thoughts as directly as possible and to allow readers to reach their own conclusions—frequent occurrences of *être* and of repeated words, and infrequent occurrences of connectives, especially logical, subordinating conjunctions. The next step was to find passages where these features occur and do not occur, analyze them, and use the results to reach a better understanding of Pascal's works. To find them, and to carry out preliminary analyses, a computer is an extremely useful tool.

We can read the *Pensées* with the three stylistic features in mind, but being human, we risk missing or misinterpreting important passages. The computer can read with these features in mind and miss nothing, but being a machine, it can recognize only what it has been told to recognize, and it can draw no conclusions about what it finds. My approach, then, has been to have the computer find as much as possible with a fairly simple program, to be aware of its limitations, and to use the results with these limitations in mind. As John Smith put it in describing his program for textual analysis, a computer system "amplifies, rather than replaces, specific perceptual and cognitive functions. It can . . . reveal subtle patterns that might be missed or only partially perceived while reading; it can help the user attain a sense of proportion, emphasis, and accuracy that is difficult or impossible to gain otherwise. The system can help manage an evolving interpretation, but it is the human being who decides what information is important, what directions the analysis should take, and what the output means."[1]

[1]"A New Environment for Literary Analysis," *Perspectives in Computing* 4, nos. 2/3 (1984): 22.

Isolating all the forms of *être* is not a problem. The occurrences of *être* as a verb have been separated from those as a noun, and the few homonyms which could confuse the computer are rare in the *Pensées*—*suis* as a form of *suivre* does not occur, nor does *été* meaning "summer." There are two or three occurrences in which *soit* might be interpreted as a conjunction rather than a verb, but this is hardly a significant number out of a total of 3,938 occurrences.

In searching for repeated words, plural and feminine forms are grouped with the masculine singular. This search is easy when the forms are regular, adding 'e' and 's'; there are not enough irregular forms to make a significant difference out of 33,761 repeated words (not counting articles, etc., as explained in part II below). It is not necessary to group all verb forms with the infinitive, since according to the *Grammaire* of Port-Royal, these forms signify the manner of our thought rather than the objects of it. The repetition of nouns, which represent these objects and form parts of *jugements,* is more important.

Searching for conjunctions is more complicated, since there are words like *si* and *comme* which are important conjunctions but which also occur frequently as other parts of speech. After considerable thought and consultation, I decided that a program could produce satisfactory results without sorting out each occurrence of such words. Searching for the conjunctions listed below yielded 6,435 occurrences, and a concordance makes it possible to look at the use of specific conjunctions such as *si.*

In all three cases (*être,* repeated words, and conjunctions), what is important is not to find every single occurrence, but to find enough to be able to determine stylistic differences and similarities among fragments and sections of the *Pensées.* Internal consistency is more important than completeness, to ensure that the same standards are applied to each fragment. My main goal is to identify stylistic differences in the *Pensées,* not to compare the *Pensées* to other texts.

Such comparisons would be of great interest but are extremely difficult to make because of the special nature of the *Pensées.* In the first place, the fragments vary from one to 2,734 words in length (not counting variants and Latin quotations), and the variations in length make it hard to compare them to texts with longer and more consistent divisions (chapters, for example, or letters such as the *Provinciales*). Second, there are different degrees of completeness in the *Pensées,* from simple lists (381/349 and 315/283, for example) to carefully rewritten "prose poems" such as 230/199 ("Disproportion de l'homme"). And third, there are many different subjects or topics in the *Pensées,* even within the fragments that we consider to have been composed with an apology in mind. How many other works of the seventeenth century have subjects ranging from the human passions to the history of the Jews to the infinity of the universe, from geometry to religion?

Within the *Pensées,* we can use the results of the computer search of the text to find passages, fragments, or groups of fragments that contain relatively large or small numbers of occurrences of certain features, either in isolation or in combination with others. Some of these passages and fragments turn out not to be interesting at all, or to be too atypical to be important (this is especially the case of unusually long and short fragments).[2] Many others, however, are excellent examples of Pascal's thought processes at work, of how he adapts his style to the subject he is treating and the method he is using.

II. Technical

The text used for the computer search is that of the Lafuma edition in three volumes, 1952; the magnetic tape was graciously furnished by Hugh Davidson and Pierre Dubé, who had used it to produce their concordances of the *Provinciales* and *Pensées* (Garland, 1980; Cornell University Press, 1975). The text was edited to correct a few errors and to identify Latin quotations; variants and homographs had already been identified. A first program, which I wrote in MS-BASIC (if only I had known about

[2]See part II below for details on the number of fragments of various lengths.

SNOBOL then!), established lists of the words in each letter and in each of the 965 fragments (out of 993) that contain French text and are not exclusively variants. A second program (which I also wrote, in MS-BASIC) checked these lists for occurrences of *être,* repeated words, and connectives. The search for repeated words ignored all definite and indefinite articles and their contractions with *à* and *de,* except when these words appear in connectives (*de peur que,* for example). It also ignored all words with fewer than two letters. Any word with a final 'e,' 's,' or both was compared to its root. The search for connectives looked for the following words and expressions and divided them into nine categories:

ET

et

LINKING

d'autre (de part et d'autre, etc.), ou, ni, tantôt

OPPOSING

au contraire, au moins, mais

COMPARING

ainsi que, à mesure que, aussi bien que, c'est-à-dire, comme si, de manière que, de même que, et même, outre que

TEMPORAL

après que, aussitôt que, avant que, depuis que, en attendant que, en même temps que, jusqu'à ce que, lorsque, quand

CAUSAL

afin que, au cas que, car, parce que, pour que, pourvu que, puisque, selon que, vu que

CONSEQUENTIAL

ainsi, alors, au point que, c'est pourquoi, de là, de sorte que, donc, or, où il est . . . que, par conséquent, par là, par où, partant, tellement que

CONCESSIVE

cependant, encore que, et en effet, même si, néanmoins, pourtant, quand même, quelque . . . [adjective] que, tandis que, toutefois

CONDITIONAL

à moins que, de peur que.

The conjunctions I call ductive come from the last four categories; those I call logical come from the last two.

The results of these searches were placed in a random file, with a value for each category established for each letter or fragment. These raw values were used to calculate percentages (i.e., a category occurring 3 times in a fragment 60 words long was given a percentage of five). These percentages were not always meaningful, however, since the lengths of the fragments vary from one to 2,734 words; the average length is 105, but the median is only 50 (half the fragments have fewer than 50 words, half more). There are very few fragments at either extreme—58 have fewer than ten words; 13 have more than 887, 96 have more than 200; 83% are thus between 10 and 200 words long. As an example of the problems in interpreting these percentages, the average percentage of repeated words for fragments 25 words long is 12%, while it is 23% for fragments 90–100 words long and as high as 51% (fragment 168/136, which is 2,695 words long) for the longest fragments. However, when we compare the percentage of repeated words for each fragment to the average percentage for fragments of that length, we find that many of the long fragments, considering their length, are not unusually high in repeated words.

In order to be able to compare fragments of different lengths, I tried several statistical procedures; I found the best results using residual values from a regression of the logarithms of the category counts (repeated words, for example) on the fragment sizes, since the logarithm of the number of repeated words in a fragment increases in a roughly linear fashion with the fragment size. The computer, using the Statistical Analysis System (SAS, 1982), computed the line that best fits this trend in the data and was thus able to predict the number of repeated words for each fragment, based on the values of fragments of similar length. The residual value for each fragment is the difference between the logarithm of the number of repeated words and the logarithm of the predicted value. This residual value is greater than zero if the number of repeated words in that fragment is greater than could be expected considering the fragment length, and less than zero if the number is less than could be expected. A frequency distribution curve was also established, which includes a point beyond which an actual value is significantly different (positively or negatively) from the norm. I am referring to this point on the curve when I describe a fragment as having a significantly high or low relative frequency of occurrence of a certain stylistic feature; "relative" refers to other fragments of similar length.

As an example, consider 614/733, 641/776, and 645/786, found in the *liasses* "pensées mélées" 4 and 5, and dealing with the Church and its controversies. Each fragment has a residual value of 0.01 (almost average) for repeated words, meaning that they have a comparable relative frequency of occurrence. However their raw number of occurrences and the percentage of occurrences vary greatly.

Fragment	Length of frag.	Raw no. of occ.	Percent of occ.	Residual value
641/776	14	1	7	0.01
645/786	50	9	18	0.01
614/733	569	237	42	0.01

These differences are less radical for occurrences of conjunctions, and even less for *être,* since the percentages do not vary as much for these categories as they do for repeated words, but the residual values are still the best means of comparing fragments of different length.

To compare the different sections of the *Pensées* according to these residual values, I used multivariate analysis of variance test criteria, using residuals.[3] These methods compare groups of frag-

[3]See Donald F. Morrison, *Multivariate Statistical Methods* (New York: McGraw-Hill, 1976).

ments (individual *liasses,* or groups of *liasses*) and determine whether the differences among the groups' means are greater than what we would expect from a random distribution of the stylistic features under consideration. If the differences are not greater, we can say that they are not significant; the results of this analysis form the basis of my comparisons of the sections of the *Pensées* in chapter 11.

A plotting procedure allows us to compare the groups at a glance. For example, the following figure shows how often *être* occurs in each of the first ten *liasses,* compared to what we might expect. The rectangles represent the range of occurrences near the norm; the '+' sign represents the mean and the hyphen the median. The zeroes outside the rectangles represent occurrences far from the norm.

Figure 1

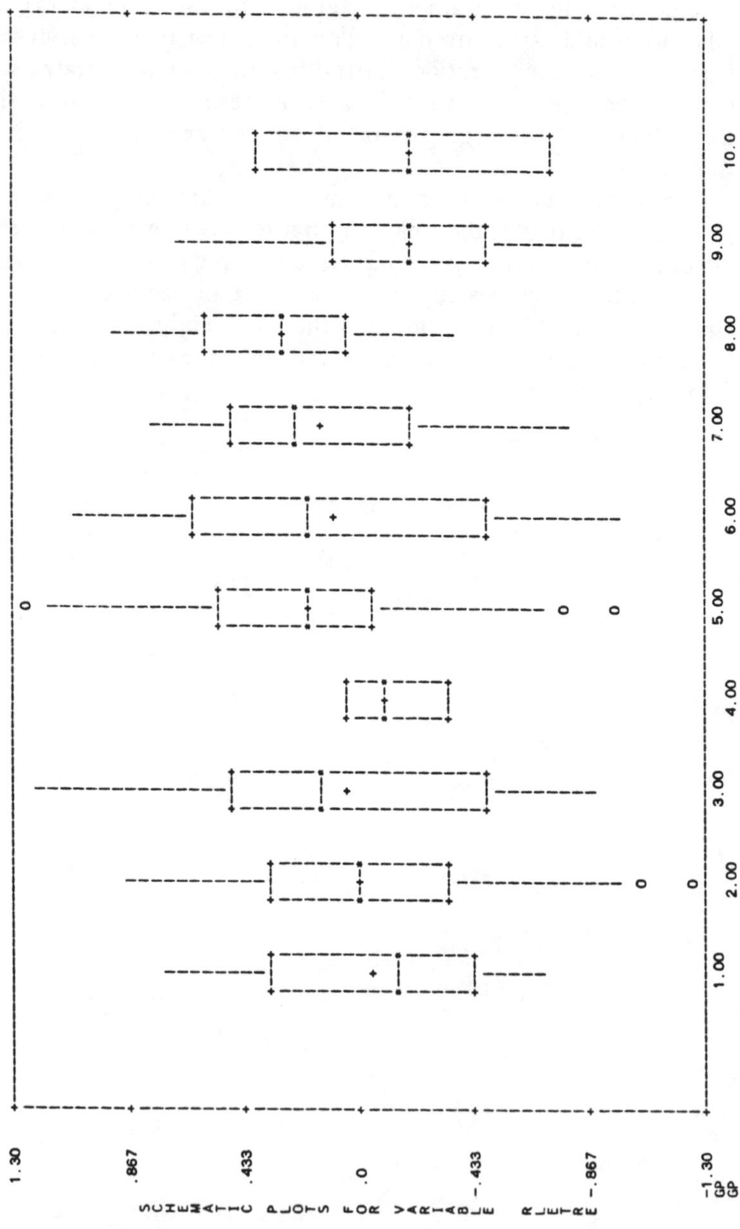

1.30
.867
.433
.0
-.433
-.867
-1.30
GP
GP
SCHEMATIC PLOTS FOR VARIABLE RLETRE
1.00
2.00
3.00
4.00
5.00
6.00
7.00
8.00
9.00
10.0

Works Cited

Académie Française. *Dictionnaire de l'Académie Française.* 2nd ed. 1695. Geneva: Slatkine, 1968.

Antoine, Gérald. "Le Langage de Pascal." *La Table Ronde* 171 (1962): 56–71.

Arnauld, Antoine. *Oeuvres.* 27 vols. Paris: Sigismond D'Arnay, 1779.

———, and Claude Lancelot. *Grammaire générale et raisonnée.* 1660. Paris: Paulot, 1969.

———, and Pierre Nicole. *La Logique ou l'art de penser.* Ed. Pierre Clair and François Girbal. 5th ed. 1683. Paris: P.U.F., 1965.

Auerbach, Erich. *Mimesis.* New York: Meridian Books, 1959.

Baudin, Emile. *Etudes historiques et critiques sur la philosophie de Pascal.* 4 vols. Neuchâtel: La Baconnière, 1946–47.

Baudouin, Charles. *Blaise Pascal, ou l'ordre du coeur.* Paris: Plon, 1962.

Booth, Wayne. *A Rhetoric of Irony.* Chicago: University of Chicago Press, 1971.

Broome, John. *Pascal.* London: Edward Arnold, 1965.

Brown, Harcourt. *Science and the Human Comedy.* Toronto: University of Toronto Press, 1976.

Brunet, Georges. *Le Pari de Pascal.* Paris: Desclée de Brouwer, 1956.

Brunschvicg, Léon. *Blaise Pascal.* Paris: Vrin, 1953.

Caturelli, Alberto. *En el corazón de Pascal.* Córdoba, Argentina: U. Nacional de Córdoba, 1970.

Charles, Michel. *La Rhétorique de la lecture.* Paris: Seuil, 1977.

Chatman, Seymour, and Samuel R. Levin, eds. *Essays on the Language of Literature.* Boston: Houghton-Mifflin, 1967.

Chinard, Gilbert. *En lisant Pascal.* Geneva: Droz, 1948.

Croll, Morris Wm. "The Baroque Style in Prose." *Studies in English Philology.* Ed. Kemp Malone and Martin B. Rund. Minneapolis: University of Minnesota Press, 1929. 427–56.

———. *Style, Rhetoric and Rhythm.* Ed. J. Max Patrick et al. Princeton: Princeton University Press, 1966.

Cruickshank, J. "Knowledge and Belief in Pascal's Apology." *Studies . . . Presented to H. W. Lawton.* Ed. J. C. Ireson, et al. Manchester: Manchester University Press, 1968. 89–103.

Davidson, Hugh M. *Audience, Words and Art: Studies in Seventeenth-*

Century French Rhetoric. Columbus: Ohio State University Press, 1965.

———. *Blaise Pascal.* Twayne's World Authors Series. Boston: G. K. Hall, 1983.

———. *The Origins of Certainty.* Chicago: University of Chicago Press, 1979.

Davidson, Hugh M. and Pierre H. Dubé, eds. *A Concordance to Pascal's* Les Provinciales. New York: Garland, 1980.

———. *A Concordance to Pascal's* Pensées. Ithaca: Cornell University Press, 1975.

De Man, Paul. *Allegories of Reading.* New Haven: Yale University Press, 1979.

———. *Blindness and Insight.* 2nd ed. Minneapolis: University of Minnesota Press, 1983.

———. "Pascal's Allegory of Persuasion." *Allegory and Representation: Selected Papers from the English Institute, 1979–80.* Ed. Stephen J. Greenblatt. Baltimore: Johns Hopkins University Press, 1981.

Demorest, Jean-Jacques. *Dans Pascal: Essai en partant de son style.* Paris: Minuit, 1953.

———. *Pascal écrivain: étude sur les variantes de ses écrits.* Paris: Minuit, 1957.

Duchêne, Roger. "D'Arnauld à Pascal ou l'art de faire 'plus court': l'exemple de la dix-septième *Provinciale.*" *Méthodes chez Pascal.* Paris: P.U.F., 1979. 253–65.

———. *L'Imposture littéraire dans les* Provinciales *de Pascal.* Aix-en-Provence: Université de Provence, 1984.

Du Marsais, César Chesnau. *Des Tropes.* Paris: Brocas, 1730.

Dumonceaux, Pierre. *Langue et sensibilité au XVIIe siècle: L'Evolution du vocabulaire affectif.* Geneva: Droz, 1975.

Dupriez, Bernard. *Gradus: Les procédés littéraires.* Paris: 10/18, 1984.

Edelman, Nathan. *The Eye of the Beholder.* Ed. Jules Brody. Baltimore: Johns Hopkins University Press, 1974.

Ernst, Pol. *Approches pascaliennes: l'unité et le mouvement, le sens et la fonction de chacune des 27 liasses titrées.* Gembloux, Belgium: J. Duculot, 1970.

Eustis, Alvin. *Seventeenth Century French Literature . . . A Critical Anthology.* New York: McGraw-Hill, 1969.

Fish, Stanley E. *Self-Consuming Artifacts: The Experience of Seventeenth-Century Literature.* Berkeley: University of California Press, 1972.

Fontanier, Pierre. *Les Figures du discours.* Ed. Gérard Genette. 1830. Paris: Flammarion, 1977.

Foucault, Michel. *Les Mots et les choses.* Paris: Gallimard, 1966.
Furetière, Antoine. *Dictionnaire universel.* 1690. Paris: Robert, 1978.
García, J. Perdomo. "El corazón come fuente de conocimiento en Pascal." *Revista de Ideas Estéticas* 11 (1953): 253–72.
———. "Los incomprensibiles del pensamiento en Pascal y las antimonías kantianas." *Revista de filosofía* 9 (1950): 605–42.
———. *La teoría del conocimiento en Pascal: Filosofía crítica Pascaliana.* Madrid: Consejo Superior de Investigaciones científicas, 1956.
Greenblatt, Stephen J., ed. *Allegory and Representation: Selected Papers from the English Institute, 1979–80.* Baltimore: Johns Hopkins University Press, 1981.
Handwerk, Gary. *Irony and Ethics in Narrative: From Schlegel to Lacan.* New Haven: Yale University Press, 1985.
Harrington, Thomas More. "Pascal et la philosophie." *Méthodes chez Pascal.* Paris: P.U.F., 1979. 37–43.
———. *Vérité et méthode dans les* Pensées *de Pascal.* Paris: Vrin, 1972.
Hentsch, Guy. "La Poésie de Pascal." *Etudes de Lettres, Université de Lausanne.* 2nd ser. 6 (1963): 29–58.
Houston, John Porter. *The Traditions of French Prose Style.* Baton Rouge: Louisiana State University Press, 1981.
Humbert, Pierre. *L'Oeuvre scientifique de Blaise Pascal.* Paris: Albin Michel, 1947.
Ireson, J. C. et al., eds. *Studies . . . Presented to H. W. Lawton.* Manchester: Manchester University Press, 1968.
Jungo, Dom Michel. *Le Vocabulaire de Pascal.* Paris: Editions d'Autrey, 1950.
Lamy, Bernard. *La Rhétorique ou l'art de parler.* 4th ed. 1699. Brighton: Sussex Reprints, 1969.
Lanham, Richard. *The Motives of Eloquence: Literary Rhetoric in the Renaissance.* New Haven: Yale University Press, 1976.
Laporte, Jean. *Le Coeur et la raison selon Pascal.* Paris: Elzévir, 1950.
Le Guern, Michel. *L'Image dans l'oeuvre de Pascal.* Paris: Armand Colin, 1969.
Lefebvre, Henri. *Pascal.* 2 vols. Paris: Nagel, 1949, 1954.
Lubbock, Percy. *The Craft of Fiction.* 1921. New York: Viking Press, 1957.
Madou, Jean Pol. "Ironie socratique, ironie romanesque, ironie poétique." *French Literature Series* 13 (1987): 62–73.
Maggioni, Sister Maria. *The* Pensées *of Pascal: A Study in Baroque Style.* Washington: Catholic University Press, 1950.
Magnard, Pierre. *Nature et Histoire dans l'apologétique de Pascal.* Paris: Belles Lettres, 1975.

———. "Pascal dialecticien." *Pascal présent.* Clermont-Ferrand: G. de Bussac, 1962: 257–89.

Marin, Louis. *La Critique du discours: étude sur la* Logique *de Port-Royal et sur les* Pensées *de Pascal.* Paris: Minuit, 1975.

Maynard, Abbé M. U. *Pascal, sa vie et son caractère, ses écrits et sa gloire.* 2 vols. Paris: Dezobry et E. Magdeleine, 1850.

Melzer, Sarah E. *Discourses of the Fall.* Berkeley: University of California Press, 1986.

Mercanton, Jacques. "Pascal: De la parole au silence." *Etudes de Lettres, Université de Lausanne.* 2nd ser. 6 (1963): 21–28.

Mesnard, Jean. *Les* Pensées *de Pascal.* Paris: Société d'Edition d'Enseignement Supérieur, 1976.

———. "Pourquoi les *Pensées* de Pascal se présentent-elles sous forme de fragments?" *Papers on French Seventeenth Century Literature* 19 (1983): 635–49.

———, Thérèse Goyet, et al., eds. *Les* Pensées *de Pascal ont trois cents ans.* Clermont-Ferrand: G. de Bussac, 1971.

Méthodes chez Pascal. Paris: P.U.F., 1979.

Miel, Jan. *Pascal and Theology.* Baltimore: Johns Hopkins University Press, 1969.

———. "Pascal, Port-Royal and Cartesian Linguistics." *Journal of the History of Ideas* 30 (1969): 261–71.

Moles, Elizabeth. "Three Categories of Intelligence in Pascal." *Australian Journal of French Studies* 8 (1971): 259–68.

Morel, Jacques. "Réflexions sur le sentiment pascalien." *Revue des Sciences Humaines* 97 (1967): 21–29.

Mornet, Daniel. *Histoire de la clarté française.* Paris: Payot, 1929.

Morot-Sir, Edouard. "Du Nouveau sur Pascal." *Romance Notes* 18 (1977): 272–79.

———. *La Métaphysique de Pascal.* Paris: P.U.F., 1973.

———. *Pascal.* Paris: P.U.F., 1973.

Morrison, Donald F. *Multivariate Statistical Methods.* New York: McGraw-Hill, 1976.

Muecke, D. C. *The Compass of Irony.* London: Methuen & Co., 1969.

Nelson, Robert. *Pascal: Adversary and Advocate.* Cambridge: Harvard University Press, 1981.

Newman, John Henry Cardinal. "Literature, a Lecture in the School of Philosophy and Letters" (1858). *The Idea of a University.* Ed. Martin J. Svaglic. New York: Holt, Rinehart and Winston, 1907. 201–21.

———. *Essay in Aid of a Grammar of Assent.* Ed. Charles Frederick Harrold. 1870. New York: Longmans, Green and Co., 1947.

Nicole, Pierre. "Dissertation contre le P. Hilarion, 'Sur les pensées imperceptibles.'" Chinard, Gilbert. *En lisant Pascal.* Geneva: Droz, 1948. 126–30.

———. "Preface to the *Recueil de poésies chrétiennes." Oeuvres diverses de La Fontaine.* Ed. Pierre Clarac. Paris: Gallimard, 1958. 779–85.

Norman, Buford. "Chez les Jésuites et chez les honnêtes gens: Methods and Styles in the *Provinciales." Biblio 17* 21 (1984): 57–78.

———. "Editing and Interpreting Fragmentary Texts: A Justification of Pascal's Text in MSL 527–Br 40." *TEXT. Transactions of the Society for Textual Scholarship.* New York: AMS Press, 1985. 197–208.

———. "L'Idée de règle chez Pascal." *Méthodes chez Pascal.* Paris: P.U.F., 1979. 87–99.

———. "Logic and Anti-Rhetoric in Pascal's *Pensées." French Forum* 2 (1977): 22–33.

Pascal, Blaise. *Le Manuscrit des* Pensées. Ed. Louis Lafuma. Paris: Les Libraires Associés, 1962.

———. *Oeuvres complètes.* Ed. Jean Mesnard. 2 vols., at least three others to follow. Bruges: Desclée de Brouwer, 1964–70.

———. *Oeuvres complètes.* Ed. Louis Lafuma. Paris: Seuil, 1963.

———. *L'Original des* Pensées *de Pascal.* Ed. Léon Brunschvicg. Paris: Hachette, 1905.

———. *Pensées de M. Pascal sur la religion et sur quelques autres sujets.* Ed. Georges Couton and Jean Jehasse. 1670. Saint-Etienne: Universités de la Région Rhône-Alpes, 1971.

———. *Pensées.* Ed. Ernest Havet. 2nd ed. Paris: Delagrave, 1866.

———. *Pensées.* Ed. Michel Le Guern. Paris: Gallimard, 1977.

———. *Pensées.* Ed. Philippe Sellier. Paris: Mercure de France, 1976.

———. *Pensées.* Ed. Zacharie Tourneur. Edition paléographique. Paris: Vrin, 1942.

———. *Pensées.* Ed. Zacharie Tourneur and Didier Anzieu. Paris: Armand Colin, 1960.

———. *Les Provinciales.* Ed. Louis Cognet. Paris: Garnier, 1965.

Petitot, Henri. "Comment Pascal acquiert la certitude." *Revue des Sciences Philosophiques et Théologiques* 3 (1909): 682–709.

———. "Théorie de la connaissance chez Pascal." *Revue Thomiste* 17 (1909): 574–86.

Polanyi, Michael. *The Tacit Dimension.* New York: Doubleday, 1966.

Prigent, Jean. "La Réflexion pascalienne sur les principes." *Mélanges de littérature française offerts à monsieur René Pintard.* Strasbourg: Centre de Philologie et de Littérature Romanes de l'Université de Strasbourg, 1975. 117–28.

Racine, Jean. *Oeuvres complètes.* Ed. Pierre Clarac. Paris: Seuil, 1962.

Reisler, Marsha. "Persuasion through Antithesis: An Analysis of the Dominant Structure of Pascal's *Lettres Provinciales.*" *Romanic Review* 69 (1978): 172–85.

Richelet, Pierre. *Dictionnaire françois.* 1680. Geneva: Slatkine, 1970.

Russier, Jeanne. *La Foi selon Pascal.* Paris: P.U.F., 1949.

Sagan, Carl. *The Dragons of Eden.* New York: Random House, 1977.

Sainte-Beuve, Charles-Augustin. *Port-Royal.* Ed. Maxime Leroy. 3 vols. Paris: Gallimard, 1954.

Sévigné, Marie de Rabutin-Chantal. *Correspondance.* Ed. Roger Duchêne. 3 vols. Paris: Gallimard, 1972–78.

Smith, John. "A New Environment for Literary Analysis." *Perspectives in Computing* 2/3 (1984): 20–31.

Stanton, Domna C. *The Aristocrat as Art: A Study of the* Honnête Homme *and the Dandy in Seventeenth- and Nineteenth-Century French Literature.* New York: Columbia University Press, 1980.

———. "Pascal's Fragmentary Thoughts: Dis-order and its Overdetermination." *Semiotica* 51 (1984): 211–35.

Taton, René. "L'Oeuvre de Pascal en géométrie projective." *Revue d'Histoire des Sciences* 15 (1962): 197–252.

———, ed. *L'Oeuvre scientifique de Pascal.* Paris: P.U.F., 1964.

Topliss, Patricia. *The Rhetoric of Pascal.* Leicester: Leicester University Press, 1966.

Vamos, Maria. *Pascal's* Pensées *and the Enlightenment: The Roots of a Misunderstanding.* Geneva: Studies in Voltaire and the Eighteenth Century, 1972.

Wimsatt, W. K., Jr. "Style as Meaning." *Essays on the Language of Literature.* Ed. Seymour Chatman and Samuel R. Levin. Boston: Houghton-Mifflin, 1967. 362–73.

Wittgenstein, Ludwig. *Philosophical Investigations.* Ed. G. E. M. Anscombe. 3rd ed. New York: Macmillan, 1958.

General Index

Index of *Pensées* Fragments

Fragment numbers (given in bold face) are those of the Sellier edition (Paris: Mercure de France, 1976), except for four fragments from the Lafuma edition (Paris: Seuil, 1963) which are either grouped together in the Sellier edition (L421–L426) or omitted (L1000). This index includes only fragments about which I have made some kind of interpretative comment, from a simple comparison to an extended discussion. It does not include the numerous fragments quoted to support arguments.